CW00819101

African MiGs, Volume 2 | Madagascar to Zimbabwe
MiGs and Sukhois in Service in Sub-Saharan Africa

Tom Cooper and Peter Weinert, with Fabian Hinz and Mark Lepko

African MiGs

Volume 2 Madagascar – Zimbabwe

MiGs and Sukhois in Service in Sub-Saharan Africa

Tom Cooper and Peter Weinert, with Fabian Hinz and Mark Lepko

HARPIA
PUBLISHING+

Copyright © 2011 Harpia Publishing L.L.C. and Moran Publishing L.L.C. Joint Venture
2803 Sackett Street, Houston, TX 77098-1125, U.S.A.
africanmigs@harpia-publishing.com

Consulting and inspiration by Kerstin Berger
Artwork and drawings by Tom Cooper
Maps by Tom Cooper and Mark Lepko
Editorial by Thomas Newdick
Layout & typesetting by Norbert Novak, www.media-n.at

Printed at Grasl Druck & Neue Medien, Austria

ISBN 978-0-9825539-8-5

Harpia Publishing, L.L.C. is a member of

Contents

Introduction

The first volume of this book provided an operational history of MiG and Sukhoi fighters, and their Chinese variants (including Shenyang, Nanchang, Guizhou and Chengdu models) in service with 12 sub-Saharan African air forces, comprising Angola, Burkina Faso, Congo-Brazzaville, Democratic Republic of Congo, Eritrea, Ethiopia, Guinea-Bissau, Guinea-Conakry, and Ivory Coast, over the last 45 years.

Continuing this fascinating story, Volume 2 details the history of these Soviet-made fighters, and their Chinese variants, in service in Madagascar, Mali, Mozambique, Namibia, Nigeria, Somalia, Sudan, Tanzania, Uganda, Zambia and Zimbabwe.

In contrast to the situation faced by many of the countries described in Volume 1, superpower rivalry and interests during the Cold War years remained limited in the countries described in this volume. Cold War realities did, however, serve as the primary fuel for the conflicts in Mozambique, Somalia, Sudan and Uganda, where various MiG designs in particular saw extensive combat service. Meanwhile, it was the rivalry between the People's Republic of China and the Soviet Union that usually dictated – often near-simultaneous – deliveries of Soviet-made MiGs and their Chinese variants to countries like Sudan, Tanzania and Zambia. Despite many announcements to this end, Zimbabwe never obtained any Soviet-made MiGs, but opted for Chinese-made variants. Despite the country's involvement in several armed conflicts in the 1980s and the 1990s, these Zimbabwean aircraft saw no combat service. In part influenced by positive Zimbabwean experiences, but primarily due to Beijing's readiness to provide fighter jets on favourable terms, several Sub-Saharan African air forces – primarily Namibia, Nigeria and Tanzania – followed this pattern following the end of the Cold War. In recent years these three nations acquired Chinese-made fighters equipped to a very advanced standard.

The story of the MiG and Sukhoi fighters in this volume is therefore notably diverse, and is characterised by even more problematic relation to first-hand sources. As was the case in Volume 1, many chapters herein originally existed as separate overviews of selected African air forces, assembled during years of often troublesome research. Some of these chapters were published on the ACIG.org website, others in printed media. They were based on a wide range of sources, including numerous reputable publications, but also interviews with participants and eyewitnesses, as well as some official documentation. Except for Ethiopia and Somalia, original documentation concerning sub-Saharan air forces is practically inaccessible. Indeed, even in the case of these two countries and their air forces, all that is available are fragments from official archives released to various scholars (in the case of Ethiopia), or the few papers that survived nearly complete destruction and anarchy (in the case of Somalia). Many of these documents are meanwhile fiercely disputed by surviving participants.

The authors carefully collected new information from first-hand sources, cross-examined various second- and third-level information, correcting and updating their findings with the aim of offering the most detailed and dependable insight possible. Included within each chapter are comprehensive texts describing the services' histories, often based on communication with first-hand sources. There follow photographs and detailed artworks of the aircraft, many of which were involved in various air wars. Accompanying maps depict all major air bases as well as airfields that have been used by MiG and Sukhoi fighter aircraft (or their Chinese variants) over the years.

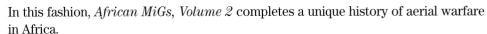

In this fashion, *African MiGs, Volume 2* completes a unique history of aerial warfare in Africa.

While preparing the second edition of this work (previously published as a single volume), the authors went to great lengths in order to 'depoliticise' the manuscript. This meant avoiding the use of terms such as 'regime', 'rebels', 'terror' or 'terrorist'. Clearly, one man's 'freedom fighter' is another's 'terrorist'. In particular, the term 'regime' is used by the media as a broad description for all too many governments in Africa, irrespective of their true nature. Through our research and travels, the authors are uncomfortably familiar with the many bloody wars fought in Africa over the last 50 years. We consider any source to be relevant until it can be proven beyond doubt to be without merit. It is a matter of fact that governments, national and private organisations, private companies and certain individuals face harsh ramifications when their influence and/or participation in such conflicts become public. However, this book does not aim to judge the politics of different countries. Having no political axe to grind, the authors instead concentrated on describing the military history of the region, and have thus made all efforts to maintain a non-partisan narrative that remains readable and easy to understand.

Similarly, in order to simplify the use of this book, all names, locations and geographic designations are as provided in *The Times World Atlas*, or other traditionally accepted major sources of reference.

Six additional years of research and the increased availability of the internet in Sub-Saharan Africa have provided much more in-depth and valuable information to this topic. We hope that our readers will find this second volume a unique point of reference, and at least as enthralling to read as the first.

Tom Cooper, Peter Weinert, Fabian Hinz and Mark Lepko
September 2011

Acknowledgements

As was the case with the first volume of this book, the authors relied greatly on cooperation with a number of individuals from around the world, who generously helped collect relevant information and photographs.

The Addenda to Volume 1 contains the unique recollections of Teniente-Colonel Eduardo Gonzalez (Air Defence and Air Force of Cuba, ret.), himself a highly experienced MiG-21 and MiG-23, who not only served three tours of duty in Angola, but authored two books of his own. Gonzalez previously provided information that proved crucial for the final form and authoritativeness of the Angolan chapter in Volume 1, and additional observations can be found in this volume, too. The authors are deeply indebted to his kind cooperation.

Albert Grandolini and Jean-Luc Debroux kindly shared some photographs from their extensive collections, or otherwise helped establish contacts to photographers of various 'African MiGs'.

Jacques Guillem kindly provided a number of exclusive photographs, as well as some fascinating recollections from his trips to various African countries.

We would also like to thank Greg Swart for his tireless efforts and kind help in pursuing research on the Angolan air arm, and Ben Wilhelmi for his provision of photographs from Tanzania.

The Addenda to Volume 1 also provides fascinating recollections from Chris Gibbson, who visited Angola and Congo-Brazzaville on a number of occasions in the late 1980s, when MiG operations in these two countries reached their apogee.

Many other persons provided invaluable support in the course of the work on this volume. Some, like Christian Pappenberg, helped with translation and establishing Russian-language contacts. Others, like Chuck Canyon, Willem Das, Herve Desallier, Ron C., Richard E. Flagg, Roberto Gentilli, Gérard Gaudin, Alexander Golz, Alexander Guk, Kenneth Iwuelmo, Michail Kishkin, Luis Laranjeira, Tom Long, William Marshall, Misha Medvedev, Vladimir Moshalov, Marco Moutinho, Holger Müller, Andrei N., Sascha Nait, Antona Pawel, Alvaro Ponte, Jürgen Roske, Pavel Shevchenko, Gerd Prieß, Phil Scoggins, Lukàs Syrovy, Andrey Timonkin, Chris Thornburg, Claudio Tosselli, Steve Touchdown and Dr Jürgen Willisch provided expertise in regard to aircraft types and their equipment, and assisted in the provision of photographs and other information. There is little doubt that this book would have been impossible without their kind help, and the authors would like to express their gratitude to every one of them.

We would also like to again extend our thanks to our families, who accompanied us through a period of intensive work, at all times providing the support we needed to complete this exhaustive volume.

Abbreviations

AA-1 Alkali	ASCC codename for RS-2US, Soviet AAM
AA-2 Atoll	ASCC codename for R-3S and R-13M, Soviet short-range AAMs
AA-7 Apex	ASCC codename for R-23/R-24, Soviet medium-range AAM
AA-8 Aphid	ASCC codename for R-60, Soviet short-range AAM
AA-10 Alamo	ASCC codename for R-27, Soviet medium-range AAM
AA-11 Archer	ASCC codename for R-73, Soviet short-range AAM
AA-12 Adder	ASCC codename for R-77, Soviet medium-range AAM
AA	anti-aircraft
AAA	anti-aircraft artillery
AAG	Armée de l'Air Guinée (Air Force of Guinea [Guinea Conakry])
AAM	air-to-air missile
AAM	Armée de l'Air Malgache
AAT	Armée de l'Air Tchadienne (Chadian Air Force)
AB	air base
AB	Agusta-Bell (Italian helicopter manufacturer)
AdA	Armée de l'Air (French Air Force)
AdAB	Armée de l'Air Burkinabé (Air Force of Burkina Faso)
AdAC	Armée de l'Air du Congo (Air Force of Congo [Brazzaville])
AdAM	Armée de l'Air Malgache (Air Force of Madagascar)
AFZ	Air Force of Zimbabwe
AGL	above ground level
AN	Anya-Nya (armed opposition group in Sudan during the 1960s; also known as the Land Freedom Army)
ANA/DAA	Armadas Nacional Aérea/Defesa Anti-aérea (Air Force and Air Defence Force of Guinea-Bissau)
ANC	African National Congress
APG	l'Armée Populaire de Guinée (People's Army of Guinea [Guinea Conakry])
APC	armoured personnel carrier
ARZ	Aviacioniy Remontniy Zavod (Aviation Repair Plant)
AS-7 Kerry	ASCC codename for Kh-23, Soviet air-to-surface missile
ASCC	Air Standardisation Coordinating Committee (US, UK, Australian and New Zealand committee for standardisation of designations for foreign [primarily Soviet] armament; its standardisation codenames are usually known as 'NATO designations')
ATGM	anti-tank guided missile
AWACS	Airborne Warning and Control System
AWNG	Air Wing of the National Guard (Air Force of Equatorial Guinea)
BAe	British Aerospace, later BAE Systems
BiAF	Biafran Air Force
Bort number	aircraft identification number, usually applied on the front fuselage of Soviet-made aircraft
Brig Gen	brigadier general (military commissioned officer rank)
CAP	combat air patrol
Capt	captain (military commissioned officer rank)
CAS	close air support

CASA	Construcciones Aeronáuticas SA (Spanish aircraft manufacturer)
CBU	cluster bomb unit
CCS	Ciidanka Cirka Soomaaliyed (Air Force of Somalia)
C-in-C	commander in chief
c/n	construction number
CO	commanding officer
COIN	counter-insurgent or counter-insurgency
Col	colonel (military commissioned officer rank)
Cor	coronel (Spanish for colonel)
CoS	Chief of Staff
CSAR	combat search and rescue
CzL	eskoslovenské letectvo (Czechoslovakian Air Force)
DAAFAR	Defensa Anti-Aérea y Fuerza Aérea Revolucionaria (Air Defence and Air Force of Cuba)
DAMEC	Dejen Aviation Maintenance and Engineering Complex (Ethiopian aircraft maintenance facility)
DHC	de Havilland Canada (Canadian aircraft manufacturer)
DRC	Democratic Republic of the Congo
ECOMOG	Economic Community of West African States Monitoring Group (military monitoring mission of ECOWAS in Liberia)
ECOWAS	Economic Community of West African States (includes 16 West African States)
ECM	electronic countermeasures
ELF	Eritrean Liberation Front
ENHV	Escadrille Nationale de Haute-Volta (National Squadron of Upper Volta – the original name of the Air Force of Burkina Faso)
EO	Executive Outcomes Ltd (South African commercial military enterprise)
ENDF	Ethiopian National Defence Force
EPLA	Eritrean People's Liberation Army, armed wing of the EPLF (see below)
EPLF	Eritrean People's Liberation Front (main Eritrean political organisation during the war against Ethiopian occupation)
EPRDF	Ethiopian People's Revolutionary Democratic Front (armed group opposing Mengistu regime in Ethiopia, 1980s)
ERAF	Eritrean Air Force
EtAF	Ethiopian Air Force
FAA	Forças Armadas Angolanas (Angolan military since 1992)
FACI	Force Aérienne de la Côte d'Ivoire
FAE	fuel-air explosive (type of weapon)
FAG	Force Aérienne de Guiné (Air Force of Guinea-Conakry)
FAGE	Fuerza Aérea de Guinea Ecuatorial
FAGB	Força Aérea da Guiné-Bissau (Air Force of Guinea-Bissau, since 1998)
FANA	Força Aérea Nacional (Angolan Air Force, since 1992)
Fantan	ASCC codename for Nanchang A-5 attack aircraft (Chinese-made fighter-bomber)
FAP	Força Aérea Portuguesa (Portuguese Air Force)

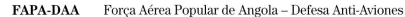

FAPA-DAA	Força Aérea Popular de Angola – Defesa Anti-Aviones (Angola People's Air Force and Air Defence Force, 1976–92)
FAPLA	Forças Armadas Populares de Libertação de Angola (Angolan military, 1976-92)
FAPM	Força Aérea Popular de Moçambique (Air Force of Mozambique)
FARM	Force Aérienne de la République du Mali (Republic of Mali Air Force)
Farmer	ASCC codename for MiG-19 fighter (also for its Chinese variant, J-6 or F-6)
FAZA	Force Aérienne Zaïroise (Zaire Air Force)
Fencer	ASCC codename for Su-24 strike aircraft
FDREAF	Federal Democratic Republic of Ethiopia Air Force (official title since 1998)
FIM-92A	US-made MANPADS (full designation FIM-92A Stinger)
Fishbed	ASCC codename for MiG-21 fighter (also for its Chinese-made variant, J-7 or F-7)
Fitter	ASCC codename for Su-7, Su-20 and Su-22 fighter-bombers
Flanker	ASCC codename for Su-27 fighter
FLEC	Frente de Libertaçâo do Enclave da Cabinda (Liberation Front of Cabinda Enclave, separatist movement fighting for separation or autonomy from Angola, in 1970s and 1980s)
Flg Off	flight officer (military commissioned officer rank; usually equal to lieutenant)
Flogger	ASCC codename for MiG-23 and MiG-27 fighters and fighter-bombers
Flt Lt	flight lieutenant (military commissioned officer rank)
FM	field marshal (top military commissioned officer rank)
FNLA	Frente Nacional de Libertaçâo de Angola (National Front for the Liberation of Angola, armed group opposing Portuguese rule in Angola in 1960-75, later fighting against MPLA government in 1970s and 1980s)
FRELIMO	Frente da Libertaçâo de Moçambique (Liberation Front of Mozambique, armed opposition to Portuguese rule in Mozambique, in 1960-75; later the ruling party in Mozambique)
Fresco	ASCC codename for MiG-17 fighter (also for its Chinese-made derivatives, including F-5 and FT-5)
Fulcrum	ASCC codename for MiG-29 fighter
GAF	Gambian Air Force
GCI	ground control interception
Gen	general (military commissioned officer rank)
GP	general-purpose (bomb)
HAS	hardened aircraft shelter
HE	high explosive (bomb)
Hind	ASCC codename for Mil Mi-24 assault helicopter (also for its Mi-25 and Mi-35 export variants)
HQ	headquarters
IAI	Israel Aircraft Industries (since 2006 Israel Aerospace Industries)
IAP	international airport

IAP	Istrebitelniy Avia Polk (Fighter Aviation Regiment, from Soviet Air Force terminology)
IDF	Israeli Defence Force
IDF/AF	Israeli Defence Force/Air Force
IEAF	Imperial Ethiopian Air Force
IP	instructor pilot
IR	infra-red
IrAF	Iraqi Air Force
IRGC	Islamic Revolutionary Guards Corps (Iranian militia originally organised in support of the newly emerging Islamic government of Iran; popularly known as 'Pasdaran', but also includes other militias and branches)
IRIAF	Islamic Republic of Iran Air Force
JWTZ	Jeshi la Wananchi la Tanzania (Tanzania People's Defence Force)
KIA	killed in action
Kh-23	Soviet air-to-surface missile, ASCC codename AS-7 Kerry
km	kilometre
LAAF	Libyan Arab Air Force
LGB	laser-guided bomb
LRA	Lord's Resistance Army (armed opposition group in south-western Sudan and northern Uganda)
LSK/LV	Luftstreitkräfte/Luftverteidigung (Air Force of the former German Democratic Republic)
Lt	lieutenant (military commissioned officer rank)
Lt Col	lieutenant colonel (military commissioned officer rank)
LTS	Light Training/Transport Squadron
Maj	major (military commissioned officer rank)
Maj Gen	major general (military commissioned officer rank)
MANPADS	man-portable air defence system(s) – light surface-to-air missiles that can be carried and deployed in combat by a single soldier
MBB	Messerschmitt-Bölkow-Blohm (German helicopter manufacturer)
MBT	main battle tank
MFDC	Mouvement des Forces Démocratiques des Casamance (Movement of Democratic Forces in Casamance; armed opposition group in Senegal)
MHz	megahertz, millions of cycles per second
Mi	Mil (Soviet/Russian helicopter designer and manufacturer)
MIC	Military Industrial Complex (in Sudan)
MiG	Mikoyan i Gurevich (the design bureau led by Artem Ivanovich Mikoyan and Mikhail Iosifovich Gurevich, also known as OKB-155 or MMZ 'Zenit')
MILAN	Missile d'infanterie léger antichar (French infantry anti-tank missile)
MLC	Movement for the Liberation of Congo (armed opposition group in central DRC, late 1990s)
MoD	Ministry of Defence (UK)
MPLA	Movimento Popular de Libertaçâo de Angola (People's Movement for the Liberation of Angola; leftist anti-colonial movement in Angola since 1970s)

NAF	Namibia Air Force (formerly the Namibia Defence Force Air Wing)
NAF	Nigerian Air Force
nav/attack	systems installed in aircraft and used for navigation and to aim weapons
NCO	non-commissioned officer
NDF	Namibia Defence Force
NDFAW	Namibia Defence Force Air Wing
NL	Namibiese Lugmag (unofficial designation often used for Namibian Air Force in everyday communications)
NORINCO	China North Industries Corporation
NRSCC	National Salvation Revolutionary Command Council (the official designation of the body governing Sudan since 1989)
NVA	Nationale Volksarmee (National People's Army, former Army of the German Democratic Republic, or East Germany)
OAU	Organisation of African Unity
OCU	Operational Conversion Unit
OGMA	Oficinas Gerais de Material Aeronáutico (formerly a Portuguese government-owned company specialising in the maintenance of aircraft and aircraft engines; now a consortium, OGMA Indústria Aeronáutica de Portugal, SA, partially owned by Embraer and EADS)
PAF	Pakistan Air Force
PAIGC	Partido Africano da Independência da Guiné a Cabo Verde (African Party for Independence of Guinea and Capo Verde, armed group opposing Portuguese colonial rule in the then Portuguese colony of Guiné, later Guinea-Bissau)
PDF	People's Defence Forces (Sudanese militia, similar in organisation and function to IRGC in Iran)
PGM	precision-guided munition (guided bombs and air-to-surface missiles)
PLAN	People's Liberation Army of Namibia (armed wing of SWAPO)
Plt Off	pilot officer (military commissioned officer rank)
PoW	prisoner of war
PRS	Partido Renovação Social (Party of Social Renewal, ruling party of Guinea-Bissau)
QJJ	al-Quwwat al-Jawwiya al-Jaza'eriiya (Algerian Air Force)
RS-2US	Soviet AAM, ASCC codename AA-1 Alkali
R-3S	Soviet short-range AAM, ASCC codename AA-2 Atoll
R-13M	Soviet short-range AAM, improved variant of R-3S, ASCC codename AA-2 Atoll
R-23/R-24	Soviet medium-range AAM, ASCC codename AA-7 Apex
R-27	Soviet medium-range AAM, ASCC codename AA-10 Alamo
R-60	Soviet short-range AAM, ASCC codename AA-8 Aphid
R-73	Soviet short-range AAM, ASCC codename AA-11 Archer
R-77	Soviet medium-range AAM, ASCC codename AA-12 Adder
RAF	Royal Air Force (UK)
RENAMO	Resistência Nacional Moçambicana (National Resistance of Mozambique, armed opposition group in Mozambique, 1980s)

RFDG	Rassemblement des Forces Démocratiques de Guinée (Rally of Democratic Forces of Guinea, supposed armed opposition group in Guinea-Bissau; actually a rebel group run by the RUF)
RCAF	Royal Canadian Air Force, until 1968, thereafter part of unified Canadian Forces
RLB	'Russian Light Blue' (colour frequently applied to various types of MiG and Sukhoi fighter jets; this shade of blue-grey is roughly between FS35550 and FS36329)
RPF	Rwanda Patriotic Front (armed opposition group in Rwanda, in mid-1980s)
RUF	Revolutionary United Front (armed opposition group in Sierra Leone)
SA-2 Guideline	ASCC codename for S-75 Dvina, Soviet SAM system
SA-3 Goa	ASCC codename for S-125 Neva, Soviet SAM system
SA-6 Gainful	ASCC codename for ZRK-SD Kub/Kvadrat, Soviet SAM system
SA-7 Grail	ASCC codename for 9K32 Strela-2, Soviet MANPADS
SA-8 Gecko	ASCC codename for 9K33 Osa, Soviet SAM system
SA-9 Gaskin	ASCC codename for ZRK-BD Strela-1, Soviet SAM system
SA-13 Gopher	ASCC codename for ZRK-BD Strela-10, Soviet SAM system
SA-14 Gremlin	ASCC codename for 9M36 Strela-3, Soviet MANPADS
SA-16 Gimlet	ASCC codename for 9M313 Igla-1, Soviet MANPADS
SA-18 Grouse	ASCC codename for 9M39 Igla, Soviet MANPADS
SAAF	South African Air Force
SAC	Somali Aeronautical Corps (in Somalia) or Safat Aviation Complex (in Sudan)
SADF	South African Defence Force
SALF	Somali-Abo Liberation Front (Somali-supported paramilitary force active within Ethiopia in 1977)
SAM	surface-to-air missile
SAS	Special Air Service
SEAMA	Sociedade de Exploracao de Aerodromos e Manutencao de Aeronaves (Portuguese company for aircraft maintenance, based at Tires)
s/n	serial number
SNA	Somali National Movement (armed opposition group in Somalia, 1980s)
SPAF	Sudan People's Armed Forces
SPLA	Sudanese People's Liberation Army (armed opposition group in southern Sudan)
Sqn Ldr	squadron leader (military commissioned officer rank)
SSLF	Southern Sudanese Liberation Front (armed opposition group in southeast Sudan during the 1980s and 1990s)
Su	Sukhoi
SuAF	Sudanese Air Force
SWA	South-West Africa (former German colony; administered by UK and then South Africa until 1990; now Namibia)
SWAPO	South-West African People's Organisation (group opposing South African administration in the former South West Africa, now Namibia)
TAAG	Transportes Aéros de Angola (Military Air Transport of Angola)

TAM	Tbilisi Aerospace Manufacturing
TAP	Transportes Aéros Portugueses (national Portuguese airline)
TASA	Tbilisi Aircraft State Association (Georgian aircraft manufacturer)
TPDF	Tanzania People's Defence Force (military of the United Republic of Tanzania)
TPLA	Tigray People's Liberation Army (military wing of the TPLF)
TPLF	Tigray People's Liberation Front (armed opposition group of Ethnic Tigreans fighting against Ethiopian central government, 1980s)
Tte	Teniente (Spanish for lieutenant)
Tte Cor	Teniente coronel (Spanish for lieutenant colonel)
UAAF	Ugandan Army Air Force
UAF	Uganda Air Force
UARAF	United Arab Republic Air Force (official designation of the Egyptian Air Force from 1958 until 1969)
UAV	unmanned aerial vehicle
UK	United Kingdom
UN	United Nations
UNITA	União Nacional para a Independência Total de Angola (National Union for the Total Independence of Angola; armed group opposing Portuguese Colonial rule in the 1960s and 1970s, then opposing MPLA until 2003)
UNLA	Uganda National Liberation Army (armed opposition group in Uganda, established in 1979 in Tanzania)
UPDF	Uganda People's Defence Force
UPDF/AW	Uganda People's Defence Force/Air Wing
UPDAF	Uganda People's Defence Air Force
USAF	United States Air Force
USD	United States Dollar
USSR	Union of Soviet Socialist Republics
VIP	very important person
V-TA	Soviet Military Transport Aviation
wfu	withdrawn from use
WSLF	Western Somali Liberation Front (armed opposition group comprising Somalis living in the Ogaden Province, in Ethiopia)
w/o	written off
WLiOPL OK	Wojska Lotnicze i Obrony Przeciwlotniczej Obszaru Kraju (Polish Air and Air Defence Forces, name in use until 2004)
WSLF	Western Somali Liberation Front (armed opposition group comprising ethnic Somalis in Ogaden, Ethiopia, in 1970s and 1980s)
ZAF	Zambian Air Force (full designation ZAF/ADC, standing for Zambian Air Force and Air Defence Command)
ZANLA	Zimbabwe African National Liberation Army (armed wing of ZANU)
ZANU	Zimbabwe Africa National Union (armed group of ethnic Shona Africans opposing white Rhodesian government in the 1970s)
ZAPU	Zimbabwe Africa People's Union (armed group of ethnic Ndele Africans opposing white Rhodesian government in the 1970s)
ZDF	Zimbabwe Defence Forces
ZIPRA	Zimbabwe Africa People's Liberation Army (armed wing of ZAPU)

ADDENDA/ERRATA TO VOLUME 1

The publication of *African MiGs, Volume 1* drew a number of positive reactions from many readers in many different parts of the world. The authors would like to thank all those who contacted them, and are using this opportunity to present some of the amendments and corrections to *African MiGs, Volume 1*, as provided by readers.

Chapter 1, Angola

Perhaps the best summary for the motivation behind the research that resulted in this book was provided by Chris Gibbson, who supplied the following recollection about his trip to Angola in early 1987:

"I'm not going for three months. No chance. Not again'. That was my initial reaction to being asked to work in Angola in early 1987. The oil exploration business had suffered one of its periodic downturns in 1986 and the only area that was providing steady work was West Africa. I had opted for the short-sleeve overalls and had just spent three months working in the Congo.

'Angola. Admittedly, my first thought was Hinds! – and a menagerie of Soviet types. An odd reaction perhaps, but remember this was during the Cold War. It is difficult to describe the situation 20 years ago. Today, Russian aircraft such as Indian Air Force Su-30s are a routine sight in Western Europe … However, before 1988, Soviet types had to be sought out in overseas garden spots. That was a period during which the sight of a Soviet aircraft of any description was a rarity. A few photos in the ROC Journal were about as close as you could get. Not even at airshows, and airshows don't count in my book as types must be seen in the 'wild' …

'I had seen MiG-15UTIs, MiG-17s and MiG-21s plus a few Mi-8s in the Congo. My colleagues and I used to go on trips around the Pointe Noire area, including a train journey to a place called Lubomo (I think). It was on this trip that the train passed the airport and I saw the MiGs. But, they were parked up and looking somewhat forlorn. Angola was in the process of a civil war and air power was playing a vital role in its conduct. I relished the chance of seeing some of this kit in the air – Hinds!

'We flew from Paris Charles de Gaulle International Airport on a battered old Boeing 707 of the French airline UTA that plied the Moscow-Paris-Luanda route. Given the political climate in Angola, the passengers were either Soviet advisors or oilfield types. In a rather bizarre situation the Russians were segregated at the back of the plane and we Westerners were kept at the front with what appeared to be a cordon of suited gents in between …

'*After what seemed like an age, our 707 landed at Luanda International Airport. Being late evening I could see nothing during the taxi to the terminal. As we traipsed down the stairs from the Boeing, I was struck by the sound of loud engines. Nothing unusual in that, it was an airport after all, but these had the districting note of high-performance aircraft. As I wandered over to the bus, the jet noise became louder and a series of white lights and strobes approached. As the first of these lights turned off the ramp and onto the taxiway, I got my first look at a Flogger. A 'G' model, to be exact, with the shorter fin fillet. The MiG-23ML was a front-line Soviet type back then, only recently supplied to other Warsaw Pact allies, so a most unexpected sight in Africa.*

'*Given my whereabouts, I suppressed my excitement and kept schtum as three more Floggers taxied out into the darkness, took off and headed south to the war, the night sky lit up by their reheat … So, not bad: less than 10 minutes in the place and I had seen more than I had ever hoped for!*'

After working for a month on an oil rig off the coast of northern Angola, in the course of which he frequently saw Angolan Mil Mi-8s and Mi-24s passing by at tree-top level (in order to avoid ground fire), Mr Gibbson and his colleagues travelled back to Luanda for their trip back home. As the crew boat arrived in the local port, they saw T-62 MBTs and BTR-60 APCs being unloaded from Soviet merchant ships, while MiG-23s were flying around in the circuit. Gibbson was to witness a similar scene immediately after his arrival in Luanda at the start of his second tour in Angola, several months later:

'*Next trip … The client had a nice shinny new Dauphin to fly us direct from Luanda to the rig … We drove to the airport and were due for a 14.00 lift. We had just chucked the bags in the hold when the captain appeared and said, 'Sorry lads, they've shut the airport. Indefinitely. That could be a couple of hours or a couple of days, but given the tower radio chatter I think it will be a couple of hours …*

'*I soon heard jet engines firing up and after about 10 minutes two pairs of MiG-23s taxied out and took off to the south. They turned north and disappeared in the haze …*

'*I settled down for one of those famous long African waits. Nothing had moved on the airport since the Floggers departed and after about half an hour I noticed hazy lights in the distance to the north: three shimmering sets in line abreast, coming closer. Well, the ramp of Luanda IAP wasn't the place to whip out the binos and have a squint, so I had to bide my time. Eventually, the dark shapes of the aircraft begin to materialise out of the haze: an Ilyushin Il-76 with a MiG-23 keeping station on each wingtip. As the Il-76 touched down, the MiGs peeled off in unison and turned to the north, where I could see another triptych of shimmering lights. Same again: an Aeroflot Il-76 with its minders, who, having shepherded their charge onto the runway, headed off north to repeat the process. In all it happened another 12 times and the Il-76s made an impressive sight lined up on the ramp …*'

What Chris Gibbson experienced on this and a number of other occasions was the arrival of arms shipments from the USSR, each of which was heavily protected by MiG-23MLs of the FAPA-DAA, although these fighters actually lacked the means of defending these lumbering transports from the threat of MANPADS.

Response from Cuba

Teniente-Colonel Eduardo Gonzalez (DAAFAR, ret.), himself an acknowledged author (his book *Angola – Tales from Heights* was published in Cuba in 2004), and who provided considerable help during the research for Chapter 1 of *African MiGs, Volume 1*, kindly recalled flying similar missions for transport aircraft hauling arms and supplies elsewhere in Angola:

'I personally provided top cover for Soviet Antonov An-22s arriving in Lubango. Our MiG-23MLs were not fitted with decoy flare launchers … and lacked light strips for formation flying by night. We therefore never practiced night formation flying and could not provide such cover by night. But, the Il-76s did have decoy flare dispensers and I saw them in Menongue spiralling down for landing or climbing to leave, and launching those flares … Many times I also provided top cover for Sukhois delivering ordnance on targets in the Mavinga region. The first batch of these, easily identifiable by an undernose fairing that carried a Doppler navigation radar, was designated 'Su-22M-4' by the Angolans. The second batch carried the same equipment but internally. I don't know how the FAPA-DAA named this variant.'[1]

Chapter 1, Angola, pp19–21

Further to the topic of deliveries of MiG fighter-bombers to Angola, Eduardo Gonzalez explained:

'The batch of 10 MiG-17F and two MiG-15UTI trainers was provided from the USSR. I think these aircraft had been diverted to Angola, and that some French-speaking country was their original destiny. We did not have the type: the DAAFAR flew the MiG-17AS, without afterburner, but Cuba sent flying and groundcrews and a reduced staff for coordination.[2]

'MiG-21MFs arrived in January 1976 and I was there for my first tour of duty in Angola. That batch included two MiG-21UM trainers. At that time Cuba was in the process of receiving its first squadron of MiG-21bis – more advanced than MiG-21MFs. Some pilots of the MiG-17F squadron transitioned to the MiG-21 after their arrival. We flew air-to-ground strikes and CAPs (armed with four R-3S air-to-air missiles), provided top cover for convoys, and flew visual reconnaissance (carrying three external tanks) … Our main armament consisted of a cannon and rocket pods of 57mm [2.24in] calibre. Up to four of them, each with 16 rockets. Sometimes our aircraft were armed with two 500kg [1,102lb] bombs for attacks from minimal level, and less heavy ones for operations from 'hot and high' runways, other times with S-24 unguided rockets, 240mm [9.45in] calibre. The latter was a tricky weapon able to flame-out the engine when launched … Attacks on South African forces were absolutely prohibited: one guy once violated this on his own and was almost de-winged, catching all kinds of hell from the Cuban mission commander (Rafael del Pino) … Around 1980, a counter-insurgency group with some MiG-21PFMs and MiG-17F was created, but the MiG-21 was not suited for such a task.

'I arrived in Angola for my second tour of duty in July 1985, to serve as operational commander of a MiG-23ML squadron. At the time I was CFI (certified flight instructor), 1st Class, with no limitations on day or night flying … There was

another ML squadron with Angolan pilots. Most of them were novices and they were flying hard with Soviet instructors because of that. A year later, enough MLs arrived for two more squadrons …

'MiG-23UB trainers were serialled from I-20 upwards. All the instructions in their cockpits were in English. My unit operated two of them: I-20 and I-21 …'

Chapter 1, Angola, p39

The artwork below reconstructs a MiG-17F installed as a gate guard at an unknown Angolan military base in recent years, and as seen on a privately filmed video. The aircraft wears a camouflage pattern with at least two shades of green and brown on the upper surfaces, and RLB on the lower surfaces, as well as the red serial number C26 – applied in the usual size, format and style in the usual position. Curiously, it also wears the old insignia of the FAPA/DAA, indicating that the team behind the restoration work was well-versed in the history of their service. Nevertheless, it remains unknown whether this camouflage was ever worn by any Angolan MiG-17 during the fighting in the 1980s.

Tom Cooper

Chapter 1, Angola, p40 and p66

Since several readers of Volume 1 requested additional information regarding the DAAFAR MiG-23BNs deployed to Angola in 1987, we asked Ten-Col Eduardo Gonzalez (DAAFAR, ret.) to offer a corresponding commentary:

'During the Cuito Cuanavale stalemate, we shipped a full squadron of MiG-23BNs to Angola. All the aircraft were left in their original camouflage colours and wore DAAFAR serials. The unit began flying but saw no action. The MiG-23BN carried 1,200 litres [317 US gal] of additional fuel in its fuselage and could easily reach Grootfontein if launching from Menongue. Therefore, they proved a strong dissuasive factor – because they could raid SAAF bases in Namibia – as an 'ace up the sleeve' of our top commanders.

'The Soviets refused to deliver drop tanks for our MiG-23MLs. The MiG-23ML is a short-range flier, needing three drop tanks if we wanted to hit any place in Namibia. But the MiG-23BN could raid all SAAF bases there – except Ohopoho, as I

*recall – while carrying only the 800-litre [211-US gal] drop tank under the centreline.
Thus, when the Soviets said 'nyet' to our requests for drop tanks, our C-in-C threw
a hidden ace on the table: he shipped out a squadron of MiG-23BNs from Cuba. The
shipment included their drop tanks. That's the whole story.'*

Chapter 1, Angola, p46

A MiG-23ML still wearing the old FAPA/DAA markings as well as the serial number C441 was photographed in an abandoned condition - together with an unidentified Su-22M-4K - at Cuito Cuanavale in May 2011. This indicates that the aircraft was not among those donated to Cuba in 1989, or that the Cuban example wearing the serial number 441 received the same code for different reasons. (via Greg Swart)

Chapter 1, Angola, p58

In regard to the presence of Soviet and other instructors from the former Warsaw Pact,
Gonzalez explained:

*'We had four Soviet advisors/instructors who flew with my 'green' pilots, day
and night, to shape them before any was sent over enemy territory. As members of
the Warsaw Pact, the Soviet pilots could not fly combat sorties, but I asked them to
go with me and they did fly a few – without the Soviet top brass being informed.
They were ready to go with me to hell if necessary and I was very pleased with
their attitude. During Operation Second Congress, in 1985, we were flying out of
Menongue and I provided cover to Su-22s flown by a mix of Angolan and Soviet
pilots too ...*

*'In my three tours in Angola, I never met any Romanians or East Germans,
or other specialists form communist countries. I only saw an Ilyushin Il-18 cargo
aircraft from East Germany in Luanda, in 1976, and another one from Poland.
They were bringing in stuff for the struggle, but no people.'*

Chapter 1, Angola, p58

Regarding the interception of two SAAF C-130 transports on 4 April 1986, Ten-Col
Gonzalez corrected our description as follows:

*'My missile never hit that Hercules' left wing. The thud the crew felt was the shock
wave of the missile passing by at supersonic speed.'*

Chapter 1, Angola, p63

Gonzalez further offered the following, particularly interesting commentary about the handling of the MiG-23ML, based upon his first-hand experience:

'I looked up the remark on p63 of your book, about the poor manufacturing standard of Soviet-made Plexiglas. Here is a quote from the flying manual for the MiG-23ML:

'Warning: sustained and repeated flying at low altitude at speeds higher than 1,100km/h [684mph] can lead to canopy's silvering.'

'This was something that happened almost every day during the Cuito Cuanavale battle and yes, those canopies started to take on a brownish colour with a sort of web of many tiny silver 'scars' that created a misty glare on every light observed from the cockpit when night flying ... Visibility through that glass became poor. The term 'silvering' is a literal translation (of mine) from the Russian word.'

Chapter 1, Angola, p66

Regarding the South African claim of 300 Cuban casualties and 30 damaged and destroyed tanks during the clash near Tchipa on 26 June 1988, Gonzalez commented wryly:

'That goes into the same ditch as those claims for '40 South African aircraft shot down' claimed by the Angolans. From wherever they come, I cannot stand lies – even those cooked in my backyard!'

Chapter 1, Angola, p68

Arthur Ricketts, co-pilot of the Botswanan BAe 125-800 that was intercepted and damaged by an Angolan fighter in August 1988, kindly provided the following narrative regarding that incident, and for which the authors would like to extend their special thanks:

'On 7 August 1988, the Botswana Defence Force Air Wing BAe 125-800 (serial number OK-1) was tasked to fly His Excellency J. K. Quett Masire, President of Botswana, and eight other government officials from Gaborone to Luanda. The aircraft was crewed by Col Albert Scheffers, CO of the Air Wing and me, Arthur Ricketts, employed as a transport and training captain with British Aerospace. Col Scheffers had completed his type conversion in the UK and I was continuing his line training in Botswana. I had been employed on the test programme of the 125 series of aircraft for the previous eight years.

'The aircraft was cruising at FL 350 [10,668m] and had just passed a position report to Luanda after crossing over Kuito Bie. Without warning, the starboard engine of the aircraft was hit by what was later discovered to be an AA-2 Atoll missile fired from a MiG-21 of the Angolan Air Force. A second missile fired was assumed to have hit the engine after it departed the airframe. When hit, the aircraft was on autopilot. This tripped out with the impact of the missile and the aircraft pitched violently upwards, a shower of turbine and fan blades being seen by myself before I instinctively took control of the aircraft manually, rolling it off the top of a stall.

BAe 125-800 carrying the president of Botswana after emergency landing at Cuito Bie. Almost the entire mount of the right engine was shot away by a missile fired from an Angolan fighter, but Arthur Ricketts saved the aircraft and its passengers.
(Courtesy *Aviation Week & Space Technology*)

'At the point of impact Col Scheffers was rendered incapacitated by the instantaneous application of approximately 33g (calculated by the BAe stress engineers later on, based on damage to the fuselage frames), which threw him hard against the port cockpit wall, and he played no further part in the recovery of the aircraft. Also at this time the engineer travelling with us was thrown into the cockpit from the cabin. The aircraft sustained damage to the pressure cabin that resulted in an explosive decompression. At least one window was shattered by shrapnel from the engine, approximately a ton and a half of fuel was lost from the damaged starboard wing tanks, all radio navigation systems failed, and the cabin oxygen masks failed to deploy automatically.

'My first instinct was to regain control of the aircraft by rolling it away from the vertical and establishing a stable descent, which I achieved by the time we reached FL 280 [8,534m]. Initially we were descending at about 6,000ft [1,829m] a minute, which gave me almost six minutes to sort everything out before arriving very hard in Africa! In that six minutes I managed to transmit two Mayday calls, one to Luanda, which was apparently not received or understood, and the other on HF radio which was picked up and acted upon by Santa Maria in the Azores.

'I had substantial previous experience of flying in Africa and assessed that there was probably an airstrip of sorts at Kuito Bie, some 25 miles [40km] behind the point at which we were hit. During the descent I had assessed the aircraft systems remaining and had made the decision to leave selecting flaps and landing gear until shortly before landing, not expecting them to work. However, when the engine departed the airframe, the quick release couplings on the hydraulic pump, starter/generator and alternator did their job and I was able to have the use of flaps, undercarriage and brakes, certainly necessary as the damage demanded a landing speed of approximately 150–160kt.

'Several passengers received injuries in addition to the crew, and these were attended to at the hospital in Kuito Bie, before we were eventually uplifted by a Gulfstream III (registration D2-ECB), to Luanda. President Masire was injured by a fan blade that penetrated the cabin and then his seat back. He was subsequently flown to England by the RAF for treatment.

'The captain's name on the flight to Luanda was Pereira, and he kindly allowed me to fly the aircraft from the co-pilot's seat. I was repatriated to Botswana by Beech King Air 200 (registration D2-ESO) via Luena Air Base in Angola, where I saw various MiG-17s and MiG-21s, but no MiG-23s as I remember. The base was a shambles, with hangars flattened and aircraft upside down all over that very large area. But, that – as they say – is yet another story!

'The aircraft that intercepted us was said to us to have been a MiG-21. It should have fired two AA-2 Atoll missiles. The information I have about that plane and the missiles is current as of the time when this happened. I can't recollect the source, but have never seen anything different quoted.

'This is the first and only account that has been written … As you can imagine, this was a 'hot potato' at the time, which is why I never commented on various reports of the incident. The only other account I am aware of is the record of an interview I gave to Air International News at the NBAA [National Business Aviation Association] show in Dallas, in 1989 …

'I was subsequently awarded the Diploma of Outstanding Airmanship, in 1989, by the Fédération Aéronautique Internationale, an honour which is awarded only once a year. I still regularly fly and still hold a valid ATPL [Airline Transport Pilot License] at the age of 72!'

Response from Cuba

Eduardo Gonzalez offered the following commentary concerning the same incident:

'During Operation Second Congress, in 1985, I personally intercepted (with GCI support), twice a month and in broad daylight, a huge Douglas DC-10 from Mozambique, flying over Mavinga and bound for Luanda. We were very pissed off because that airway was closed for all commercial traffic – or at least we asked a number of times for it to be closed to the ATC authorities in Luanda, since it was a combat zone. Documents on this matter were signed, but to no avail.

'I do not want to act as a 'prophet of the past' now, but at those times I was sure an incident involving a civilian airliner would happen sooner or later, because violations of the war zone occurred almost on a daily basis. Remember that only two years earlier, the Soviets had shot down the South Korean Boeing 747, and only three years later – i.e. in the same year the interception of that BAe 125 occurred – an US cruiser shot down an Iranian Airbus. A responsible aircrew will never accept a flight plan that overflies a combat zone. I was terrified that if a passenger aircraft would enter that zone at night, my pilots and I could not establish a visual ID.

'We [Cubans], as the 'world's black sheep', could not afford such a mistake. That's why I instructed my pilots already in 1985 that before launching their missiles at any such target in daylight, they always had to establish a visual ID. Thus, I feel it must be told to Mr Ricketts that it was a gross mistake for them to fly across a location known by every newspaper in the universe as a war zone. Even more so with a VIP on board.

'The aircraft in question first came under fire from an Angolan SAM site near Cuito Cuanavale. They were on full readiness and attempted to identify the 'bogie'. There was no 'friendly' answer and a 'clear to fire' order was issued. They fired

Better photographs of Su-22s recently overhauled by the 558th ARZ have also appeared recently. This Su-22UM-3K two-seat conversion trainer is operated by the Esquadra de Caça-bombardeiros of the Regimento Aéro de Caça-bombardeiros from Base Aérea N°5, Catumbela.
(via D. Z.)

four missiles but all missed: they were out of tune with the fire-control radar… Meanwhile, the information was forwarded to Menongue AB and a Cuban pilot, Capt Albert Olivares Horta, scrambled in MiG-23ML C-479. He accelerated to Mach 1.9 to catch the intruder but never established a visual ID of the BAe 125 before opening fire… Horta fired two missiles. The first was an R-24T from the left-wing station no. 3. This scored a hit, and that was when Horta sighted his target for the first time. He then fired an R-24R from the right-wing station no. 4. To the luck of the crew and passengers in the targeted aircraft, this missile went astray…

'The name of the doctor who took care of all the injured was Ransin Cruz Mendez… I was not in Angola at the time, otherwise, I would keep hammering those cabrones ['bastards' in Cuban slang] *to insist on visual ID before launching…*

'C-479 was later lost due to engine-related problems. 1st Lt Eladio Avila ejected safely.'

Chapter 1, Angola, p75

The latest photos and videos of FANA MiG-23MLs overhauled and upgraded to MiG-23MLD standard by the Ukrainian company Odesaviaremservice show the aircraft armed with R-24R air-to-air missiles, possibly indicating that Angola did not purchase any R-77s, as previously reported.

This photograph of a MiG-23ML (upgraded to MiG-23MLD standard) was taken when the jet was put on display at Luanda IAP in early 2011. It shows to advantage the details of the camouflage pattern applied at the Odesaviaremservice.
(via D. Z.)

Chapter 1, Angola, p77

Further to the topic of the camouflage patterns and serial numbers of the two Angolan Sukhoi Su-27s, during recent years various scale modelling companies have issued decals for FANA Su-27s, including serial number C605 for the sole single-seater and I51 for the sole two-seater, with claims that these are based on sightings of the original aircraft. Since *African MiGs, Volume 1* was published, the authors have obtained a number of photos from various sources, showing the true serials of these aircraft, and they are included here, together with an additional artwork, for illustration.

Showing four Russian technicians that helped prepare the aircraft for delivery, this photograph was taken in front of the sole single-seat Angolan Su-27 apparently shortly before its delivery in 1998, and clearly shows the actual serial number of that aircraft: C110. (Pctcrmann Collection)

It seems that soon after its delivery, the sole Angolan Su-27 single-seater lost its serial number. This video still, taken once the aircraft entered service with the FANA, seems to be the confirmation. (Petermann Collection)

Latest photographs of the sole two-seat Angolan Su-27UB reveal details of the serial number applied – apparently in quite a crude manner and using a brush – under the forward cockpit: I100. This can be seen on all three photographs presented here, and is still present in its place. The serial number previously associated with this aircraft, namely I51, is worn by an L-39 jet trainer. (Alexander D. & Petermann Collection)

Chapter 3, Chad, pp95–97

Deliveries of Su-25s to Chad continued into 2010, with two additional examples arriving and entering service. Both are single-seaters, serialled TT-QAO and TT-QAN. The Armée de l'Air Tchadienne therefore now operates six Su-25s (see Appendix I for full information on the AAT order of battle).

Chadian Su-25 TT-OAN rolls after a post-delivery test-flight at N'Djamena IAP in 2010. (via G. Z.)

Chapter 5, Democratic Republic of the Congo, pp121-139

This photograph of a Congolese Su-25, taken inside a hangar on the military side of N'Djili IAP in 2010, shows one of two aircraft of this type that are still in service with the local air force, while being disassembled pending an overhaul. It appears that both Su-25s have since received a new camouflage pattern, and are now back in operational condition.

(via Y. T.)

This extremely rare photograph of an ex-Libyan MiG-23MS (serial number 8301) was likely taken at Kamina in around 2009, by a UN helicopter crew. It confirms deliveries of this variant to the Congo and their probable operational status during the war of 1998–2001, when Kamina was exclusively under Zimbabwean control. (Petermann Collection)

Chapter 8, Federal Democratic Republic of Ethiopia, pp182–185

Since 2010, the Ethiopian Su-27 fleet is in the process of undergoing overhauls at DAVEC. One of the aircraft appears to have received a completely new camouflage pattern while there. Notable is the fake cockpit painted on the underside of the front fuselage.

Patch of No. 5 Squadron, FDREAF

Taken at an unknown date at Debre Zeit air base, this photograph shows previously unknown Su-27UB with serial number 1907. It documents the presence of the new FDREAF roundel on the fin.
(via Pit Weinert)

Chapter 10, Republic of Guinea (Conakry), pp198–205

Photographs that recently surfaced on the internet show up to four MiG-21s that remain in service with the AAG. Two of these wear the new camouflage pattern, applied during the overhaul by Odesaviaremservice in 2007, while two others reveal the previous camouflage pattern as applied in the mid-1980s, but still quite fresh and applied in a slightly different form than on MiG-21bis serial number 662, illustrated on p205 of Volume 1. This indicates that the AAG operates more than 'at least three' MiG-21s, as previously reported.

Another photograph that recently surfaced shows the front section of the AAG MiG-21UM serial number 120:

(Pit Weinert Collection)

Chapter 11, Guinea-Bissau, pp207–211

Jacques Guillem, who kindly provided a series of exclusive photographs showing ANA/DAA MiG-15s, MiG-17s and MiG-21s, added the following commentary about the circumstances under which these were taken, as well as about various other aircraft he saw at Bissalanca IAP at the same opportunity:

'All the photos were taken on 5 November 1995. I found a total of three MiG-17Fs in shelters, plus a MiG-15UTI, two MiG-21bis, wreckage of one Alouette II and an intact Mi-8 around the apron (where some wreckage of another Mi-8 could be found too: that helicopter was set on fire during start-up and burned out). In another, closed hangar, I had a glimpse of a third MiG-21bis (same colours as the one with the serial number 75), and a MiG-21UM in light grey and medium green camouflage. Both aircraft were in much better condition than the other ones.'

Jacques Guillem provided reference for this illustration of an ANA/DAA MiG-21UM as sighted by him at Bissalanca IAP in November 1995:

Tom Cooper

Chapter 11, Guinea-Bissau, p210

A reader who prefers to remain anonymous provided the following information regarding the latest known operations by MiGs in Guinea-Bissau:

'In June 1998, an attempted coup d'état against the government of President João Bernardo Vieira led by Brig Gen Ansumane Mané triggered a civil war in Guinea-Bissau that was to last until November of the same year. Nearly all of Guinea-Bissau's armed forces defected to join the rebel junta, and they brought most of the military bases in Bissalanca under their control in the process, including the international airport, prompting the government to request support from Senegal and Guinea-Conakry. Although 1,300 Senegalese and 400 Guinean troops arrived to support the government, they were unsuccessful in regaining control of rebel-held areas. Following unsuccessful negotiations between the government and rebels in Abidjan, Côte d'Ivoire, in September 1998 the rebels began work on returning some of the aircraft and helicopters of the former ANA/DAA stored at Bissalanca IAP to operational condition. A Mi-8 was made operational with the help of spares from Libya, acquired via Gambia, followed by at least one MiG-21. I do not know who flew these aircraft nor if they ever took part in the fighting, but I saw the MiG-21 flying over Bissalanca on 22 September 1998.'

Chapter 12, Republic of Côte d'Ivoire, pp216–217

The following photograph shows one of two MiG-23MLDs – the example registered as TU-VCH – purchased by Côte d'Ivoire from Bulgaria in April 2003 and air-freighted to Lome IAP, in Togo:

(Pit Weinert Collection)

As reported in Volume 1, the two aircraft in question were exchanged for two additional two-seat Su-25UBs from Belarus, while the Togolese authorities subsequently seized both MiG-23s and they remain 'stored' at Lome until this day.

Chapter 12, Republic of Côte d'Ivoire, p222

In spring 2011, Côte d'Ivoire experienced the culmination of years of internal struggle. Widespread unrest, violence and human rights violations erupted in late 2010, after President Laurent Gbagbo refused to accept his electoral defeat and leave the presidency. The reorganised insurgent forces from the north of the country sided with election winner Alassane Outtara and in late February advanced beyond the ceasefire lines dating from the civil war in 2004-05. During the following month, the insurgents captured all of western Côte d'Ivoire, thus severing links between the forces that remained loyal to Gbagbo and Liberia.

In late March, insurgents launched a major offensive on Abidjan, reaching the city within barely a week. The fighting that culminated in chaotic firefights through the streets of Abidjan ended with arrest of the former President Gbagbo on 11 April 2011.

While the rebel forces appear to have received some support from French and UN combat helicopters deployed in Côte d'Ivoire, and which destroyed a number of vehicles (including several BMP-2s) operated by the forces loyal to the former President Gbagbo, the latter appear not to have managed to reactivate any FACI assets, left in a state of disrepair following the end of the First Civil War in 2005.

1   The Su-22s that received the local 'Su-22M-4' designation in Angolan service were of the variant designated S-32-92 by the manufacturer, and exported under the designation 'Su-22'.

2   For details about the MiG-17AS and its service with the Air Defence and Air Force of Cuba, see Guevara y Moyano, *Latin American Fighters: a History of Fighter Jets in Service with Latin American Air Arms*, Harpia Publishing, 2009, pp113–114.

Chapter 13

MALAGASY REPUBLIC (MADAGASCAR)

Overview

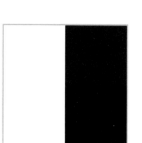

Granted independence by France on 26 June 1960, the Malagasy Republic concluded mutual defence and military assistance agreements with France. These agreements provided aid for maintaining internal security and also covered basing rights, transit and overflight privileges, and military training and aid. Under the arrangement France maintained headquarters for Overseas Zone 3 (Indian Ocean) and a garrison of about 2,500 men at the Diego-Suarez naval base, plus detachments at Ivato and Antsirabe air bases. French forces in the Malagasy Republic also included one squadron of Douglas A-1D Skyraider attack aircraft and six Nord Noratlas transport aircraft. West Germany also provided military assistance during the mid-1960s, while the country allowed Britain's Royal Air Force to use its airfields while patrolling the Mozambique Channel against tankers smuggling oil to Rhodesia, from 1966 until 1971.

The Malagasy Republic established a sizeable air transport arm, equipped with different types left behind or supplied by the French. As of 1970, the air arm included 400 men and operated 10 transport aircraft, 11 liaison aircraft, 3 trainers, and 10 helicopters. These were operated from air bases at Arivonimamo (Tananarive), Ivato (Tananarive), Diego-Suarez, Fort Dauphin, Tamalave, Majunga and Tulear.[1]

In the early 1970s there was a radical change in Franco-Malagasy relations, after the government in Antananarivo requested the withdrawal of French forces, this being completed in 1975. During the same year, Ivato air base was constructed and the High Command of the future air force was established. During the following years, Madagascar gradually began acquiring air defence equipment, followed by aircraft and helicopters, from North Korea and then the USSR, resulting in the acquisition of MiG-17s and MiG-21s.

During the 1980s, relations with France improved again, but in 1991 France was requested to withdraw its troops again in the face of internal unrest. Since then the condition of the Armée de l'Air Malgache (AdAM) has declined considerably. Most of the surviving MiGs were put into storage at Ivato, and the AdAM was reoriented towards maritime patrol tasks, pilot training and VIP transport.

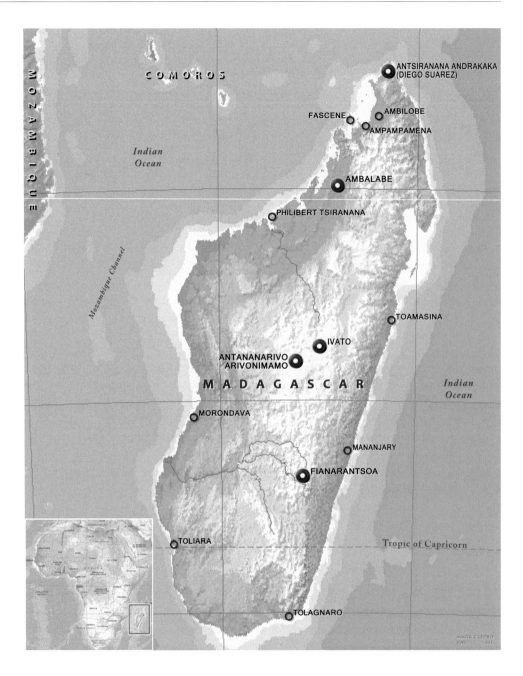

Map of Madagascar

Deliveries of MiG fighters to Madagascar and force structure

Reports of deliveries of up to eight MiG-21PFMs from the USSR (sometimes reported as 'MiG-21FLs') cannot be confirmed, even although Madagascar is known to have received its first Mi-8 helicopters in 1976, followed by two An-26 transports in 1980. North Korea provided four MiG-17Fs to the AdAM in 1979, and these were first shown in public in summer 1980, by which time the single Escadrille de Chasse had become operational.

Although manufactured in the early 1950s, and despite years of service with the Democratic People's Republic of Korea Air Force (DPRKAF), MiG-17F serial number 113 arrived in Madagascar in near-pristine condition – and still bearing traces of DPRKAF insignia. (Albert Grandolini Collection)

The most curious marking applied on ALM MiG-17F serial number 242 was the red star in front of the left side of the cockpit. This might commemorate an unknown kill scored by this aircraft while it still served with the DPRKAF. (Philip Colin)

The last known photograph of Malagasy MiG-17s shows three examples in a derelict condition at Arivonimamo. (Sobika)

MiG-21bis serial number 138 as seen in the late 1990s, after several years in open storage and already with some spares removed.
(via Albert Grandolini)

Despite reports of the delivery of the improved MiG-21bis to Madagascar by around 1980, as well as the establishment of the Fighter School at Base Aérienne Tactique Arivonimamo (BATAC) in 1984, the presence of 10 MiG-21bis and two MiG-21UMs can first be confirmed in the period between 1990 and 1995, their operational status continuing until 2001. Generally, the MiGs were flown during various official celebrations and most were eventually put into 'active storage' at Arivonimamo and Ivato. Plans for their eventual upgrade in Russia or Israel were discussed in 2003, but were never realised, since Madagascar lacks the finances and the infrastructure required to maintain supersonic aircraft.

National markings

Adopted in 1959, the national marking consists of the three colours of the national flag: red, white and green, outlined in yellow. This device was introduced as a fin flash on the MiG-17Fs, which wore no roundels. In contrast, the MiG-21bis acquired in the 1990s did not wear fin flashes, but received roundels in the same colours, also outlined in yellow. These were applied on the forward fuselage below the cockpit, as well as on the lower surfaces of both wings (although not on the upper surfaces).

Malgasy MiG-21s flew seldom and spent most of their careers stored. This is a front view of MiG-21bis serial number 169 inside a hangar at Ivato, near Antananarivo.
(Christophe Gasztych via Albert Grandolini)

Some dozen MiG-21s were finally stored under spartan conditions at Ivato (in the foreground is MiG-21UM serial number 339). Announcements concerning possible overhaul and modernisation with European or Israeli support were made, but never realised. (Christophe Gasztych via Albert Grandolini)

Camouflage colours and serial numbers

AdAM MiG-17s provided by North Korea were left in overall natural metal colours. The previous North Korean markings were relatively crudely removed, and their traces could be seen on most aircraft. Reportedly, at least one MiG-17F had its nose painted red, and also wore the AdAM crest on the forward fuselage, but various corresponding artworks that appeared since the 1990s cannot be confirmed by sightings or photographic evidence.

MiG-21bis and MiG-21UM jets arrived in an overall 'air superiority grey' scheme. Serial numbers were applied on the fin, in black, or sometimes in dark blue. In addition, the title 'TAFIKA ANABAKABAKA' ('Air Force') was applied on the forward fuselage. Known serial numbers are as follows:

Table 25: Serial numbers of AdAM MiGs, 1975-99

Aircraft type	Serial number	c/n	Remarks
MiG-17F	113		Ex-DPRKAF; AdAM insignia on the nose; last seen 1990s at Arivonimamo
MiG-17F	242		Ex-DPRKAF; AdAM insignia on the nose; open storage at Arivonimamo, 2005
MiG-17F	933		Ex-DPRKAF; AdAM insignia on the nose; open storage at Arivonimamo, 2005
MiG-17F			Ex-DPRKAF; last seen at Ivato, 1990s
MiG-21bis	108		Stored in 1997; to scrap yard at Ivato in 2007
MiG-21bis	138		Stored in 1997; to scrap yard at Ivato in 2007
MiG-21bis	164		Stored in 1997; to scrap yard at Ivato in 2007
MiG-21bis	169		Stored in 1997; to scrap yard at Ivato in 2007
MiG-21bis	173		Stored in 1997; to scrap yard at Ivato in 2007
MiG-21bis	204		Stored in 1997; later donated to City Kindergarten at Arivonimamo
MiG-21bis	211		Stored in 1997; to scrap yard at Ivato in 2007
MiG-21bis	233		Stored in 1997; to scrap yard at Ivato in 2007
MiG-21bis	255		Stored in 1997; to scrap yard at Ivato in 2007
MiG-21bis	266		Stored in 1997; to scrap yard at Ivato in 2007
MiG-21UM	291		Stored in 1997; later donated to Technical School at Arivonimamo
MiG-21UM	339		Stored in 1997; to scrap yard at Ivato in 2007

This insignia (left) was applied on the forward fuselage of all AdAM MiG-17s, and appears to have been the patch of the Commandement de la Premiére Escadron Malgache (1er ESCAMA). However, a similar insignia, though with the number 1 in orange, is known to have been applied on at least one AdAM C-47, too.

MiG fighter operations in the Malagasy Republic

Malagasy MiG fighters are sometimes said to have seen combat service during one of the small-scale insurgencies in the country, in the 1990s, but no specific details are known. Overall, the aircraft were rarely flown and spent most of their careers in 'active storage'.

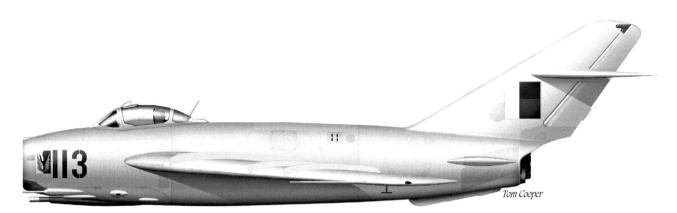

The first of four MiG-17Fs delivered to Madagascar by North Korea in 1979. The aircraft probably retained its North Korean serial number, and had the insignia of the 1er ESCAMA applied on the forward fuselage.

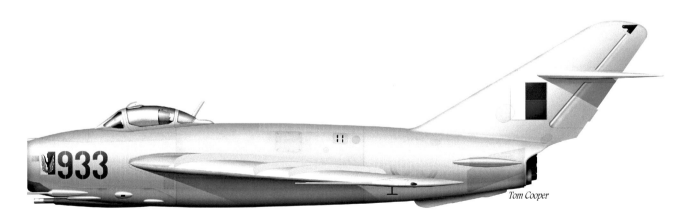

Like the other two known MiG-17Fs of the AdAM, the third example – serial number 933 – also clearly showed traces of Democratic People's Republic of Korea Air Force insignia on the rear fuselage.

Last seen while still operational at Ivato in 1997, this is the second of two MiG-21UMs delivered to the AdAM. It saw only brief service and was put into 'open storage' at Ivato a few months later.

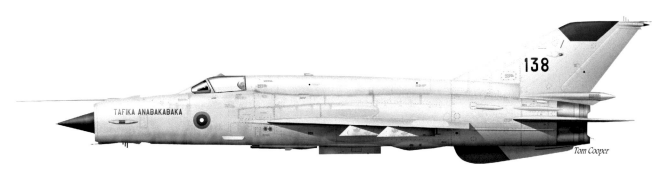

MiG-21bis serial number 138 was the second aircraft of this variant received by the Escadrille de Chasse during the mid-1990s. In addition to the title 'TAFIKA ANABAKABAKA' ('Air Force') and the serial number applied in black on the fin, it wore roundels in six positions.

Like all AdAM MiG-21s, MiG-21bis serial number 355 was painted in 'air superiority grey' overall and wore the usual service title and markings (including roundels in six positions).

1   Dupuy, *The Almanac of World Military Power*, p225.

Chapter 14

REPUBLIC OF MALI

Overview

Originally formed as a component of the French colony then known as French Sudan, this territory was reorganised into the then autonomous Federation of Mali in 1959. The Republic of Mali separated from Senegal and was released into independence by France on 22 September 1960.

An air arm was formed in 1961, initially with some French help, but subsequently foremost with assistance from Czechoslovakia. This was equipped with two Douglas C-47s, two MH.1521M Broussards, and five Aero 145s.[1] The government then severed its ties with Paris and remained outside the French Community, establishing relations with Czechoslovakia and then the USSR instead. The first two Mil Mi-4 helicopters were delivered from the USSR in 1962, and by 1971 the Republic of Mali had received military assistance from Moscow worth over USD20 million, including Yakovlev Yak-18 training aircraft, MiG-17 jet fighters and armament, five Antonov An-2s, and training of personnel, plus small arms, military vehicles and artillery.[2]

Throughout the 1970s, and particularly following the first confrontation with Burkina Faso over the Agacher Strip, the Republic of Mali continued to acquire small numbers of Soviet aircraft, including two Antonov An-24s and one An-26 transport. These deliveries enabled an expansion of the air arm into the Force Aérienne de la République du Mali (FARM; according to other sources, the correct designation is 'Armée de l'Air du Mali'), on 6 February 1976. The FARM saw an intensive first combat deployment during the Agacher Strip War of 1985. In reaction to that conflict, the air arm was then expanded through the acquisition of MiG-21 fighters and several SA-3 SAM sites.

In the early 1990s the Malian Army was briefly deployed in the north of the country to quell a Tuareg rebellion over land, cultural and linguistic rights. On this occasion, FARM involvement was limited to providing support through helicopter operations.

In recent years, the FARM has mainly flown helicopters with the purpose of suppressing rebels operating from Niger. Operations against terrorists associated with al-Qaeda have often been reported as taking place in the north of the country. However, these seem to be more related to government attempts to obtain financial aid from the US.

One of at least three MiG-15UTIs delivered to Mali is now on display as a gate guard at Bamako-Sénou air base, wearing a camouflage pattern consisting of colours recently applied on FARM MiG-21s and the fake serial number 'TZ-001'.

Deliveries of MiG fighters to Mali

Mali received five MiG-17Fs and one MiG-15UTI in around 1965, the aircraft being provided by the USSR and/or Czechoslovakia. Several replacement aircraft, including at least 1 MiG-15UTI, followed sometime between 1971 and 1974, before a batch of 12 MiG-21bis and at least 4 MiG-21UMs was provided by the USSR, probably in 1985 or 1986. One MiG-21UM is known to have crashed on 12 July 1989, and the majority of the fleet was stored inside a hangar at Bamako air base by 1991. Despite this, at least a portion of the fleet remained operational, since another MiG-21 reportedly crashed on 6 March 1996, killing its pilot. The small FARM MiG-17 fleet was abandoned during the early 1990s and was largely left to rust in the open at Sévaré air base, near Mopti. A few aircraft have meanwhile reappeared as gate guards. Two MiG-21bis appear to have been overhauled (they at least received a fresh coat of paint and new cockpit canopies) in around 2002, but have seldom been flown.

The second FARM MiG-15UTI, the serial number of which is known to be TZ-366, photographed within the military compound at Mopti/Sévaré air base (originally Barbé, later Hambodedjo International Airport) in 1999.
(Jacques Guillem)

FARM MiG-17F serial number TZ-346 was photographed in an abandoned condition at the former Base Aérienne 101, in Bamako-Sénou, in 2008. Contrary to usual practice, this aircraft wore relatively small roundels in six positions.
(E.B. via Jean-Luc Debroux)

By 1999, FARM MiG-17F serial number TZ-339 was in a derelict condition after spending several years in open storage at Base Aérienne 102 in Mopti-Sévaré. (Jacques Guillem)

When photographed at Mopti-Sévaré in 2008, FARM MiG-17F TZ-360 wore only the sad remnants of its former camouflage pattern, but at least the serial number and national marking applied on the fin, as well as the Soviet-made underwing pylon, were still to be seen to some advantage. (E.B. via Jean-Luc Debroux)

In 2005 an unnamed Czech company exported two disused MiG-21MFs and a single MiG-21UM to Mali. One of the single-seaters made an emergency landing in a field outside Gao on 10 October 2007, and its current status is unknown. The other two MiGs are reportedly still operational, and have meanwhile been reinforced through the addition of at least four Mil Mi-24 assault helicopters purchased from Bulgaria.

MiG-17F TZ-365, and all other MiG-15s and MiG-17s with higher serial numbers, have received camouflage in the same colours (although applied in varying patterns), with light grey (or caramel), light or azure blue and dark blue on the upper surfaces, and light blue on the lower surfaces. (Jacques Guillem)

Obviously camouflaged according to a similar pattern as TZ-365, MiG-17F TZ-367 appears to have had a dark green colour applied in place of the dark blue.
(E.B. via Jean-Luc Debroux)

It was probably TZ-367 that was subsequently patched up, painted in an entirely new camouflage pattern and installed as a gate guard at Bamako-Sénou.
(E.B. via Jean-Luc Debroux)

MiG-17F TZ-368 was one of the most intact examples found at Mopti-Sévaré as of 1999. Of special interest are the details of the pylon usually used for carrying UB-16-57 pods for unguided rockets of 57mm (2.24in) calibre, and widely installed on Soviet MiG-17Fs in the early 1960s.
(Jacques Guillem)

Force structure

The FARM is known to have established three air bases over the years, including Base Aérienne 100 in Bamako (no longer operational), Base Aérienne 101 in Bamako-Sénou (which remains the major air base to this day), and Base Aérienne 102 in Mopti-Sévaré. Several minor airfields were (or still are) under military control, including Base Aérienne Dogofry (mainly used for agricultural flying), Base Aérienne Tombouctou (at the international airport), Base Aérienne Gao and Base Aérienne Kayes.

In terms of organisation, four transports originally delivered by France in 1961 entered service with the Escadrille de Transport, based at Senou air base. Initially flown and maintained by Soviet personnel while Malian personnel received training, MiG-17s entered service with an Escadrille de Chasse, also stationed at Base Aérienne 100, in the mid-1960s. Since the mid-1980s the same unit has flown the MiG-21s from the new main air base at the international airport of Bamako-Sénou. In 1983 an Ecole de Pilotage (Flight School) was established at Sénou AB.

Map of Mali

MiG-21bis TZ-372 entered service with the FARM in the mid-1980s but was in storage by the mid-1990s and was never flown again. Serving as an interceptor and fighter-bomber, the type was equipped with the usual, simplest arsenal consisting of R-3S and R-13M AAMs, as well as UB-16-57 rocket pods.
(E.B. via Jean-Luc Debroux)

Although delivered around the same time as MiG-21bis TZ-372, TZ-377 sported a very different camouflage pattern. The aircraft also displayed the original form of serial application when photographed for the last time, in 2008.
(E.B. via Jean-Luc Debroux)

In this photograph from 2008, TZ-378 can be seen in a camouflage pattern applied relatively recently, indicating that this aircraft was locally overhauled and saw some additional service in more recent times.
(E.B. via Jean-Luc Debroux)

Right-hand view of MiG-21bis TZ-381, which shows the opposite side of the same camouflage pattern applied on TZ-378.
(E.B. via Jean-Luc Debroux)

National markings

FARM national markings consist of the pan-African colours of red, yellow and green. Most combat aircraft received a roundel applied on the fin instead of a fin flash. Roundels were also applied on the upper and lower surfaces of each wing, but not necessarily on all aircraft. There appears to have been at least one MiG-17F on which roundels were applied on the upper surface of the starboard (right) wing and – apparently – the lower surface of the port (left) wing only.

When it comes to the MiG-21bis, the situation is entirely unclear, since there are no photographs showing the upper or lower surfaces of either wing. More recently acquired MiG-21MFs seem to have received national markings in six positions (including the upper and lower surfaces of both wings).

Port view of the front of MiG-21bis TZ-382. Notable is the relatively large roundel applied on the fin, as well as remnants of up to 10 R-3S and R-13M AAMs, and a single RS-2US (lying on the ground): such old weapons were seldom exported to Africa, and were mainly used for training purposes.
(E.B. via Jean-Luc Debroux)

Taken at Bamako-Sénou in 1991, this photo shows six FARM MiG-21bis – including TZ-377, TZ-385 and TZ-381 – already in storage, but still wearing their original camouflage patterns.
(US DoD)

Slightly more than 10 years later, MiG-21bis TZ-385 looked much the worse for wear. Even though receiving some fresh brown paint in several areas in the meantime, it was hardly ever flown after 1991.
(E.B. via Jean-Luc Debroux)

Camouflage colours and serial numbers

In terms of camouflage colours and serial numbers, the small fleet of FARM MiG-15UTIs and MiG-17Fs is one of the best-documented in all of sub-Saharan Africa, even though these aircraft were painted in several different camouflage patterns.

One of the patterns applied included irregular stripes of light blue or caramel, blue and azure blue (or dark green, in one instance); another comprised irregular stripes of yellow sand or light earth and dark green, and a third consisted of light green, olive green and chocolate brown.

Malian MiG-21bis originally wore a variant of the standardised camouflage pattern for exported examples of this version. This consisted of beige, dark brown and dark olive green, applied in a wavier pattern than was the case with most MiG-21bis exported to countries like Congo-Brazzaville or Mozambique. MiG-21UMs arrived painted in beige or dark tan, various shades of green and/or green and brown, applied in very varied patterns. Sometime in the first half of the 1990s, the FARM introduced its

Starboard view of MiG-21UM TZ-358 as seen in 2007, while the aircraft was still stored inside a hangar at Bamako-Sénou.
(E.B. via Jean-Luc Debroux)

Port (above) and starboard views of MiG-21UM TZ-384, which was overhauled and repainted sometime in the 2000s, and saw several additional years of service before being replaced by additional examples acquired from the Czech Republic.
(E.B. via Jean-Luc Debroux)

own camouflage pattern on at least two MiG-21bis that underwent local overhaul, this consisting of light green, dark green and two shades of brown. A similar pattern was applied on one MiG-21MF and the sole MiG-21UM acquired from Czechoslovakia, more recently.

The three ex-Czech Air Force aircraft delivered in 2005 arrived each painted in a different colour: TZ-356 was camouflaged in pink sand, dark blue-green, dark brown and apple green; TZ-357 wears light grey overall; and TZ-375 is camouflaged in sand, green, dark blue/green and brown.

Table 26: Known serial numbers of FARM MiGs, 1964-2009

Aircraft type	Serial number	c/n	Remarks
MiG-15UTI	TZ-001		Serial number is fake; gate guard at Bamako/Senou as of 2009
MiG-15UTI	TZ-337?		White overall, stored at Bamako-Sénou as of 2005
MiG-15UTI	TZ-366		Open storage in Mopti/Sévaré, last seen November 1999
MiG-17F	TZ-339		Open storage in Mopti/Sévaré, last seen November 1999
MiG-17F	TZ-346		Open storage at Bamako-Sénou, last seen April 2008
MiG-17F	TZ-348		
MiG-17F	TZ-360		Open storage at Bamako-Sénou, last seen 1999
MiG-17F	TZ-365		Open storage in Bamako-Sénou, last seen November 1999
MiG-17F	TZ-367		Gate guard at Musée de l'Armée, Bamako, 2008
MiG-17F	TZ-368		Open storage at Bamako/Senou, last seen November 1999
MiG-21UM	TZ-002		Serial number is fake, now gate guard at Bamako-Sénou, formerly TZ-377?
MiG-21MF	TZ-356	96005512	Formerly CzL 5512, last seen at Bamako-Sénou, 2005; reportedly non-operational due to technical problems
MiG-21MF	TZ-357	96005508	Formerly CzL 5508, last seen at Bamako-Sénou, 2006
MiG-21UM	TZ-358		Open storage at Bamako/Senou, last seen April 2008
MiG-21UM	TZ-364		Apparently overhauled around 2001; open storage at Bamako-Sénou, last seen April 2008
MiG-21bis	TZ-371		Open storage at Bamako-Sénou, last seen 2005
MiG-21bis	TZ-372		Open storage at Bamako-Sénou, last seen April 2008
MiG-21UM	TZ-375	516999341	Formerly CzL 9341, last seen at Bamako-Sénou in 2006
MiG-21UM	TZ-376		Last seen May 2006 at Bamako-Sénou
MiG-21bis	TZ-377		Open storage at Bamako-Sénou, last seen April 2008; to gate guard TZ-002?
MiG-21bis	TZ-378		Apparently overhauled around 2001; open storage at Senou, last seen April 2008
MiG-21bis	TZ-381		Apparently overhauled around 2001; last seen around that time
MiG-21bis	TZ-382		Open storage at Bamako-Sénou, last seen April 2008
MiG-21bis	TZ-383		Open storage at Bamako-Sénou, last seen April 2008
MiG-21bis	TZ-385		Open storage at Bamako/Senou AB, last seen April 2008

Crest of the Force Aérienne de la République du Mali

Patch FARM MiG-21

Patch FARM RightShoulder

One of the FARM MiG-21UMs withdrawn from service – probably the former TZ-377 – is now serving as a gate guard at Base Aérienne 101 in Bamako-Sénou, wearing an entirely new camouflage pattern that closely resembles that of MiG-21s operated in recent years. (E.B. via Jean-Luc Debroux)

MiG fighter operations in the Republic of Mali

Malian MiGs appear to have seen no combat service before 25 November 1974, when the first short conflict erupted with Burkina Faso over the Agacher Strip. In the course of a few border skirmishes, registered on 25 November, as well as on 14, 16 and 18 December, one FARM MiG-17 crashed under unknown circumstances, sometime in late November, killing the pilot. Subsequently, a ceasefire was agreed and fighting stopped.

Tensions began to increase again in 1985, during another lengthy period of drought, just like the one that preceded the conflict in 1974. The drought came to an end in October 1985, but when the rain began to fall it washed away most of the roads and led to the outbreak of a cholera epidemic, adding to the misery and making it impossible to distribute food to the population. Midway through this catastrophe, the government of Burkina Faso organised a general population census, in the course of which census agents visited some camps inside Mali by mistake. The government of Mali protested against this violation of its sovereignty and immediately prepared a military response. The situation escalated and by 20 December the Malian military was gearing up for a war, deploying a number of truck patrols along the border, while MiGs flew combat air patrols and reconnaissance missions high over the border. Eventually, on 25 December 1985, the Malian military launched several local attacks against Burkinabe border posts and police stations.

The FARM was relatively well equipped by this time and was in possession of some reserves of spares and weapons. It could also call upon six major airfields with runways longer than 2,500m (8,202ft), as well as no fewer than 22 unpaved strips around the country. The air arm operated a reasonably well-developed radar network that could support MiG-21 operations. Despite some problems faced when operating in hot climatic conditions, the radar network proved capable of supporting navigation over the relatively featureless and flat terrain of the Agacher Strip. In addition to interceptors, the FARM operated two SA-3 batteries for the protection of Sénou air base. Malian defence doctrine envisaged waiting for the first strike to be delivered by a foreign aggressor, with the FARM then reacting with air defence – and perhaps a few interdiction – sorties. However, the presence of the SA-3s probably precluded the AdAB (Armée de l'Air Burkinabé – Air Force of Burkina Faso, see Volume 1, Chapter 2 for details) from even attempting to fly anywhere near Sénou.

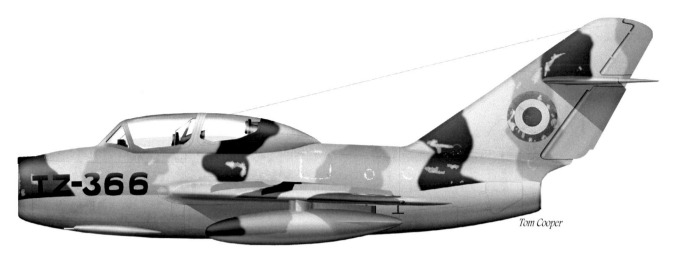

The sole FARM MiG-15UTI that remained intact long enough for its original camouflage pattern to be photographed was TZ-366. Colours included light blue-grey (or caramel), light blue and dark blue on the upper surfaces. The aircraft is known to have had roundels applied in six positions.

MiG-17F TZ-339 was unusual in having received particularly large roundels on the fin, but apparently none on the wings. The exact reason for this measure is unknown.

While wearing a very similar camouflage pattern to MiG-17F TZ-368, shown below, the darkest colour applied on TZ-367 was apparently dark green, rather than dark blue. It is unclear if any roundels were applied on the wings of this aircraft.

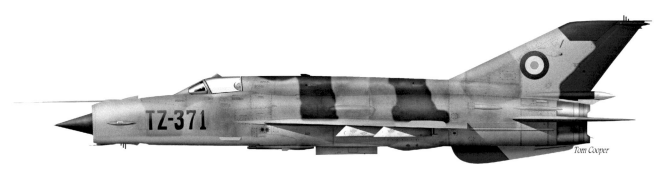

Shown in its original camouflage pattern – the same as applied on most the aircraft of this variant exported in the mid-1980s – MiG-21bis TZ-371 had its serial number applied in a quite unusual fashion.

A reonstruction of the camouflage as applied on the port side of MiG-21UM TZ-376, based on a relatively poor photograph from the late 1990s, when it was already in 'open storage' at Bamako-Sénou.

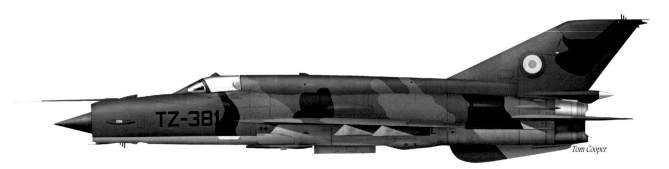

Also overhauled in the late 1990s was MiG-21bis TZ-381. Curiously, it seems the aircraft received a fresh coat of paint only on the upper surfaces and sides, as well as on the underwing pylons.

MiG-21bis TZ-383 is shown still in its original – albeit already worn-out – camouflage colours, and with the weapons known to have been supplied to the FARM, including (from left to right): R-3S and R-13M air-to-air missiles, the UB-16-57 pod for unguided rockets and a 400-litre (106-US gal) drop tank.

The second ex-Czech MiG-21 delivered to Mali was TZ-357. It arrived painted in overall air superiority grey. Latest photographs show it overpainted in the same camouflage pattern as a number of MiG-21bis subjected to local overhaul in the late 1990s, and wearing a serial number applied in white.

Most recent photographs of this MiG-21UM delivered from the Czech Republic show it overpainted in the same pattern as MiG-21MF TZ-357. Interestingly, the cartoon on the forward fuselage was retained even after the entire aircraft had been repainted.

The military of Burkina Faso was still in the process of mobilisation and Army units were rushed into the Agacher Strip. In response to the first few counterattacks, and using the airfields in Gao, Mopti and Ségou to stretch the critically short range of its MiGs, the FARM then deployed MiG-17s for strikes against a number of selected targets. The sole AdAB MiG-17 was scrambled several times, but due to poor radar coverage never managed to intercept any of the intruders. Much more importantly, both sides employed their transport aircraft and helicopters for troop deployment along the border, as well as to haul supplies.

The first ceasefire had been negotiated by Libya by 26 December, but collapsed almost immediately. Correspondingly, Burkinabe counterattacks into Mali continued, the situation culminating with a strike by FARM MiG-17s against the marketplace in Ouhigeouya, in which a number of civilians were killed. This attack came as a complete surprise to Burkina Faso and demonstrated not only the capabilities but also the determination of its opponent.[3] Considering the fact that this town is at least 80km (50 miles) inside Burkina Faso, as well as over 300km (186 miles) from the nearest FARM air base in Mopti, it is evident that the MiGs operated at the limits of their combat endurance.

Nigeria and Libya then negotiated another ceasefire, to take effect on 29 December, under the auspices of the Organisation of African Unity (OAU). This failed, and fighting continued as the Army of Burkina Faso attempted to recover some of the ground lost previously. Finally, the next ceasefire, agreed for 30 December, held and eventually the two governments reached an agreement and stopped fighting.

The Agacher Strip War lasted only five days. Nevertheless, fighting was bitter and resulted in between 59 and 300 killed, and a similar number of injured soldiers and civilians on both sides. (Mali never provided its casualty figures, while Burkina Faso declared that it lost 'more than 40, including many civilians'.) The eventual resolution for the conflict was reached during further negotiations in early 1986, followed by a judgement concerning the demarcation of the common border by the International Court of Justice in September 1983.[4]

Malian MiG-21s remain operational, and sometimes fly combat sorties against the rebels in the north of the country, despite frequent technical problems. The MiG-21MFs purchased from the Czech Republic have also suffered from maintenance issues and one of them made a safe emergency landing near Gao on 9 October 2007.

1 Information on Czechoslovak assistance kindly provided by Martin Smisek on the basis of original Czechoslovak documentation. This indicates that the Aero 145s were paid for in kind (by peanuts), but that the type did not prove particularly well suited to African conditions. In September 1965, Mali officially requested the three surviving aircraft to be bought back by Czechoslovakia. Prague offered five L-200 Moravas modified for military purposes, and training for Malian pilots and technicians instead, but it remains unknown if any related deal was reached.

2 Dupuy, *The Almanac of World Military Power*, p229. According to information provided by Martin Smisek, Mali initially had only two crews (each consisting of three) for the DC-3s, and four technicians qualified on that type. Additionally, four pilots and four technicians were trained by four Czechoslovak instructors, the last of which left Mali in 1967.

3 It is not entirely certain if this attack was indeed flown by FARM MiG-17s, MiG-21s, or by transport aircraft.

4 Based on contemporary media reports as well as Maj Sory Ibrahim Kone (FARM), *Doctrine for a Smaller Air Force: Mali and the Question of Unique Air Doctrine*, a research paper presented to the Research Department Air Command and Staff College, USAF, 1997 (AU/ACSC/97-0604I/97-03).

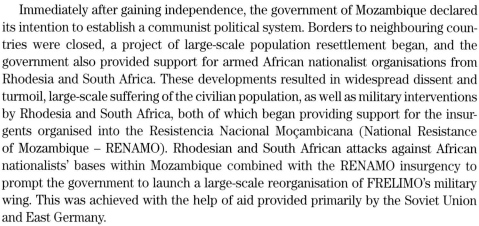

Chapter 15

REPUBLIC OF MOZAMBIQUE

Overview

Colonised by the Portuguese in 1505, the Republic of Mozambique became independent from Portugal on 25 June 1975, following almost 10 years of bitter COIN warfare waged by insurgents of the Frente de Libertaçâo de Moçambique (Liberation Front of Mozambique – FRELIMO). The fighting resulted in the departure of almost the entire Portuguese population.

Immediately after gaining independence, the government of Mozambique declared its intention to establish a communist political system. Borders to neighbouring countries were closed, a project of large-scale population resettlement began, and the government also provided support for armed African nationalist organisations from Rhodesia and South Africa. These developments resulted in widespread dissent and turmoil, large-scale suffering of the civilian population, as well as military interventions by Rhodesia and South Africa, both of which began providing support for the insurgents organised into the Resistencia Nacional Moçambicana (National Resistance of Mozambique – RENAMO). Rhodesian and South African attacks against African nationalists' bases within Mozambique combined with the RENAMO insurgency to prompt the government to launch a large-scale reorganisation of FRELIMO's military wing. This was achieved with the help of aid provided primarily by the Soviet Union and East Germany.

The Portuguese left behind a small but relatively well-developed infrastructure in Mozambique. This included one major air base, three large and three smaller airfields, and around a dozen landing strips. Portugal also left behind several North American T-6G Texans as well as a few other light aircraft and helicopters, including seven Noratlas and five C-47s. Some of these aircraft were pressed into service as the initial equipment of the Força Aérea Popular de Moçambique (People's Air Force of Mozambique – FAPM), established in 1976. Immediately afterwards, the first groups of FAPM personnel were sent to the USSR for training.

Rumours concerning the delivery of the first fighter jets to Mozambique surfaced as early as 1977, but cannot be confirmed. However, South Africa took the affair very seriously and constructed an extensive air base at Hoedspruit, near the mutual border. It was only in 1979 that the FAPM began receiving its first large shipments of combat aircraft and helicopters, as well as transport aircraft, which were almost immediately rushed into the COIN war against RENAMO.

Throughout the 1980s the FAPM was expanded through additional deliveries of aircraft and equipment from the USSR. However, by 1986 it had become clear that

Three East German Air Force technicians with one of the MiG-15UTIs delivered from their country to Mozambique in September 1981.
(Jürgen Roske)

the government could not prevail in the war against RENAMO, and the expected acquisitions of more modern aircraft were put on hold following changes within the government in Maputo, as well as a large-scale reorganisation of the military. Although foreign troops, including Zimbabweans, remained deployed in the country, the last Soviet advisors were withdrawn in 1988, and the war gradually came to an end by 1992, by which time most of the FAPM combat fleet was already grounded.

Deliveries of MiG fighters to Mozambique

According to Russian sources, the first 24 or 25 MiG-15UTI and MiG-17 jets were delivered to Nacala in late 1979. They arrived together with a group of Soviet technicians who assembled them, and five pilots who test-flew them.[1] By summer 1980, 2 MiG-15UTIs and 24 MiG-17s could be counted in Maputo. In August 1980, East Germany delivered a further 12 MiG-17Fs (many of which were actually Polish-built Lim-5s, all adapted as fighter-bombers) and 2 MiG-15UTIs. All were overhauled and had their remaining service lives lengthened through appropriate measures before delivery to 'Country 58', as Mozambique was designated by former East German Intelligence.[2] The assembly and training of Mozambican pilots for ex-East German aircraft were actively supported by a contingent of East German Air Force (LSK/LV) technicians and pilots that assembled and flight-tested all the MiGs at the facility formerly occupied by the Portuguese OGMA, in Maputo, prior to their handover to the FAPM in Beira.

In November 1981, Mozambique requested from Czechoslovakia the delivery of L-39s, MiG-17s and MiG-21s, as well as instructors. This request was turned down by Prague, which donated a sizeable shipment of infantry weapons and ammunition instead. A similar request was issued to the Czechoslovak defence minsiter during his visit to Maputo in February and March 1983, but was once again turned down.[3]

Reports concerning the delivery of an additional batch of MiG-17s and MiG-15UTIs in 1981, and another in 1983, cannot be confirmed, but it seems that Mozambique did receive some additional aircraft of either type as attrition replacements and to serve as advanced trainers, in 1984. Despite relatively light losses in the course of the

Colour photographs of former East German MiG-17Fs and Lim-5s in FAPM service appear to be non-existent. This recently taken photograph shows the forward part of a surviving example that appears to have ended its days as a gate guard at Beira.
(via Petermann)

war against RENAMO, only a handful of FAPM MiG-15UTIs and MiG-17s remained operational by 1991.

The first examples of the MiG-21bis arrived from the USSR between 1983 and 1984. Available reports indicate deliveries of no fewer than 48 aircraft of this type from 1983, mostly based at Beira, but also including a small number of MiG-21Rs based at Nacala. Plans for the delivery of four MiG-21UMs and four MiG-21Rs were agreed with Moscow in 1989, but were never realised, even although some Soviet instructors for these aircraft arrived in the country.[4] Fuel shortages resulted in most of the fleet being grounded by 1990, and most MiG-21s had become unserviceable by 1992. The few airframes that remained operational were concentrated within a hangar at Nacala, although the building was in a terrible condition only two years later.

Force structure

The organisational structure of the FAPM apparently closely followed that of the Soviet Air Force. Over time, the FAPM established two fighter regiments, one equipped with MiG-17s and the other with MiG-21s.[5]

Based at Beira, the first fighter regiment became operational after Mozambican pilots returned from training in the USSR in 1981, and was expanded through the addition of a squadron flying ex-East German MiG-17Fs, in late 1981.[6] The same regiment subsequently re-equipped with MiG-21s and its remaining MiG-15s and MiG-17s were gradually phased out.

A second regiment was formed upon the arrival of additional MiG-21s, operating a squadron of the type at Nacala and Maputo respectively. Each of these units included at least two, or perhaps even three fighter squadrons of between six and eight aircraft. The different squadrons were apparently indicated by the manner in which serial numbers were applied, as discussed below. Sadly, the exact designations of specific FAPM units remain unknown.

In addition to Beira, Maputo and Nacala, MiGs were operated from Luabo, and possibly from Quelimane.

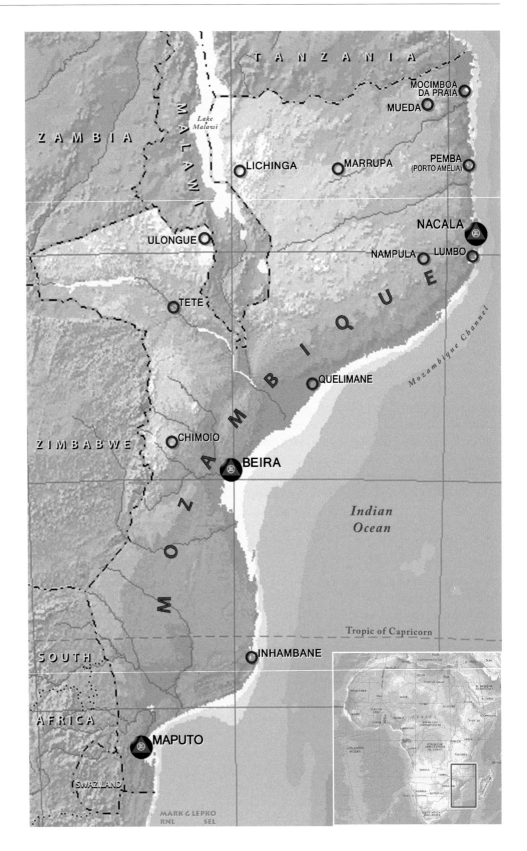

Map of Mozambique

A rare top-view of a FAPM MiG-17 (photographed during testing of an aircraft flown to South Africa by a defecting pilot, in 1981), showing to advantage the position of the national markings as applied on the upper surfaces of the wing. (Claudio Tosselli Collection)

National markings

Most, although by no means all, FAPM combat aircraft usually wore roundels applied in six positions (including the fin) on MiG-15UTIs and MiG-17Fs, and in at least two positions (generally on the fin) on MiG-21s.

The roundel consisted of a black field on which a red triangle was superimposed, and included various devices applied in yellow: a book, a hoe, and a rifle, all within a yellow gearwheel.

Camouflage colours and serial numbers

The majority of FAPM MiG-15UTIs and MiG-17Fs received an overall coat of RLB before their delivery from the USSR. All MiG-15UTIs were painted grey overall, and some might have had their wingtips painted orange. They usually wore large, Soviet-style Bort numbers on the forward fuselage, applied in red and outlined in black.

MiG-17Fs and Lim-5s delivered from the LSK/LV were primarily distinguishable from Soviet-delivered MiG-17s on account of their large inboard underwing pylons for Mars unguided rocket pods (a Polish-made variant of the Soviet UB-16-57 rocket pod), as well as the RV-UM radio altimeter antennae, which replaced the small T-shaped antennae normally mounted under the wings, as well as their 'afterburner cans'. The former LSK/LV aircraft arrived in their original camouflage, consisting of earth brown and olive drab on the upper surfaces (patterns differed from aircraft to aircraft) and light blue undersides. The aircraft retained maintenance and warning stencils characteristic of the LSK/LV, albeit applied in Portuguese. Such stencils were particularly evident in the cockpit area. Following their transfer to Beira in 1981, at least one former LSK/LV aircraft was over-painted in RLB overall, and it is possible that the same colour was applied on other ex-East German MiGs in subsequent years.

All FAPM MiG-21bis received the same standardised camouflage pattern for exported aircraft of this variant, as applied before delivery during the mid-1980s.

Although of poor quality, this rare photograph showing several FAPM MiG-21bis inside a hangar at the former Beira air base, in the early 1990s, shows the application of serial numbers in several different colours, as well as the fact that many of these aircraft never received national markings on their fins.
(AM via Alvaro Ponte)

This consisted of beige, light green and dark green. FAPM MiG-21s with lower serial numbers apparently received red Bort numbers, consisting of three digits applied in red and outlined in white (or yellow). Higher serial numbers were usually applied in blue, outlined in black. It is possible that the final batch received their Bort numbers in yellow, again outlined in black, but it is at least as likely that reports about sightings of such aircraft are actually based on sightings of MiGs that had their camouflage colours and markings practically 'washed out' by the sun and rain.

Table 27: Known serial numbers of FAPM MiGs, 1978-91

Aircraft type	Serial number	c/n	Remarks
MiG-17	01		Derelict in Beira, 1997
MiG-17	02		Derelict in Beira, February 1997
MiG-15UTI	04	922259	Ex-LSK/LV
MiG-17	07		Last seen in Beira, 1991
MiG-17	16		Last seen in Beira, 1991
MiG-17	17		Last seen in Beira, 1991
MiG-15UTI	20		Ex-LSK/LV, last seen in Beira, 1980
MiG-17	21	5238	Flown to South Africa, 8 June 1981; returned; last seen derelict in Beira, February 1997
MiG-17F	23		
MiG-17	24		Last seen in Beira, 1991
MiG-17	26		Derelict in Beira, February 1991
Lim-5	128	1C08-22	Formerly LSK/LV 210; delivered in August 1981
MiG-17F	129	0619	Formerly LSK/LV 211
Lim-5	130	1C06-14	Formerly LSK/LV 314; delivered in August 1981
Lim-5	131	1C06-22	Formerly LSK/LV 322; delivered in August 1981
MiG-17F	132	0479	Formerly LSK/LV 393
Lim-5	133	1C06-19	Formerly LSK/LV 519; delivered in August 1981
Lim-5	134	1C06-28	Formerly LSK/LV 528; delivered in August 1981
Lim-5	135	1C09-19	Formerly LSK/LV 569; delivered in August 1981
Lim-5	136	1C08-24	Formerly LSK/LV 757; delivered in August 1981; derelict in Beira, 1991
Lim-5	137	1C06-16	Formerly LSK/LV 886; delivered in August 1981
MiG-17F	138	7134	Formerly LSK/LV 910; delivered in August 1981; derelict in Beira, 1991
Lim-5	139	1C08-16	Formerly LSK/LV 911; delivered in August 1981
MiG-15UTI	150	922259	Czech-Built, ex-LSK/LV; delivered in August 1981
MiG-15UTI	170		Derelict in Beira, February 1997
MiG-15UTI	180		Derelict in Beira, February 1997
MiG-21bis	201		
MiG-21bis	202 red	75095084	
MiG-21bis	203	75095095	
MiG-21bis	204	75095103	
MiG-21bis	205		
MiG-21bis	206		

MiG-21bis	207		
MiG-21bis	208 red		Derelict in Beira since early 1990s
MiG-21bis	209		
MiG-21bis	210		
MiG-21bis	221	75096037	
MiG-21bis	222	75096055	
MiG-21bis	223 blue		Derelict in Beira since early 1990s
MiG-21bis	225 blue		
MiG-21bis	226	75096105	
MiG-21bis	227	75096124	
MiG-21bis	228	75096176	
MiG-21bis	229	75096182	
MiG-21bis	231 blue	75096189	
MiG-21bis	232		
MiG-21bis	233 blue		
MiG-21bis	236		
MiG-21bis	237		
MiG-21bis	238		
MiG-21bis	239		
MiG-21bis	240		
MiG-21bis	241 blue	75096524	Derelict in Beira since early 1990s
MiG-21bis	242	75096601	
MiG-21bis	243		
MiG-21bis	244	75096608	
MiG-21bis	245	75096624	
MiG-21bis	246		
MiG-21bis	247 blue	75096782	Derelict in Beira since early 1990s
MiG-21bis	249	75096782	

MiG fighter operations in the Republic of Mozambique[7]

FAPM MiGs saw extensive combat service in the course of the Mozambican Civil War, which erupted in 1977 after a Rhodesian-instigated RENAMO insurgency spread through the country. Over time, RENAMO expanded into a powerful insurgent force, stronger even than FRELIMO at its peak during the war against the Portuguese. The regular Mozambican military lacked training, equipment, motivation and leadership, and was completely unable to defeat the opposition. The situation became even more obvious after the Rhodesian Air Force bombed the headquarters of the 3rd Mozambican Brigade, where Soviet instructors were also stationed. As a result, the government in Maputo requested help from the USSR and several Warsaw Pact countries, and later from several of its neighbours.

The Soviets were first to react, providing training and equipment. However, it took the FAPM some time to establish, organise and prepare for combat operations. Even although Moscow originally granted fighter aircraft and advisors to Mozambique on the condition that Soviet personnel would not become involved in combat operations,

Crest of FAPM

One of two MiG-15UTIs that crashed in shortly after delivery to Mozambique, in 1981, while flown by Soviet pilots. Although the aircraft was completely wrecked, the crew escaped without major injuries. (Michail Chmyhov Collection)

Soviet and other foreign 'advisors' did fly at least some operational sorties during the first phase of this conflict in the late 1970s and the early 1980s. At this time, the majority of Mozambican personnel were still undergoing training in the USSR.[8]

With the exception of various adventures by Soviet pilots, and the experiences of East German personnel that helped with the introduction of the MiG-17, very little is known about FAPM activities during this period. Among the facts that are known, two MiG-15UTIs were written off during their post-assembly test flights, while flown by Soviet pilots.[9] The remaining four Soviet instructors took part in the fighting against RENAMO, some of them completing up to 250 combat sorties, and often in conjunction with the FAPM An-26s, equipped with bomb shackles for four 500kg (1,102lb) bombs. One of the reasons was that the armament of the MiG-17s delivered from the USSR was limited to the three internal cannon: the two underwing hardpoints were usually reserved for drop tanks.[10] Most MiG-17 operations proved very limited in terms of duration and were undertaken at flight levels between 1,200 and 1,800m (3,937-5,906ft), mainly because the MiG-15 and MiG-17 suffered from excessive fuel consumption when operated at lower levels.

In 1979, together with Zambia, Mozambique found itself on the receiving end of a series of South African and Rhodesian raids undertaken against camps belonging to various insurgent movements. The FAPM was clearly in no condition to react to these, and the appearance of its MiGs was reported only once, by the crew of a South African Air Force (SAAF) Canberra, under way on a reconnaissance mission. Similarly, no SAAF raids against Mozambican SAM sites were reported before March 1983, even although at least one South African UAV was shot down by a SAM while flying a reconnaissance mission over the Maputo area later that year.

Zimbabwean aid, provided from 1982, proved much more important, both in terms of troop deployment and operations by the highly experienced Air Force of Zimbabwe (AFZ; see Chapter 23 for details). Between 1982 and 1986, the Zimbabwe

On 8 June 1981, FAPM Lt Ty Bomba defected to South Africa while flying MiG-17 serial number 21. The South African Air Force subjected the aircraft to an extensive series of test-flights before returning it to Mozambique – by road (this photograph shows Bomba's MiG-17 accompanied by a SAAF Mirage F.1AZ).
(Albert Grandolini Collection)

Defence Forces (ZDF) deployed almost 12,000 troops in Mozambique, primarily along the strategically important Beira corridor – a land, rail and pipeline link along which most imports and exports flowed into and out of landlocked Zimbabwe. However, even more important than the troop presence itself was the fact that the Zimbabwean forces – and the AFZ in particular – not only possessed extensive training and experience in COIN operations, but also operated suitable equipment. The AFZ mainly deployed helicopters, but also Reims-Cessna FTB-337G and SIAI-Marchetti SF.260W Gannet light attack aircraft into Mozambique. These aircraft played a significant role in local COIN operations, usually closely coordinated with Zimbabwean SAS, the Parachute Battalion and the Commando Group of the ZDF.

By 1984 the first FAPM MiG-21s had also become available. These jets were almost immediately involved in fighting in the Beira and Mutare areas. Reports subsequently surfaced implying that Ethiopian or even Zimbabwean pilots flew some of these aircraft. This cannot be confirmed, although it seems that a fair quantity of FAPM combat sorties were still undertaken under the full leadership of Soviet advisors.

Nevertheless, by that time the Mozambican military had been defeated in several major engagements with RENAMO, and then weakened by large-scale defections. Under pressure, the government in Maputo entered negotiations with South Africa, reaching an agreement (known as the Nkomati Treaty) under which the two countries would withdraw their support from insurgent organisations operating against each other.

In early 1985 the Soviets delivered additional arms and equipment, and the ZDF contingent in Mozambique was significantly increased. On 25 August of that year, Zimbabwe launched a major COIN operation against insurgent bases in the Gorongosa area, the main RENAMO stronghold. In the weeks leading up to this operation, the AFZ and Zimbabwean SAS conducted several reconnaissance operations, which helped them establish a very precise order of battle of their opposition.

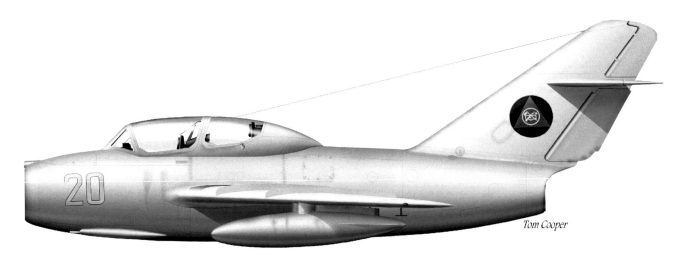

Tom Cooper

An ex-East German MiG-15UTI, as seen immediately after reassembly following delivery to Beira in September 1981. The type appears to have been painted in RLB overall, and to have worn only the national markings and a serial number.

Tom Cooper

The majority of ex-Soviet MiG-17s delivered to Mozambique in the early 1980s were painted in RLB overall and wore large, Soviet-style Bort numbers in red, outlined in black, on the forward fuselage. The MiG-17 flown by Lt Bomba, depicted in this artwork, was no exception to this rule.

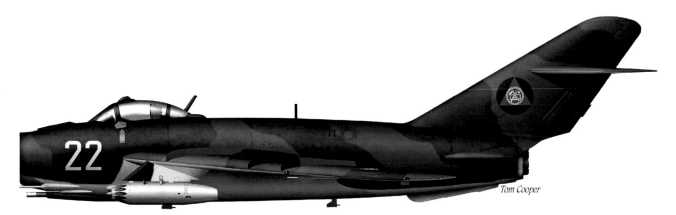

Tom Cooper

A reconstruction of one of the former East German MiG-17Fs delivered to Mozambique in 1981. While still in service with the LSK, the aircraft was upgraded to Lim-5 standard in Poland through the addition of underwing hardpoints for Mars-5 rocket pods or FAB-100 bombs. It retained the camouflage pattern as applied long before delivery, although the serial number 22 was assigned in Mozambique.

Before South Africa discontinued aid to RENAMO, it supplied the insurgents with a number of heavy machine guns and even some MANPADS. The new offensive began with a series of fierce strikes by AFZ Hawker Hunters and BAe Hawks, flown out of Thornhill air base in Zimbabwe, against RENAMO AAA positions. Zimbabwean and Mozambican helicopters were then used for the heliborne deployment of the Zimbabwean 1st Parachute Group, which was delivered directly into insurgent strongholds. This was followed by a ground advance by the Mozambican Army from Vila Paiva de Andrada, supported by yet additional attacks flown by FAPM fighter jets. The insurgents fought bitterly and claimed at least two Mozambican fighter-bombers and several helicopters as shot down, but proved unable to hold their ground in the face of this onslaught. Casa Banana, RENAMO's HQ with an 800m (2,625ft) airstrip, was captured on the first day of the operation, and by 2 September the government in Maputo was able to declare this offensive successful.

Prior to the Zimbabwean offensive of August 1985, RENAMO operated in larger groups from bases that were relatively easy to reach. In the aftermath, only smaller insurgent groups remained active, these being organised depending on their task. A series of minor attacks against Indoro, Nhamatanda, and Vuruca in mid-September 1985 proved that RENAMO was back in action. Undaunted, Zimbabwe and Mozambique then launched another major attack against Xichocoxa, some 60km (37 miles) north of Pnada, and Matungame, some 50km (31 miles) from Maputo. In the process, the last remaining major insurgent bases were destroyed.

In early 1986 the ZDF contingent in Mozambique was significantly decreased in size. Gorongosa was soon back in the hands of RENAMO, which also overran the garrison in Vila Paiva da Andrada. Once again, help was requested from Zimbabwe, but also from Malawi, Tanzania and Zambia. Correspondingly, the ZDF – in cooperation with the Zambian and Tanzanian militaries – launched another offensive. However, the insurgents learned of this operation – reportedly supported by no fewer than 17 FAPM MiG-17s and MiG-21s, in addition to Zambian Air Force MiG-21s and AFZ fighter-bombers – in advance and withdrew from Gorongosa. As a result, the attack hit an empty base. This time, Zimbabwe constructed an airstrip in Vila Paiva de Andrada to ease the flow of supplies for its troops, but also for potential use in future deployments.

One of at least six MiG-21s operated from Beira in the late 1980s was 'Blue 223'. Although still nearly new and in excellent condition, it was abandoned, together with all the other aircraft inside the same hangar, only a few years later. (via Pit Weinert)

The FAPM reportedly acquired up to 48 MiG-21bis, practically all of which were painted in different variations of the camouflage pattern usually applied on examples of this variant exported in the mid-1980s. 'Red 202' was one of the earliest examples in service, operated by the first of two FAPM fighter regiments, and thus had its serial number applied in dark red. It is shown carrying a single FAB-250ShN parachute-retarded GP bomb.

Either the second FAPM regiment, or the second squadron of the first regiment operating MiG-21s, used to apply serial numbers in dark blue, outlined in black, on its aircraft. This MiG-21bis is shown carrying a ZB-500 napalm tank, as frequently used during the fighting with RENAMO insurgents in the mid-1980s.

Another weapon commonly used by the FAPM was the omni-present UB-16-57 rocket pod. Note that the use of 800-litre (211-US gal) drop tanks under the centreline and up to two 400-litre (106-US gal) drop tanks on the outboard underwing pylons (not shown on this artwork) was obligatory in Mozambique, due to the considerable distances over which these aircraft had to operate. Most centreline drop tanks were painted in beige on the upper surfaces, with RLB lower surfaces.

The war remained relatively static until October 1986, when the first president of the Republic of Mozambique was killed in the crash of a Tupolev Tu-134 airliner. In the course of the next few weeks, RENAMO fighters entered Sambesia Province and overran all the local garrisons. Indeed, the insurgents considered their position strong enough to declare war on Zimbabwe, and launch attacks against ZDF outposts along the Beira corridor. The year 1987 thus began with the government in Maputo reorganising and retraining its army to make it more capable of conducting COIN operations. Meanwhile, military contingents from Malawi, Tanzania, Zambia and Zimbabwe were reinforced once again. The allies then launched a series of small-scale operations – all proceeded by air raids flown by the AFZ and FAPM, and perhaps also by ZAF fighter-bombers. These strikes hit RENAMO almost simultaneously in several parts of Mozambique, eventually turning the tide of the war against the insurgents.

In August 1987 a further large-scale offensive was launched against insurgents in Sambesia Province, this being followed by another operation in November, targeting the RENAMO base in Matsenquenha. These two attacks inflicted such heavy losses on the insurgents that they never recovered. Thereafter the government retained control of most of the vast country even after the withdrawal of some 800 Soviet advisors in 1988.

Although the civil war in Mozambique was to last for another five years, political reforms introduced by the government in the late 1980s removed the reason for the existence of RENAMO. Correspondingly, most of the remaining FAPM MiG-17s and MiG-21s had been deactivated by 1991, and were subsequently put into storage, never to fly again.

Table 28: Confirmed and reported attrition of FAPM MiG fighters, 1977–91[11]

Date	Aircraft	Serial number	Pilot/crew	Remarks
1979	MiG-15UTI		Mikhail V. Chmyhov (Soviet advisor) and FAPM student recovered	Engine failure during post-assembly test flight near Nacala; crash landed and w/o
1979 or 1980	MiG-15UTI			W/o during post-assembly test flight
9 February 1983	MiG-17		Capt O. A. Muthemba KIA	W/o under unclear circumstances
16 April 1985	MiG-17			Claimed shot down by RENAMO
16 April 1985	MiG-17			Claimed shot down by RENAMO
28 August 1985	MiG-17			Claimed shot down by RENAMO during engagement in Casa Banana area
28 August 1985	MiG-21bis		Pilot, supposedly Ethiopian, reported as KIA	Claimed shot down by RENAMO during engagement in Casa Banana area
6 October 1985	MiG-17			Claimed shot down by RENAMO during engagement near Majanga de Costa
6 October 1985	MiG-17			Claimed shot down by RENAMO during engagement near Majanga de Costa

9 October 1985	MiG-17	Tte M. Muiambo KIA	Crashed into sea off Beira
10 October 1985	MiG-21bis		Claimed shot down by RENAMO during engagement near Luabo
12 April 1986	MiG-21bis		Claimed shot down by RENAMO during engagement near Gorongosa
20 November 1988	MiG-17		
13 June 1989	MiG-21bis		Claimed near Beira IAP
26 July 1989	MiG-21bis	Pilot KIA	Crashed into Nacala Bay

Entries in bold signify confirmed losses.

1   *Russia (USSR) In the Wars in the Second Half of XX Century*, Chapter 4: The Armed Struggle of the Mozambican People for Freedom and Independence (1965–1979).

2   'NVA Flugzeuge in Afrika; Einstmals streng geheim', *Fliegerrevue*, Volume 6/1992, pp16–19.

3   Information based on official Czechoslovak documentation, kindly provided by Martin Smisek.

4   *Russia (USSR) In the Wars in the Second Half of XX Century*, Chapter 4: The Armed Struggle of the Mozambican People for Freedom and Independence (1965–1979). Note that available Russian sources usually cite 1985 as the year in which the first FAPM MiG-21 unit was established.

5   In addition to two fighter regiments, the FAPM operated one transport regiment (including a squadron of An-26s and Mi-17s each, and a flight of Mi-25s, manned by Soviet crews), and at least one SAM brigade equipped with S-125/SA-3 SAMs, which became operational as early as 1982.

6   'NVA Flugzeuge in Afrika; Einstmals streng geheim', *Fliegerrevue*, Volume 6/1992, pp16–19. According to the same report, the Soviets were not especially happy with the East Germans helping the Mozambicans establish an entire fighter-bomber squadron manned by FAPM pilots within the shortest possible time. This success caused some jealousy on the part of the Soviet advisers and prompted them to discourage Mozambican pilots – already limited by the higher stick-forces and more complex weapons system of the MiG-17F when compared to those of the MiG-17 – from deploying these aircraft to their full potential.

7   Largely based on Turner, *Continent Ablaze*, pp126–150 and Flintham, *Air Wars and Aircraft*, p122, and expanded through addition of reference materials from subsequently published works and some first-hand sources.

8   Indeed, even as of 1984, the C-in-C FAPM was still a foreigner: the (North) Vietnamese Maj Gen Hama Thai.

9   'I crashed a Military Aircraft in the Jungle' by Michail Chmyhov (in Russian), *Irpin Bulletin* (Ukraine), April 2009

10 'NVA Flugzeuge in Afrika; Einstmals streng geheim', *Fliegerrevue*, Volume 6/1992, pp16–19.

11 This list is based on all available sources, including various printed periodicals, books, TV and other media reports, the internet, and also some first-hand sources. The list should not be considered complete, and only the entries marked in bold can be considered as confirmed.

Chapter 16

REPUBLIC OF NAMIBIA

Overview[1]

The Republic of Namibia came into existence as the German colony of South West Africa (SWA). The country came under British and then South African supervision during and after World War I, and was then administered by South Africa until released into independence on 21 March 1990.

In 1966 the South-West Africa People's Organisation (SWAPO) established its military wing, the People's Liberation Army of Namibia (PLAN). This force then launched an insurgency against South African rule, demanding direct responsibility over the territory. SWAPO changed the name of SWA to Namibia in 1968, and in 1973 was recognised by the UN as the official representative of the Namibian people. However, the South African security forces and military, later supported by locally recruited security forces under South African control (South West African Territorial Force – SWATF), prevented SWAPO from establishing itself within the territory and kept it out of the country until 1989.

Upon independence, the PLAN and SWATF were largely disarmed, but some of their elements were integrated into five battalions and a small headquarters element that became the basis of the emerging Namibia Defence Force (NDF). During the 1990s the NDF was carefully and patiently developed into a highly professional and capable force, reinforced through an air wing operating a miscellany of light transport and liaison aircraft, as well as helicopters. The development of the Namibian Defence Force Air Wing (NDFAW) was somewhat hampered by losses suffered during the country's intervention in the Second Congo War (for details, see Volume 1, Chapter 5). However, the air arm subsequently received a boost through material aid supplied by Angola and Libya. In particular, this assistance was provided in reaction to the outbreak of an insurgency in the Caprivi Strip, clearly supported by the Angolan insurgent organisation UNITA, as well as the Zambian government.

On 13 March 2005 the Namibian Air Force (usually referred to by its unofficial designation 'Namibiese Lugmag' – NL), was officially established at Grootfontein air base. Its mission involves support of NDF ground and naval forces, as well as protecting the territorial integrity of the country and national interests.

Deliveries of Chengdu F-7 fighters to Namibia

In late 1999, apparently in reaction to reports of the arrival of MiG-23s scheduled to enter service with an air arm maintained by UNITA insurgents in Angola, up to four MiG-23s were reportedly delivered to Grootfontein under very strict security. The exact details of this affair remain unknown, and it is possible that it was based on fake reports, since it is certain that no MiG-23 ever entered service with the NDFAW.

Instead, a major project for NDFAW expansion was launched in 2000, apparently in reaction to first-hand experiences from the war in the Democratic Republic of the Congo, where the Namibian military was actively involved in fighting on the side of the government, and against several insurgent groups, as well as troops from Rwanda, Uganda and Burundi.

Groups of Namibians were sent for training in China, and at the same time the Namibia Aviation Training Academy (NATA) was established at Eros airport, near the Namibian capital Windhoek, with German support. Most cadets sent to China began their study with ground courses organised by the Chinese CATIC company, within the framework of paramilitary training on Nanchang CJ-6 trainers. This was followed by advanced training on the Hongdu K-8 Karakorum jet trainer. Indeed, the Chinese are known to have developed a K-8 simulator with a special programme for Namibia.

As the training of future pilots and ground personnel progressed, in late 2004 Namibia ordered 12 Chengdu F-7NMs and a pair of two-seat FT-7NM conversion trainers. The first five NDFAW jet pilots officially completed a three-month conversion course in early March 2005, immediately after arrival of the first two F-7NMs. These initial jets were delivered by CATIC to Grootfontein direct from China on board chartered Antonov An-124 transports. The fighters arrived on 23 February 2005, and were then assembled by Chinese technicians. The second group of Namibian student pilots for the F-7, including one female, completed training on 12 August 2005. Two additional groups graduated in 2006, by which time all the remaining F-7NMs had arrived in Namibia.

The F-7NM with serial number 0313 during pre-delivery testing in China in early 2005. (via Pit Weinert)

The F-7s delivered to Namibia belong to a variant of the J-7MG as built for Chinese People's Liberation Army service, and include a single-piece windshield and a cranked delta wing (the most obvious feature of this version), as well as extensive Western avionics, including a nav/attack system centred around the Italian-made Grifo NG radar.

The Namibian F-7s were officially inaugurated into service on 23 June 2006, during festivities for Namibia's Independence Day. The first two FT-7NM two-seaters were delivered on 23 October 2006, and it is possible that the NL fleet was subsequently reinforced through further aircraft from Chinese production.

Force structure

Originally constructed by South Africa in the 1970s, Grootfontein air base is not only the largest airfield in Namibia, but is currently also the primary NL base and is home to the F-7 fleet – operated by No. 23 Squadron of the Air Defence Wing. The Chinese are meanwhile constructing a new airfield at Karibib, which should become the future base of the NL's Flying School (which operates one Air Wing Training Squadron). The latter unit was established at Grootfontein in 2005, with Chinese support.

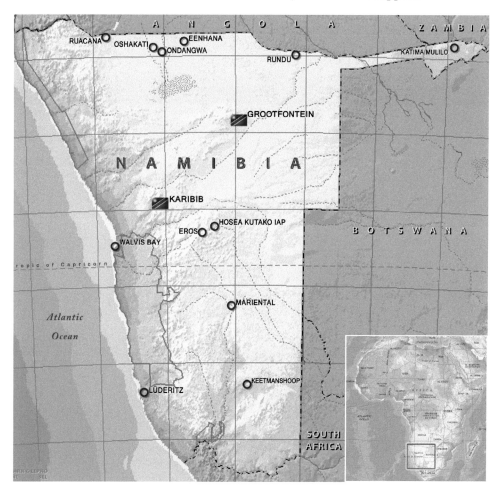

Map of Namibia

National markings

Aircraft and helicopters operated by the NDFAW formerly wore the national flag as a fin flash. The colours of the flag include red, white, green, blue and golden-yellow. A small light-blue roundel with white and dark blue devices was sometimes also applied on the rear fuselage.

In line with the creation of the NL in 2005, all K-8s and F-7s have ever since worn a new and much more complex roundel. This consists of a pair of blue wings over a large golden wreath (all outlined in black), with the official crest of Namibia at the top. It is currently unclear as to whether these roundels are also applied on the wings.

Camouflage colours and serial numbers

F-7NM fighters delivered to Namibia wear a camouflage pattern consisting of yellow sand and light green colours on the upper surfaces, and a dark variant of RLB on the lower surfaces. The jets are marked with sizeable, four-digit serial numbers on the forward fuselage, and also have an anti-glare panel applied in black, in front and around the cockpit.

The latest photographs and videos show that the 'F-7NM' titles, applied before delivery on the upper surfaces of the mid-fuselage, have since been removed.

Table 29: Known serial numbers of NL F-7s, 2005–09

Aircraft type	Serial number	c/n	Remarks
F-7NM	0310	0310	Last seen Grootfontein, 2006
F-7NM	0311	0311	Last seen Grootfontein, 2007
F-7NM	0313	0313	Last seen Grootfontein, 2006
F-7NM	0314	0314	Last seen Grootfontein, 2006
F-7NM	0315	0315	Last seen Grootfontein, 2010
F-7NM	0316	0316	Last seen Grootfontein, 2006
F-7NM	0317	0317	Last seen Grootfontein, 2010
F-7NM	0319	0319	Last seen Grootfontein, 2006
F-7NM	0321	0321	Last seen Grootfontein, 2010
FT-7NM	0330	0330	Delivery in 2006, last seen 2009
FT-7NM	0331	0331	Delivery in 2006, last seen 2011

MiG and Chengdu fighter operations in the Republic of Namibia

The requirement for air defence was plainly illustrated to Namibia during the short conflict with Botswana over the Kasikili Islands in October 1992. During the conflict, aircraft of the Botswana Defence Force violated Namibian airspace on several occasions without facing any opposition.

The NDFAW was first blooded during the country's intervention in the Democratic Republic of Congo, launched in cooperation with the local government, Angola and

As delivered to Namibia, the double-delta F-7NM is equipped to a very high standard, including an advanced, GPS-assisted nav/attack platform centred around the FIAR Grifo radar, Martin-Baker ejection seats, digital RWRs and an assortment of modern Chinese-made weapons, including (from left to right): PL-9 AAMs, 250kg GP bombs, and six-round pods for rockets of 80mm (3.15in) calibre.

A notable feature of the camouflage pattern of Namibian F-7NMs is the sharp edges of the light green fields and a highly polished finish, thanks to a top cover consisting of clear lacquer. Technically, the manufacturing quality of these aircraft is excellent, indicating significant advances made in China over recent years.

The FT-7 is a Chinese-made variant of the MiG-21U, stretched in length through the installation of a plug that contains the locally manufactured variant of the Soviet-made GSh-23 cannon. Contrary to F-7NMs, these aircraft retain the original (single) delta wing, but this is capable of mounting a total of four pylons, the outboard examples being plumbed for carriage of drop tanks.

Crest of NL

Zimbabwe, in August 1998. In the early days of the Namibian intervention, some 21 tons of weapons stored at Grootfontein were picked up by two Força Aérea Nacional (Angolan Air Force – FANA) aircraft. A roughly brigade-sized force of the NDF, including some 2,000 troops, was then flown by chartered transport aircraft to Lubumbashi, where they mainly fought in support of loyalist units of the Congolese Army. Two NDFAW officers are known to have lost their lives in two separate accidents in the course of the Namibian involvement in the Congo, one of which occurred in December 1998, and the other in January 1999. Five other officers and NCOs were killed in the night-time collision of two NDF helicopters, later in January 1999.

Delivery of as many as four MiG-23s to Grootfontein in late 1999 and early 2000 was widely reported, but never officially confirmed. There is no evidence that the NDF ever operated this type of fighter jet and subsequent investigation into this affair proved that most of the corresponding reports were unreliable. More likely, the reports in question were related to the delivery of two Mi-8s and two Mil Mi-25s by Libya. These helicopters were likely supplied to Namibia as part of the same project that saw Libya provide Mi-8s to the DRC and finance the acquisition of Mi-35s by Zimbabwe.

In August 2000, a previously unknown and inactive separatist group launched a series of attacks on security forces' installations in Namibia's Caprivi Strip. Apparently made possible by assistance from UNITA insurgents in Angola, as well as the governments of Botswana and Zambia, these attacks were primarily motivated by UNITA's wish to 'punish Namibia for its role in the Congo War'. In particular, this conflict had seen the demise of a government that had supported Angolan insurgents for decades. UNITA insurgents also reportedly attacked several Namibian border villages. It is possible that some FANA MiGs were deployed to Namibian bases in reaction to this crisis, as well as during subsequent Angolan military operations against the UNITA insurgency within southern Angola.

Namibian F-7s, officially introduced to service in mid-2006, are not known to have seen combat service. No. 23 Squadron is developing its capabilities relatively slowly, reports indicating that the training of the first Namibian F-7 pilots was incomplete by the time they returned from China in 2005. As a result, two Chinese pilots flew F-7s (and both the NL's K-8s) during festivities for Namibia's Independence Day on 23 June 2006. The situation improved following the delivery of the two FT-7s, which – according to Chinese reports – enable a 'systematic approach' to the training of Namibian pilots, a number of which are since known to have qualified on the type.

1   Background information acquired from reports published by republikein.com.na website, Chinese media
    reports and the Namibia Defence Force magazine.

Chapter 17

FEDERAL REPUBLIC OF NIGERIA

Overview[1]

Nigeria came under British administration in the 19th century before gaining independence on 1 October 1960. Declared a federal republic of 36 states in 1963, Nigeria was slow to develop an air arm, since the government did not see the need for a flying branch of the military.

The origins of the Nigerian military can be tracked back to 1863, when the Hausa Constabulary was formed by the British colonial authorities. The Constabulary metamorphosed into the West Africa Frontier Force and then the Nigerian Regiment, established in 1956, by which time the need to protect the long Nigerian coastline and its rich natural resources had prompted the authorities to create the Nigerian Navy.

The position of the government in regards of establishing an air force changed once the country became independent and was called upon to participate in the UN-led intervention in the Republic of the Congo in the early 1960s, and also to help quell military insurrections in Tanganyika (now Tanzania) in 1959. In the course of both operations the Army was forced to rely on civil and foreign military transport aircraft to convey its troops and logistics to these theatres.

In January 1964 the Air Force Act was enacted by parliament and accepted by the government, which meanwhile approached a number of countries for assistance in the training of Nigerian pilots and ground personnel. While negotiations were held with Canada, Ethiopia, India and West Germany, for the training of personnel, the Nigerian Air Force was established on 18 April 1964, with parliament's passage of the Air Force Act.

Work on establishing the NAF had been under way since an earlier date, however, with the first group of 10 Nigerian cadets accepted for training with the Ethiopian Air Force in July 1962. The second group of 16 was accepted by the Royal Canadian Air Force in February 1963. Six others were sent to the Indian Air Force in 1963, and a fourth – much smaller – batch meanwhile began their training in the US.

Most influential for the initial development of the NAF proved to be its cooperation with West Germany, which accepted a group of no fewer than 84 NAF officer cadets on 2 August 1963. Additionally, a 75-man German advisory group led by Col G Katz – who acted as the first Chief of the Air Staff NAF – arrived in Nigeria to help train additional personnel.

Local flying training began on 3 November 1965, when the Germans launched a course for the first 18 trainees – including a mix of cadets trained in Canada, Ethiopia

and India – at Kaduna air base. The aircraft used were Piaggio P.149 primary trainers of Italian origin, and Dornier Do 27 light transports of German origin.

On 24 November 1965, a new German team under Col Wolfgang Timming took over from Col Katz, and by May 1966 around 513 personnel had passed through training facilities in Germany. The number of trained personnel was expected to rise to 1,500 by 1967, by which time the NAF also had planned to have 100 qualified pilots.

As early as 1964 the government had decided to 'Nigerianise' the air force. For this purpose, a number of high-ranking Army officers were transferred to the NAF to understudy the Germans and form a first nucleus of indigenous staff officers, senior enough to take over. However, due to the first military coup in Nigeria on 15 January 1966, the Germans unilaterally terminated their agreement with the government and left the country, and thus the leadership of the infant NAF was assumed by Lt Col George Kurubo much earlier than originally planned, on 16 January 1966.

Considering the original motivation for the establishment of the NAF, it is little surprising that the force initially developed its transport capabilities above all. By the time the Nigerian Civil War erupted, the NAF operated 2 ex-Luftwaffe Noratlas transports, 5 Do 28B-1 and 20 Do 27A light transports, as well as 14 Piaggio P.149D basic trainers. Since the training of many Nigerian ground personnel was incomplete, in the following years the NAF was forced to contract various Western companies, which provided their services and established maintenance centres in various parts of the country.

The development of the NAF's combat component was also disturbed by the withdrawal of the German advisory group. Although originally considering the acquisition of Fiat G.91s from West Germany for some time, Nigeria was eventually forced to opt for Aermacchi MB.326 ground-attack trainers, although this order was embargoed once the civil war began.

Nigeria therefore turned to the USSR for aid, which initially provided Egyptian MiG-17s that were undergoing overhaul at works in Siberia. Moscow followed this with additional deliveries from its own stocks and from East Germany, while Sudan donated two British Aircraft Corporation Jet Provost armed trainers. The NAF thus grew significantly in size during the late 1960s and early 1970s, acquiring numerous combat aircraft from the USSR, and subsequently even more from West Germany, Italy and the UK. However, during the 1990s, much of the air force became non-operational due to a lack of funding and general negligence. In recent years, several major attempts to revitalise the NAF have been announced, evidence of corresponding funding and related work appearing only in early 2010.

Two Dornier Do 28s of the NAF can be seen parked on the apron at Kaduna in the mid-1960s. (John Fricker Collection, via Simon Watson)

Photographed at Enugu air base while operated by No. 1 Squadron, NAF, in 1969, MiG-17F NAF605 shows to advantage the underwing launch rails for Egyptian-made Sakr 76mm (3in) calibre rockets. (Keith E. Sissons via Albert Grandolini)

Deliveries of MiG fighters to Nigeria

On 13 August 1967, Kano airport in northern Nigeria was closed to all commercial traffic to permit the arrival of 15 Antonov An-12 transports in Aeroflot markings. The airlifters were carrying 2 MiG-15UTIs and 8 MiG-17Fs, together with 30 Soviet technicians and associated equipment. The jets were assembled and test flown during the following week, and entered service with No. 1 Squadron, NAF. The Soviet Union subsequently arranged for a group of between 25 and 30 Egyptian pilots and technicians to fly these aircraft, while several Nigerian pilots underwent conversion.

A second batch of MiG-17 fighters, which were required as attrition replacements, arrived in Kano during April 1968, followed by a third, larger batch delivered in autumn of the same year. By that time, the first European contract personnel had completed their conversion courses and were ready to fly these aircraft in combat. Eventually, the number of MiG-17s delivered to Nigeria amounted to at least 41 airframes. However, only some 37 of these entered NAF service, since some were destroyed on the ground immediately following their arrival.

In order to replace the tired MiG-17s, the USSR delivered 24 MiG-21MFs and 6 MiG-21UMs in 1975. Peacetime attrition of this fleet was heavy and although one additional MiG-21MF was delivered at an unknown date, only 12 MiG-21MFs and 5 MiG-21UMs remained operational by 13 October 1984, when Nigeria signed a contract for 12 MiG-21bis and 2 MiG-21UMs to serve as replacements. Eventually, most Nigerian MiGs were withdrawn from service and stored during the early 1990s.

Two Aero L-29s and a row of MiG-21MFs seen at Maiduguri air base in 1978. (Marinus Dirk Tabak Collection)

NAF-813 is one of the three FT-7NIs known to have been delivered to Nigeria by early 2011.
(Kenneth Iwelumo)

In mid-2004 reports surfaced that a Russian-Israeli consortium had offered to overhaul and return to service 'all 23 remaining NAF MiG-21s', but the inability of the government to guarantee the necessary funding prevented such a project from being launched. Instead, the government supposedly selected an offer for overhaul and upgrade by the Romanian company Aerostar Bacau and Israel's Elbit. It was apparently also for economic reasons that the Israeli-Romanian proposal was also never realised, even although it was apparently accepted.[2]

In September 2005 reports surfaced concerning a Nigerian order for 15 Chengdu F-7 fighter jets from China, comprising 12 F-7NI single-seat interceptors and at least three FT-7NI two-seat conversion trainers, worth USD251 million.[3]

Another reported contract, apparently worth USD32 million, included deliveries of 20 PL-9C AAMs, 10 PL-9 training rounds, unguided rockets and 250kg (551lb) bombs. Nigerian pilots travelled to China for training in 2008, even though the C-in-C NAF denied any related orders in January 2009, and the delivery of aircraft only began in December 2009.[4]

As of April 2010, three FT-7s had officially been introduced to service with 64 Air Defence Group at Makurdi air base, followed by delivery of the first F-7NIs.

Force structure

In accordance with a Statutory Act of Parliament of April 1964, the organisational structure of the NAF was established in order for the service to function efficiently. The first unit to become operational was the NAF Tactical and Technical Wing (NAFTW), based at Kaduna (originally a technical school, but subsequently one of the major installations of the NAF). This comprised the Military Training School (MTS), Light Transport and Liaison Squadron (LTLS), and support elements.

While other units were established before the German advisors left the country, the LTLS came into being at Kano air base only in August 1967, and was initially equipped with L-29 Delfin jet trainers, Jet Provosts, MiG-15UTIs and MiG-17s.

Following the end of the war in Biafra, the LTLS was reorganised as the Advanced Flying Training Wing (AFW), and its status was then upgraded to that of Flying Training Group (FTG). The FTG comprised two Flying Wings (the Primary Flying Training Wing based at Kaduna, and the Basic Flying Training Wing based t Kano). Meanwhile, Enugu air base became the home of the two units equipped with MiG-17s (reportedly Nos 1 and 2 Squadrons), and remained the main Nigerian fighter base until 1981, when the headquarters of the Tactical Air Command and Air Defence Group were established at Makurdi.

During the 1980s, MiG-21s and Dassault/Dornier Alpha Jets were initially operated from Kano, before their respective units became operational at Makurdi, Maiduguri and Kainji. The only unit known to have flown MiG-21s, however, was No. 21 Operational Conversion Unit, an element of No. 64 Air Defence Group (ADG), established in 1980 in Makurdi and responsible for training MiG-21 pilots. The same base was also the home to No. 33 Logistics Group (LOG), responsible for performing third- and fourth-line maintenance on MiG-21 fighters (and subsequently also on SEPECAT Jaguars).

Another MiG-21 unit – also part of No. 64 ADG – was established at Maiduguri in 1982. All surviving MiG-21s theoretically remained concentrated within No. 64 ADG at Makurdi even after they were stored and never flown again.

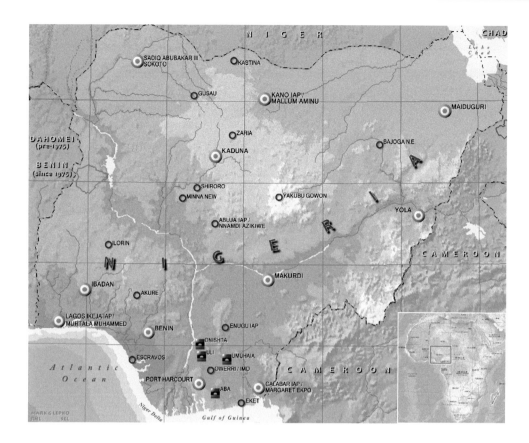

Map of Nigeria

National markings

The NAF has always used the national colours of green and white as national markings on its combat aircraft. However, the first batch of MiG-15UTIs and MiG-17s had fin flashes and roundels applied in green only, with the white fields left out. Roundels were usually – but by no means always – worn on four positions on the wings.

The second batch of MiG-17Fs, delivered in spring 1968, introduced large roundels applied on the fins instead of fin flashes, and – sometimes – also roundels applied in four positions on the wings.

Beginning in 1970, the use of roundels instead of fin flashes became standard on all MiG-17s. The same practice was subsequently applied on all MiG-21s and F-7s as well, even though the latter two types appear not to have received any roundels on their wings.

MiG-17F NAF612 (left) and NAF616, photographed at Enugu while undergoing post-flight checks during the Biafran War, received an entirely different set of national markings and serial numbers. Those applied on NAF612 appear to have served as a 'prototype' for the NAF-wide standard introduced in the 1970s.
(Keith E. Sissons via Albert Grandolini)

Camouflage colours and serial numbers

The first two batches of MiG-15UTIs and MiG-17s arrived in overall 'natural metal', although some former United Arab Republic Air Force (UARAF) aircraft showed obvious traces of the removal of their rear-fuselage identification stripes. A number of these aircraft, as well as most of those from the third batch, were subsequently camouflaged in various shades of green, primarily 'jungle dark green' (FS34227), overall. Serial numbers applied on these aircraft were all in black, some being applied very crudely, others with the aid of stencils. Serial numbers were worn on the rear fuselage only.

Nigerian MiG-21MFs were painted in the standard camouflage pattern for export aircraft, applied prior to delivery at the Znamya Truda Works. This consisted of beige and dark olive green on the upper surfaces, with RLB on the lower surfaces. MiG-21UMs were left in 'natural metal' overall. On both variants, full serial numbers were applied in red on the rear fuselage, together with the prefix 'NAF', with the 'last two' repeated in large red numerals on the forward fuselage.

MiG-21bis delivered in the mid-1980s arrived wearing the standard pattern and colours for this variant. This consisted of yellow sand and two shades of green on the upper surfaces, with RLB lower surfaces. The MiG-21bis fleet wore serial numbers applied in a similar manner to the MiG-21MF, but in a dark blue and black colour. Serials on all MiG-21UMs, regardless if arriving in Nigeria together with MiG-21MFs or MiG-21bis, were applied in red.

F-7NIs delivered in 2009 and 2010 wear the same camouflage pattern as worn by MiG-21bis in earlier times, but applied in slightly darker colours of tan, dark olive green and dark green on the upper surfaces, and a colour very similar to RLB on lower surfaces. Maintenance stencils are applied in black and dark red, with serial numbers in dark green.

Still wearing its original camouflage colours, markings and serial numbers, this MiG-21bis now serves as a gate-guard at the entrance to the NAF air base in Abuja. (Kenneth C. Iwelumo)

Table 30: Known serial numbers of NAF MiGs, 1966–2010

Aircraft type	Serial number	c/n	Remarks
MiG-15UTI	NAF601		Delivered to Kano on 18 August 1967
MiG-15UTI	NAF602		Delivered to Kano on 18 August 1967
MiG-17F	NAF603		Delivered to Kano on 13 August 1967; probably w/o prior to November 1968
MiG-17F	NAF604		Delivered to Kano on 13 August 1967; probably w/o prior to November 1968
MiG-17F	NAF605		Delivered to Kano on 13 August 1967; Sakr rocket rails; became gate guard at Kano AB
MiG-17F	NAF606		Delivered to Kano on 13 August 1967; probably w/o prior to November 1968
MiG-17F	NAF607		Delivered to Kano on 13 August 1967; probably w/o prior to November 1968
MiG-17F	NAF608		Delivered to Kano on 13 August 1967; Sakr rocket rails
MiG-17F	NAF609	0515317	Delivered to Kano on 13 August 1967
MiG-17F	NAF610		Delivered to Kano on 13 August 1967
MiG-17F	NAF611		Delivered to Kano on 27 April 1968; attrition replacement; roundel on fin

MiG-17F	NAF612	Delivered to Kano on 27 April 1968; attrition replacement; roundel on fin
MiG-17F	NAF613	Delivered to Kano on 27 April 1968; attrition replacement; roundel on fin
MiG-17F	NAF614	Delivered to Kano on 27 April 1968; attrition replacement; roundel on fin and crude serial number
MiG-17F	NAF615	Delivered to Kano between 12 October and 4 November 1968; destroyed by Biafran T-6G at Port Harcourt on 10 November 1969
MiG-17F	NAF616	Delivered to Kano between 12 October and 4 November 1968; w/o in crash landing on road near Opobo, 25 June 1969
MiG-17F	NAF617	Delivered to Kano between 12 October and 4 November 1968; no fin flash; strafed Flughjalp DC-6 during landing at Uli on 2 June 1969
MiG-17F	NAF618	Delivered to Kano between 12 October and 4 November 1968
MiG-17F	NAF619	Delivered to Kano between 12 October and 4 November 1968
MiG-17F	NAF620	Delivered to Kano between 12 October and 4 November 1968; damaged beyond repair by Biafran MFI-9B at Port Harcourt on 22 May 1969
MiG-17F	NAF621	Delivered to Kano between 12 October and 4 November 1968
MiG-17F	NAF622	Delivered to Kano between 12 October and 4 November 1968
MiG-17F	NAF623	Delivered to Kano between 12 October and 4 November 1968; crashed near Port Harcourt on 19 July 1969, British pilot KIA
MiG-17F	NAF624	Delivered to Kano between 12 October and 4 November 1968; now at War Museum in Umahia
MiG-17F	NAF625	Delivered to Kano between 12 October and 4 November 1968
MiG-17F	NAF626	Delivered to Kano between 12 October and 4 November 1968
MiG-17F	NAF627	Probably delivered to Kano between 12 October and 4 November 1968, but no visual or photographic evidence for delivery before 1970 is available
MiG-17F	NAF628	Probably delivered to Kano between 12 October and 4 November 1968, but no visual or photographic evidence for delivery before 1970 is available
MiG-17F	NAF629	Probably delivered to Kano between 12 October and 4 November 1968, but no visual or photographic evidence for delivery before 1970 is available
MiG-17F	NAF630	Probably delivered to Kano between 12 October and 4 November 1968, but no visual or photographic evidence for delivery before 1970 is available
MiG-17	NAF631	Ex-LSK/LV; delivered on unknown date in 1969; crash landing at Makurdi on 12 September 1969 and w/o
MiG-17	NAF632	Ex-LSK/LV; delivered to Kano on 13 October 1969
MiG-17	NAF633	Ex-LSK/LV; delivered to Kano on 13 October 1969
MiG-17	NAF634	Ex-LSK/LV; delivered to Kano on 13 October 1969; on display at Kaduna AB, 2010
MiG-17	NAF635	Ex-LSK/LV; delivered to Kano on 13 October 1969
MiG-17	NAF636	Ex-LSK/LV; delivered to Kano on 18 October 1969
MiG-17	NAF637	Ex-LSK/LV; delivered to Kano on 18 October 1969
MiG-17	NAF638	Ex-LSK/LV; delivered to Kano on 18 October 1969
MiG-21UM?	NAF650	
MiG-21MF	NAF651	Delivered 1975; crashed on 4 November 1981
MiG-21MF	NAF652	Delivered 1975
MiG-21MF	NAF653	Delivered 1975; gate guard at Makurdi AB

MiG-21MF	NAF654	Delivered 1975
MiG-21UM	NAF655	Delivered 1985; stored Makurdi AB, 2008, and offered for sale
MiG-21MF	NAF656	Delivered 1975
MiG-21MF	NAF657	Delivered 1975
MiG-21MF	NAF658	Delivered 1975
MiG-21MF	NAF659	Delivered 1975
MiG-21UM	NAF660	Delivered 1975; last seen Makurdi AB, early 1970s; probably crashed on 13 May 1986
MiG-21MF	NAF661	Delivered 1975
MiG-21MF	NAF662	Delivered 1985; stored Makurdi AB, 2008, and offered for sale
MiG-21MF	NAF663	Delivered 1975; wreck at Makurdi AB, 2009
MiG-21MF	NAF664	Delivered 1975
MiG-21UM	NAF665	Delivered 1975; crashed on 1 March 1978 (collision with an airliner)
MiG-21MF	NAF666	Delivered 1975
MiG-21MF	NAF667	Delivered 1975
MiG-21MF	NAF668	Delivered 1975
MiG-21MF	NAF669	Delivered 1975
MiG-21UM	NAF670	Delivered 1985; stored Makurdi AB, 2008, and offered for sale
MiG-21MF	NAF671	Delivered 1975; last seen in 1975
MiG-21MF	NAF672	Delivered 1975; w/o on 19 June 1981
MiG-21MF	NAF673	Delivered 1975
MiG-21MF	NAF674	Delivered 1975
MiG-21MF	NAF675	Delivered 1975; w/o on 1 October 1976
MiG-21MF	NAF676	Delivered 1975; wreck at Makurdi AB in 2009
MiG-21MF	NAF677	Delivered 1975
MiG-21MF	NAF678	Delivered 1975
MiG-21MF	NAF679	Delivered 1975
MiG-21UM	NAF680	Delivered 1975
MiG-21bls	NAF681	Delivered 1985
MiG-21bis	NAF682	Delivered 1985; stored Makurdi AB, 2009, and offered for sale
MiG-21bis	NAF683	Delivered 1985; stored Makurdi AB, 2009, and offered for sale
MiG-21bis	NAF684	Delivered 1985; stored Makurdi AB, 2009, and offered for sale
MiG-21UM	NAF685	Delivered 1985
MiG-21bis	NAF686	Delivered 1985
MiG-21bis	NAF687	Delivered 1985
MiG-21bis	NAF688	Delivered 1985
MiG-21bis	NAF689	Delivered 1985; stored Makurdi AB, 2009, and offered for sale
MiG-21bis	NAF690	Delivered 1985; stored Makurdi AB, 2009, and offered for sale
MiG-21bis	NAF691	Delivered 1985
MiG-21bis	NAF692	Delivered 1985; stored Makurdi AB, 2009, and offered for sale
MiG-21bis	NAF693	Delivered 1985; gate guard at Abuja, 2009
MiG-21bis	NAF694	Delivered 1985
F-7NI	NAF800	Manufactured in 2009; delivered in mid-2010
F-7NI	NAF801	Manufactured in 2009; delivered in mid-2010
F-7NI	NAF802	Photographed pre-delivery, 2009; delivered in mid-2010

F-7NI	NAF803	Manufactured in 2009; delivered in mid-2010
F-7NI	NAF804	Manufactured in 2009; delivered in mid-2010
F-7NI	NAF805	Manufactured in 2009; delivered in mid-2010
F-7NI	NAF806	Manufactured in 2009; delivered in mid-2010
F-7NI	NAF807	Photographed pre-delivery, 2009; delivered in mid-2010
F-7NI	NAF808	Manufactured in 2009; delivered in mid-2010
F-7NI	NAF809	Manufactured in 2009; delivered in mid-2010
F-7NI	NAF810	Manufactured in 2009; delivered in mid-2010
F-7NI	NAF811	Delivered 2010
FT-7NI	NAF812	Delivered 2010
FT-7NI	NAF813	Delivered 2010
FT-7NI	NAF814	Delivered 2010; last seen in April 2011

MiG-17F NAF612 seen at Enugu in 1969. Of interest are traces of the identification stripes around the rear fuselage, peculiar to the UARAF.
(Keith E. Sissons via Albert Grandolini)

Belonging to the same batch of MiG-17s delivered to Nigeria in April 1968 and photographed at Enugu in early 1969, NAF614 wore similar markings to NAF612.
(Keith E. Sissons via Albert Grandolini)

Official crest of the NAF Tactical Air Command, to which all MiG units are assigned

Patch of No. 64 ADG

MiG and Chengdu fighter operations in the Federal Republic of Nigeria

The Nigerian Civil War erupted after a prolonged period of tension culminating in Biafra's declaration of independence on 30 May 1967. The result was a massive arms build-up by both the federal military and Biafra. Originally expected to develop into little more than a short police action, the conflict turned very violent, lasting nearly three years.

Biafra established a small air arm relatively swiftly, equipped with miscellaneous combat aircraft including two Douglas RB-26 Invaders and, in late 1967, North American B-25 Mitchell light bombers, as well as a few Douglas DC-3 and de Havilland Dove transports, Aérospatiale SA.316 Alouette and Westland Whirlwind helicopters – clandestinely acquired from Austria, Belgium, France and other sources, and mainly flown by foreign contract personnel. This small air arm actually became involved in fighting even before the NAF. On the other hand, the federal government experienced considerable problems in acquiring combat aircraft from abroad. Eventually, Egypt and the USSR proved to be the only major foreign powers ready to help, and in mid-August 1967 the first batch of MiG-15UTIs and MiG-17s was delivered to Kano. Barely six days later, with most of the jets still in the process of being assembled by Soviet technicians, Kano was attacked by a Biafran RB-26. The bomber arrived only minutes after the departure of the last of the An-12s that had brought the MiGs to Nigeria. The French pilot flying the B-26 claimed to have destroyed a number of MiG-17s on the ground, but his claims remain unconfirmed. Eyewitnesses on the ground could only confirm some damage to crates containing spare parts and to the old airport terminal building.

The first of two MiG-15UTIs delivered to Nigeria in 1967 were left in 'natural metal' overall, and had only the green fields of their national insignia, as well as the serial number on the rear fuselage, applied. Both were based at Kano during the Biafran War.

As shown by the oxidised traces of two black identification stripes on its rear fuselage and launch rails for unguided rockets under its wingtips, the NAF605 was one of the ex-UARAF MiG-17Fs that represented the majority of the first batch of these aircraft delivered to Nigeria. Although equipped with launch rails for Egyptian-made Sakr rockets, these weapons were rarely used during the Biafran War.

MiG-17F NAF612 belonged to the second batch of this type, delivered to Nigeria on 27 April 1968. Starting with these aircraft, the NAF introduced the practice of applying roundels on the fins of its fighter jets, instead of the fin flash. Due to a series of raids by Biafran aircraft against NAF airfields, most MiGs were eventually camouflaged in jungle dark green (FS34079) overall. Obviously, the national markings and serial numbers were left in their original positions.

MiG-17F NAF615 belonged to the third batch of this type delivered to Nigeria between 12 October and 4 November 1968. This artwork shows it armed with a single FAB-100M GP bomb, carried instead of the more usual drop tanks. This jet was destroyed in a Biafran attack on Port Harcourt airfield on 10 November 1969.

NAF615 preparing for take-off at Enugu in 1969, had the fin flash and other markings applied in standard form. (Keith E. Sissons via Albert Grandolini)

During the early phase of the war, Biafran B-26s continued flying raids against various federal army installations and units. Although causing few losses, these proved potentially dangerous for the NAF's MiGs, at least as long as these were parked on the ground. The threat prompted the air force to camouflage most of its aircraft.

Except for raiding airfields, the Biafrans also bombed the oil storage tanks in the Niger delta, industrial areas in Lagos, and Niger River ferries, but with very little effect. The small Biafran air arm was in tatters by the end of 1967, after suffering considerable attrition, primarily to mishaps caused by a lack of spares.

The first combat sortie flown by NAF MiG-17s took place on 30 August 1967, when a single aircraft carried out a strafing attack along Biafra's northern border. These aircraft were initially piloted by Egyptians, before a few Nigerians converted to them, followed by up to 22 European, South African and Australian contract personnel. Reportedly paid between GBP800 and 1,000 per month, tax-free, plus free accommodation and bonuses for any kills recorded, most foreign contract pilots were converted to MiG-17s by Maj Usman Jibri, NAF, while most Nigerian pilots only flew ferry missions. MiG-17s and their foreign pilots were usually based at Lagos-Ikeja, Port Harcourt, Makurdi, Benin and Enugu, depending on the location of the fighting.

As the number of MiG-17s and pilots qualified to fly them increased, the NAF gradually established a form of air superiority over Biafra, even although no air-to-air combats occurred, and pilots flying for the federal air force preferred not to run the gauntlet of heavy AAA fire that protected enemy airfields. Nevertheless, the CAPs flown by NAF MiGs over Biafra, as well as a few raids by other Nigerian attack aircraft, proved decisive, and most Biafran combat aircraft were eventually knocked out in exchange for several lightly damaged MiGs.

Despite initial successes by the Biafrans on the ground, the federal army was on the advance by mid-September 1967. By May 1968 most large airfields used by the rebels had been captured, further limiting operations by Biafra's fledgling air force. Indeed, by June 1968 only one airstrip was left in rebel hands, limiting even operations by the foreign transport aircraft that delivered relief aid for the Biafran population of nearly eight million.

MiG-17F NAF624 prepares to launch for another combat sortie from Enugu AB in 1969. This photograph illustrates the original form of Nigerian national insignia applied on the fins of most NAF MiG-15s and MiG-17s: in green only, without any white fields.
(John Fricker Collection via Simon Watson)

Biafra managed to obtain several light attack aircraft in early 1969, and on 22 May 1969 these raided the airfield in Port Harcourt, posting exaggerating claims for no fewer than 11 NAF aircraft destroyed on the ground, including 3 Ilyushin Il-28s, 4 MiG-17s, 2 British Aerospace Corporarion Canberras, one Hawker Siddeley Heron and one Curtiss C-46. In fact, it is doubtful if more than two MiG-17s and two Il-28s were hit. Nevertheless, two days later, Benin City airfield was hit as well, and one MiG-17 and two Il-28s were claimed as destroyed. In reaction, NAF MiG-17s intensified their CAPs over the area remaining under rebel control, and began operating by night in an attempt to harass supply flights to Biafra. During the night of 2/3 June 1969, Flughjalp's Douglas DC-6 was attacked and damaged by two MiGs while landing at Uli. Three nights later, a Douglas DC-7 chartered by the Red Cross was attacked by a NAF MiG-17 flown by a South African contract pilot; the transport crashed after crossing the coast near Eket, killing the crew.

Biafra subsequently clandestinely purchased four Gloster Meteor NF.Mk 14 night fighters to counter this new threat. In the event, two Meteors never left Belgium while the other two ended their voyage in Guiné – then still under Portuguese rule – where the local authorities refused to allow their delivery.

Slightly more successful was another Biafran effort. In early 1964, the Armée de l'Air (French Air Force) offered for sale some 150 North American T-6s. Some 16 of these were purchased by intermediaries working on behalf of Biafra and 12 of these delivered to the SEAMA facility at Tires, in Portugal, in June 1969, for overhauls. Four of these were test-flown and then shipped to Bissalanca, in Guiné, arriving there in late September.

Following extensive problems, two were finally flown by ex-FAP reserve pilots to an airstrip near Uli, in Biafra. The operational records of the Biafran T-6s remain sketchy and at least one was captured intact at Uli by Nigerian troops. However, they did fly a number of sorties, albeit without any effect on the progress of the war. Meanwhile, in late 1969, federal troops, supported by surviving NAF MiG-17s and Il-28s, launched their final offensive, first splitting the territory under rebel control in two, and then forcing the Biafrans to capitulate on 13 January 1970.

MiG-17F NAF619 belonged to the third batch of this type delivered to Kano between October and November 1968. This jet was flown by a number of foreign contractors in combat operations during the Biafran War.

MiG-17F NAF625 received quite a large serial number, stencilled on the rear fuselage, as well as a fin flash without the white field. Whether any roundels were applied on the upper or lower surfaces of its wings remains unknown.

MiG-17F NA F633 belonged to the batch of ex-East German aircraft delivered to Kano on 13 October 1969. It was camouflaged in dark olive green overall shortly after its arrival and assembly.

During the early 1970s a number of reports surfaced concerning Nigerian MiG-17s being deployed to Guinea-Conakry, and even flying reconnaissance sorties over Portuguese Guiné (now Guinea-Bissau), but no evidence for such rumours can be found even in the official archives of the Portuguese Air Force.

From the 1970s to the 1990s the NAF operated dozens of fighter jets and attracted many new recruits via the colourful air displays staged during ceremonial events. Hundreds of NAF officers received various forms of training in China, France, Italy, Pakistan, the Soviet Union and the US. Ironically, most of these pilots were never able to put their training into practice, since the majority of Nigerian fighter jets were grounded shortly after delivery.

Time and again the NAF time spent huge sums of money on servicing the grounded aircraft, but without any success, since – for entirely unclear reasons – both successive governments and the air force lacked the commitment to maintain their aircraft in operational condition. Indeed, in the late 1980s and early 1990s, in order to cut its costs, the NAF closed seven major air bases, including Calabar, Ibadan, Ilorin, Minna and Sokoto. It is probably for this reason that the workshops of the NAF's 401 Aircraft Maintenance Depot – fully qualified to overhaul a wide range of aircraft and helicopters – have mainly stood idle ever since.

MiG-21MFs NAF651 (foreground) and NAF650 (right) seen during post-delivery assembly at Kano. (Marinus Dirk Tabak Collection)

Abandoned hulks of three NAF MiG-21MFs – including what used to be NAF676 (left) and NAF663 (centre) – as seen at Makurdi in 2009. Reportedly, all three fuselages are up for sale. (Lukàs Sirovy)

A reconstruction of the camouflage pattern applied on the port side of MiG-21MF NAF651. The aircraft was painted in one of most unusual variants of the standard camouflage pattern applied at the Znamya Truda Works in the former USSR.

MiG-21MFs were delivered to Nigeria together with a consignment of 'standard' armament for this variant, as available in the mid-1970s, and including (from left to right): R-3S and R-13M air-to-air missiles, UB-16-57 unguided rocket pods, and 400-litre (106-US gal) drop tanks.

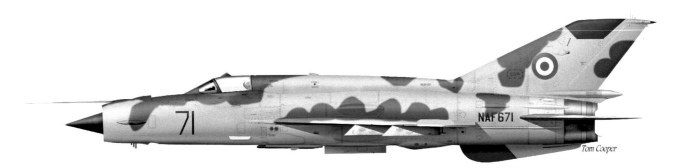

Wearing the most frequently used variant of the camouflage pattern applied at the Znamya Truda Works, MiG-21MF NAF671 is one of the best-known Nigerian MiGs, with several photographs taken of it in 1978 having been widely published.

NAF MiG-21s saw their only combat deployment during an Organisation of African Unity (OAU) operation in Chad in the early 1980s. Within the framework of Operations Harmony 1 to Harmony 4 in 1982, 'B Squadron' of No. 64 ADG was established at Maiduguri, comprising several MiG-21s and MBB Bo.105 helicopters. The unit was responsible for supporting security operations in northeast Nigeria and western Chad. MiG-21s flew several reconnaissance operations over Chad, and on several occasions landed at various dirt strips in that country. In one instance, after a dispute over fishing on Lake Chad in April 1983, Nigerian MiG-21s attacked several lakeside villages, leaving as many as 90 dead and even more wounded.[5]

Following a lengthy break in operating fighter jets, the newly delivered F-7s of the NAF began flying in late 2010. Sadly, two incidents overshadowed their early operations. One of the F-7NIs crashed at Kano following a routine training exercise on 22 March 2011, killing one of the NAF's most experienced fighter pilots. Less than two months later, on 11 May 2011, an FT-7NI crashed near Mbaniongu Mbazaam in Benue State, though the crew ejected safely and was subsequently picked up by a search and rescue helicopter from 305 Flying Training School, which flew them to Makurdi air base for medical attention. Reports concerning another possible crash in May 2011 were probably related to an Aero L-39, a number of these having been re-deployed to Makurdi in order to ease training of future F-7 pilots. Put together, these developments suggest that the NAF might be experiencing some problems in training its pilots to operate its new supersonic fighters.

Showing extensive traces of exposure to the harsh elements of the Nigerian climate, MiG-21UM NAF655 appears not to have had its full serial number applied on the rear fuselage, or perhaps this was completely worn out over time. (NAF HQ via Dr Jürgen Willisch/ Luftwaffenmuseum)

MiG-21bis were delivered to Nigeria painted in the standardised camouflage pattern for examples exported to several African countries (including Mozambique and the Guineas) in the mid-1980s. This consisted of beige, olive green and dark olive green on the upper surfaces (most of which is washed out on this example, almost becoming unrecognisable) and RLB on the lower surfaces. (NAF HQ via Dr Jürgen Willisch/ Luftwaffenmuseum)

Table 31: Confirmed and reported attrition of NAF MiG fighters, 1977–91[6]

Date	Aircraft	Serial number	Pilot/crew	Remarks
19 July 1969	MiG-17F	NAF623	Mike Thompsett (British) ejected but KIA	Ran out of fuel while approaching Port Harcourt and crashed
1971	MiG-17F		Maj D. Ato KIA	Crashed under unknown circumstances
24 September 1976	MiG			Crashed under unknown circumstances
1976	MiG-21MF		Flt Lt D. Shekoni KIA	Crashed under unknown circumstances; could be the example reported lost on 24 September
1976	MiG-17F		Flg Off J. C. Nwatarali KIA	Crashed under unknown circumstances
1 March 1978	MiG-21UM			Crashed under unknown circumstances
1 March 1978	MiG-21MF		Flg Off V. O. T. Ladoye KIA	Crashed under unknown circumstances; could be MiG-21UM
13 May 1983	MiG-21MF		Flg Off B. Yusuf KIA	Crashed under unknown circumstances at Maiduguri AB
1985	MiG-21bis		Flg Off J. Akpogu KIA	Crashed under unknown circumstances
1985	MiG-21bis		Sqn Ldr A. B. Ogboye KIA	Crashed under unknown circumstances
13 May 1986	MiG-21UM	NAF660?	Crew ejected safely	W/o under unknown circumstances
1986	MiG-21		Flt Lt K. Lawal KIA	Crashed under unknown circumstances; could be the example reported lost on 13 May
3 June 1988	MiG-21bis			W/o under unknown circumstances
1988	MiG-21bis		Flg Off F. Olubode KIA	Crashed under unknown circumstances; could be the example reported lost on 3 June
1988	MiG-21bis		Flt Lt Ogu KIA	Crashed under unknown circumstances; could be the example reported lost on 3 June
1989	MiG-21bis		Flg Off McDavid KIA	Crashed under unknown circumstances
1989	MiG-21bis		Flt Lt Shoyebi KIA	Crashed under unknown circumstances
22 March 2011	F-7NI		Capt Enny Bibinu Saleh KIA	Crashed at Kano AB following training mission
11 May 2011	FT-7NI		Two crewmembers ejected safely	Crashed near Mbaniongu Mbazaam, near Yandev, during training mission

Nearly the entire NAF MiG-21 fleet, a total of at least 20 aircraft, ended their careers essentially abandoned at the southern apron of Makurdi (at least three additional aircraft were abandoned at Maiduguri air base, in northeast Nigeria). (Lukàs Sirovy)

A long row of F-7NIs manufactured for Nigeria as seen pre-delivery, in China. Of particular interest is their camouflage pattern, based on that previously worn by the NAF MiG-21bis. (NAF via Pit Weinert)

F-7NI NAF606 seen shortly after delivery to Nigeria, in early 2011. Notably, while their serial numbers are applied in dark green and light green, the maintenance instructions on Nigerian F-7s are applied in dark red and black. (NAF via Pit Weinert)

All three Nigerian FT-7NIs identified to date (only two of which remain in service) wear the same camouflage pattern as the F-7NIs, but display slight differences in the application of their serial numbers: those on the F-7NIs are oval, while serial numbers on the FT-7s are in block script. This Chinese-developed variant has 'wet' outboard underwing pylons, capable of carrying drop tanks. (NAF via Pit Weinert)

As far as is known, all Nigerian MiG-21UMs were left in 'bare metal' overall and either did not wear full serial numbers on the rear fuselage, or lost these to wear caused by prolonged exposure to the elements.

The majority of the NAF's MiG-21bis fleet was marked in this fashion, wearing their full serial numbers – including the prefix 'NAF' – in light blue on the rear fuselage. Curiously, photographs from recent years show nearly all of them with the prefix 'NAF' removed.

NAF F-7NIs wear a camouflage pattern based on that of MiG-21bis exported in the mid-1980s, in beige, dark olive green and dark green-brown with sharp edges on the upper surfaces, and with dark RLB on the lower surfaces. According to available reports, Chinese-made PL-9 air-to-air missiles (derived from the Israeli-made Python III) should represent the major weapon of the type, in addition to internal 30mm cannon.

1 Largely based on Ruben Buhari, 'Queen of Battle Comes of Age', *This Day* (Lagos, 18 May 2010), Dupuy, *The Almanac of World Military Power*, pp.236-240 & Brent, *African Air Forces*, pp127-137.

2 'Failed Affair for the Upgrading of the Nigerian Air Force', *Nine O'Clock*, 17 October 2006.

3 'Nigeria Agrees to buy Fighter Planes from China', Reuters, 28 September 2005.

4 'Air Force Gets Chinese Jets Soon', *Daily Trust*, 14 February 2008 and 'Air Chief Denies Aircraft Contract Report', *This Day*, 10 January 2009.

5 Flintham, *Air Wars And Aircraft*, pp94.

6 This list is based on all available sources, including various printed periodicals, books, TV and other media reports, the internet, and also some first-hand sources. The list should not be considered complete, and only the entries marked in bold can be considered as confirmed.

Chapter 18

REPUBLIC OF SOMALIA

Overview

The Republic of Somalia came into existence on 1 July 1960, when the former British protectorate of Somalia and the Italian trusteeship territory of Somalia (or 'Somaliland') were united and granted independence.

By the time the original Somali Aeronautical Corps (SAC) was officially established on 30 June 1960, the air arm was a small but well organised force developed with Italian help, and including dozens of Somali personnel trained in Italy, Egypt and Iraq. By December 1960, when it received two Egyptian-made Gomhouria trainers, the SAC had been officially renamed as the Ciidanka Cirka Soomaaliyed (CCS – Air Force of Somalia).

Due to strong nationalist and expansionist tendencies in Somali foreign policy, the government soon began searching for ways of bolstering its armed forces and eventually established close ties with the USSR. The first Somali students were sent for pilot training in the Soviet Union in September 1962. Subsequently, the Soviets began providing sizeable amounts of arms and equipment, including MiG-17 fighter jets, MBTs and artillery. By the end of the 1960s the CCS had been reinforced through the delivery of the first helicopters and, in 1972, through the acquisition of four Il-28 bombers.

The CCS had reached the peak of its strength by 1976, by which time it operated over 20 MiG-17s, 30 MiG-21MFs, as well as SA-2 and SA-3 SAMs for air defence.

While Italians trained the original cadre of Somali Air Force personnel, additional cadets were subsequently trained in Somalia with the help of Egyptian advisers and using Egyptian-made Gomhouria basic trainers. Barely visible in this photograph is the original fin flash as worn by CCS aircraft in the 1960s.
(Tahsin Zaki via Dr David Nicolle)

Despite the very strained economic situation, in 1977 the Somali government instigated an irredentist insurgency in the Ogaden Province of Ethiopia, an area predominantly populated by ethnic Somalis. This eventually erupted into a full-scale war between Ethiopia and Somalia, better known as the Ogaden War. The CCS suffered heavy losses in the course of this conflict and spent most of the early 1980s rebuilding its strength with the help of combat aircraft delivered from China and various Arab countries, as well as foreign contract personnel.

The Ogaden War had extremely negative effects upon Somali society as a whole, eventually resulting in a civil war that had practically destroyed the once proud Republic of Somalia by 1991. Ever since, feuding between numerous warlords has meant that Somalia has served as a synonym for chaos and anarchy, and even the UN has given up attempts to establish any kind of order.

Deliveries of MiG and Shenyang fighters to Somalia and CCS unit structure

After signing a contract with Moscow for an unconditional loan of USD32 million in 1963, Somalia ordered 8 MiG-15UTI conversion trainers and between 24 and 30 MiG-17 fighters from the USSR, with the intention of establishing two fighter squadrons. In order to help the CCS convert to these aircraft, 300 Soviet advisors were deployed to Somalia, while over 400 Somali pilots and technicians travelled to Moscow for training. The first MiG-17s became operational with the CCS in 1964, and by 1966 Somalia had not only established two operational units, but was also able to transfer several experienced MiG-17 pilots to a squadron that was to fly four Il-28 bombers, starting in 1972.

By the time Somalia reached another agreement with the Soviets, in 1973, the CCS operated four combat units and now ordered 36 MiG-21s – including 33 MiG-21MFs (from production batches 87, 88 and 89) and 3 MiG-21US – to establish two new units. The Soviets not only delivered new MiGs, starting in early July 1974, but also helped expand the airfield at Berbera.

Interestingly, the CCS decided to field the MiG-21s in two entirely new units, manned by new pilots, fresh from basic flying training at the Flying School in Hargheisa. Even though most of these pilots successfully completed their conversion courses in the USSR, in the following two years each barely flew 50 hours, as severe drought in Somalia in 1974 and 1975 inflicted serious problems on the local economy.

Photographs of intact CCS fighter jets are as good as non-existent, and those showing full details of camouflage patterns, markings and insignia are even more seldom. This MiG-17 was ditched in a salt lake by a pilot attempting to defect to Djibouti on 11 July 1988. It appears to have had no roundels applied on the upper surfaces of the wings. (Albert Grandolini Collection)

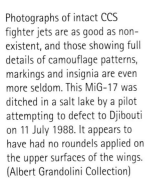
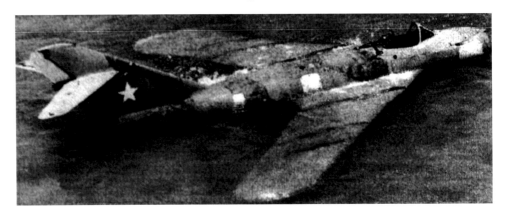

In December 1976, a Somali delegation led by the Vice-President and Minister of Defence, Gen Mohammad Ali Samantar, visited Czechoslovakia, and requested delivery of MiG-17 spare parts, in addition to several L-29 and/or L-39 jet trainers. Samantar also inquired about the possibility of training CSS pilots in that country. Not interested in donating any such equipment, the government in Prague turned down these requests.[1]

Immediately after the Ogaden War, Somalia ordered Shenyang F-6 jet fighters from China, although the manufacturer was unable to deliver any examples before 1980. Thereafter, all the remaining CCS pilots were converted to the type with the help of Chinese instructors, at Baledogle air base in Somalia. The F-6s were Somalia's last active fighter jets and remained operational until 1991.

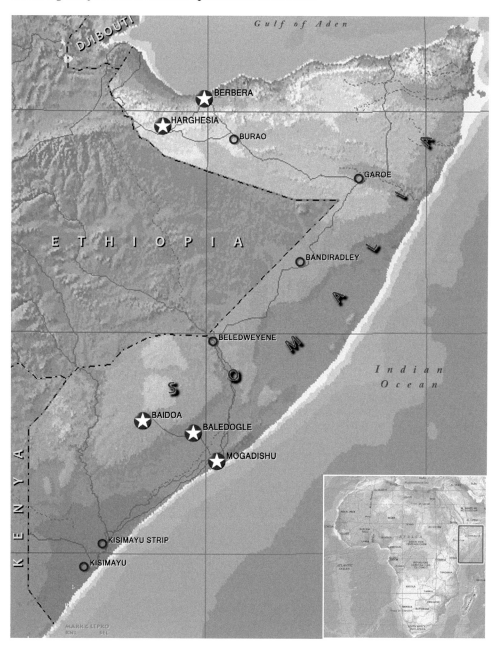

Map of Somalia

National markings

While still under Italian supervision the SAC introduced a white star superimposed over a light blue roundel as its national marking. The CCS continued to use the same insignia on its fighter jets, but added fin flashes – consisting of a light blue field with a white star and a wavy dark blue line – on some of its helicopters. While not applied on all MiG-15UTIs, MiG-17s, MiG-21UMs and F-6s, the roundels were usually applied in six positions (this was certainly the case for all CCS MiG-21MFs): four on the wings and two on the fins.

Camouflage colours and serial numbers

CCS MiG-15UTIs and MiG-17s were originally delivered in their 'natural metal' livery overall, and wore large serial numbers in black or dark blue, prefixed by the letters 'CC' (short for CCS and standing for 'Air Force') on the forward fuselage, as well as fin flashes and roundels in six positions.

It appears that the practice of applying fin flashes was abandoned in around 1973-74, when these aircraft were camouflaged – most commonly with the same colours as used for the then newly delivered MiG-21MFs, i.e. beige and olive green on the upper surfaces, and RLB on the lower surfaces. Some MiG-17s were camouflaged in different shades of yellow or sand and dark green, however. Around the same time, the practice of applying black serial numbers, prefixed by 'CC', on the fins of MiG-17s was introduced, but using much smaller digits.

MiG-15UTIs, in contrast, continued to receive very large black serial numbers (also prefixed by 'CC'), but applied on the forward fuselage, apparently in the same style as all CCS MiG-15s and MiG-17s during the 1960s.

CCS MiG-21MFs were delivered in the standard camouflage pattern applied at the Znamya Truda Works, consisting of yellow sand and dark olive green. The MiG-21MFs received relatively large serial numbers applied in blue on the forward fuselage, and without suffixes.

Chinese-made F-6Cs and FT-6s were originally delivered painted white overall. Sometime during the mid-1980s most of them received a coat of disruptive camouflage. The colours consisted of yellow, dark brown and dark olive green on the upper surfaces, with RLB on the lower surfaces, but most were of rather poor quality and rapidly began to show heavy wear.

Table 32: Serial numbers of CCS MiG and Shenyang fighters, 1965–91

Aircraft type	Serial number	c/n	Remarks
MiG-15UTI	CC114		
MiG-15UTI	CC115		Wreck in Mogadishu, 1992-93
MiG-15UTI	CC116		Wreck in Mogadishu, 1992-93
MiG-17	CC125	1025	Wreck in Mogadishu, 1992-93
MiG-17	CC126		
MiG-17	CC128		

MiG-17	CC129	1029	Wreck in Kismayu, 1992-93
MiG-17	CC130		
MiG-17	CC131		
MiG-17	CC132		
MiG-17	CC133		
MiG-17	CC134	1034	Wreck in Mogadishu, 1992-93
MiG-17	CC135		
MiG-17	CC136	1036	Wreck in Mogadishu, 1992-93
MiG-21UM	20?		
MiG-21UM	205	516963026	Wreck in Mogadishu, 1992-93
MiG-21UM	208	516909001	Wreck in Mogadishu, 1992-93
MiG-21MF	220		
MiG-21MF	222		
MiG-21MF	224		
MiG-21MF	226		
MiG-21MF	228		
MiG-21MF	230		
MiG-21MF	232		
MiG-21MF	234	8711	
MiG-21MF	236	8708	
MiG-21MF	238		
MiG-21MF	240		
MiG-21MF	242		
MiG-21MF	244		
MiG-21MF	246		
MiG-21MF	248	8811	Wreck in Mogadishu, 1992-93
MiG-21MF	250		
MiG-21MF	252	8901	Wreck in Mogadishu, 1992-93
MiG-21MF	254	8902	
MiG-21MF	256	8903	Wreck in Mogadishu, 1992-93
MiG-21MF	258	8904	Wreck in Mogadishu, 1992-93
MiG-21MF	261		Damaged during EtAF attack on Berbera AB, 27 December 1977
FT-6	403?		Wreck in Mogadishu, 1992-93
FT-6	405		Wreck in Mogadishu, 1992-93
F-6C	426	10519	Wreck in Mogadishu, 1992-93
F-6C	428		Wreck in Mogadishu, 1992-93
F-6C	430		
F-6C	432		
F-6C	434		
F-6C	436		
F-6C	438		
F-6C	440		
F-6C	442		
F-6C	444		
F-6C	446		

A reconstruction of MiG-15UTI CC116, found abandoned inside a hangar at Mogadishu air base in 1992. The aircraft was camouflaged with beige and dark olive green on the upper surfaces, but its lower surfaces were apparently left in 'bare metal', as were the original drop tanks, installed directly on the lower surfaces of the wing. Roundels were applied in six positions.

A reconstruction of the original appearance of the MiG-17 now on display in the centre of Hargheisa. Apparently camouflaged in beige and dark olive green on the upper surfaces, the lower surfaces of this aircraft were likely left in 'bare metal' overall, even though they are now painted in yellow and green. The 'winged cheetah' insignia was applied on either side of the forward fuselage and roundels were applied in six positions. The aircraft is shown as it probably appeared during the Ogaden War, carrying a single 50kg (110lb) FAB-50TsK bomb.

The wreck of MiG-17 CC125 was found by UN troops in Mogadishu in 1992, and apparently had its winged cheetah insignia applied in a slightly darker shade of yellow.

F-6C	448		Wreck in Hargheisa, 1992-93
F-6C	450		
F-6C	452		
F-6C	454		Wreck in Hargheisa, 1992-93
F-6C	456	10514	Wreck in Mogadishu, 1992-93
F-6C	458		
F-6C	460	10511	Wreck in Mogadishu, 1992-93

MiG fighter operations in Somalia, 1964–91[2]

Somali MiG-17s and MiG-21s saw very little service before becoming involved in the Ogaden War with Ethiopia in 1977-78. Former CCS personnel reported flying barely 20-25 hours a year prior to that conflict. Nevertheless, two Somali MiGs intercepted a passenger airliner of the Neckermann Travel Agency on 22 November 1970, and forced it to land in Somalia.

Several encounters between CCS MiGs and various French aircraft were reported in 1977 as well, mainly during tensions caused by the Ogaden War. On 25 March, a pair of MiG-17s attacked a Lockheed P-2H (P2V-7) Neptune reconnaissance aircraft of the Aéronavale (French Naval Aviation) that was under way over the Gulf of Aden, monitoring CCS radio transmissions. The French pilot initiated a series of evasive manoeuvres at very low level and escaped the MiGs' fire.

One CCS MiG-17 is known to have crashed, killing its pilot, in the course of a landing attempt at Berbera, after a similar action that resulted in the forcing down of an Air France airliner, in spring 1977.

Ever since Somalia's independence, it has been the stated policy of the government to promote the unity of ethnic Somali peoples living inside and beyond its frontiers. This has been conducted by legal and peaceful, but also by other means. Corresponding claims, written into the Somali constitution and on its flag, affected Kenya and – above all – Ethiopia and Djibouti. After preparing its military for action from the early 1960s, in July 1977 the Somali government seized the opportunity to invade Ethiopia, a country weakened by internal unrest and power struggles, with the aim of incorporating its State of Ogaden into a 'Greater Somalia'.

With Somalia poised to launch an invasion of Ethiopia, in spring 1977 the CCS had a strength of around 1,750 personnel and was organised into two wings, based at Hargheisa and Baida, and each operating one squadron of MiG-17s and one of MiG-21s. Additionally, Somalia could call upon a small squadron of Il-28 bombers and two transport units equipped with Antonovs and Mil helicopters. On the ground, the Somali Army prepared all 20 of its regular brigades, plus around 20 reserve brigades. The Army could also count upon around 6,000 fighters of the Western Somali Liberation Front (WSLF) and another 30,000 of the Somali-Abo Liberation Front (SALF), composed of exiles from Ethiopia and Somali Army officers and NCOs that resigned their commissions to volunteer for the upcoming task. Indeed, at the time of the Somali invasion of Ethiopia, the WSLF and SALF were already active inside Ogaden, attacking Ethiopian garrisons and forcing the EtAF to evacuate all its operational assets from local air bases.

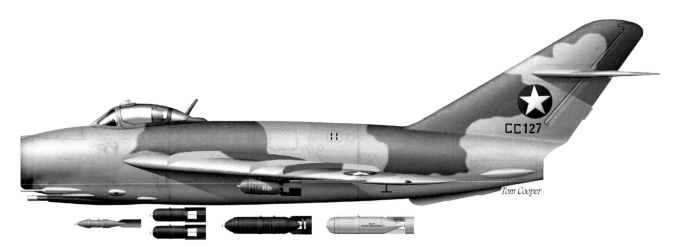

A reconstruction of the MiG-17 that was the gate guard at the military side of Mogadishu IAP, before 1992. In addition to its original camouflage, this aircraft had sizeable parts of the fuselage and wings painted in dark yellow – possibly indicating that it was overhauled and returned to service sometime in the late 1980s. The aircraft is shown with the usual arsenal of bombs delivered with the type, including (from left to right): FAB-50M-4, FAB-50M, FAB-250M-46 and the RBK-250 cluster bomb. A single FAB-100M is shown underwing.

This MiG-17 was found in Kismayu, albeit without wings. It wore a slightly darker camouflage pattern than usual, consisting of tan and dark green on the upper surfaces, with a sharp border to the lower surfaces, which were left unpainted.

Another MiG-17 found inside a hangar at Mogadishu IAP was painted in a more usual camouflage pattern of beige and dark olive green, with roundels worn only on the fin. The aircraft is shown armed with a UB-16-57 rocket pod, installed instead of the (more usual) drop tank. The MiG-17 was unable to carry both external fuel and weapons at the same time, which greatly diminished its effectiveness during the Ogaden War.

On the early morning of 13 July 1977, Somalia launched its onslaught, preceded by CCS fighter-bombers that flew some 50 combat sorties, mainly against targets in the Gode area, at the limits of their combat radius.

The invasion caught the Ethiopians by surprise: chaos reigned all around the country; Somalia had not declared war, and thus the leadership in Addis Ababa did not comprehend the situation. Ethiopian officials required no less than two weeks before they realised they were no longer facing an insurgency of the WSLF and SALF alone. Supported willingly by the local population, the Somali Army rapidly advanced westwards, capturing towns one after the other, including Aysha and Gode, the later including one of only two major local airfields used by the EtAF.

The EtAF began engaging CCS fighters under way over Ogaden on 16 July, but only a few unconfirmed reports about the results of these early air combats are available. Some available reports indicate that several Somali MiG-17s and MiG-21s crashed in the course of a number of air combats. It was only on 21 July that the EtAF launched a major operation – the aerial re-supply of garrisons besieged due to the Somali advance. In the course of this action, one EtAF C-47 transport was intercepted by two CCS MiG-17s, hit in the port wing and forced to belly-land in the desert.

Subsequently, the EtAF decided to provide all its transports under way over Ogaden with fighter escort. This decision in turn resulted in the first officially confirmed air combat between Northrop F-5E Tiger II fighters of the EtAF and CCS MiG-21MFs, on 24 July, when one Somali fighter was shot down.

A much larger air combat occurred only a day later, when three F-5Es intercepted a CCS strike package consisting of MiG-17s protected by MiG-21s led by the CO of Hargheisa air base and the CO of the locally based MiG-21 squadron. In the ensuing furball, two MiG-21MFs collided, killing both the leading Somali officers, and the Ethiopians subsequently shot down not only another MiG-21, but also two MiG-17s. Later the same day, the CCS also lost a single MiG-17 near the Karamara Pass, shot down by 40mm Bofors AAA of the Ethiopian Army. Another MiG-21 was shot down by F-5Es on 29 July, and on 2 August, four Ethiopian F-5As flew a highly successful raid against Hargheisa, destroying one MiG-21MF, one Il-28 and an An-26 on the ground. Following this debacle, the CCS never challenged EtAF air superiority over Ogaden again, and limited its operations to hit-and-run raids using small MiG formations. In turn, the EtAF was free to strike hard against Somali Army units, exposed in the open desert – with predictable results.

Due to the small number of combat aircraft available to the EtAF, it took some time until the effects of its attacks were felt by the Somalis. The latter thus initially continued their advance, assaulting Dire Dawa on 17 August, and provoking a major battle for the local airfield that lasted for the next two days. With the EtAF launching no fewer than 68 combat sorties out of Debre Zeit air base within a single day against Somali Army units exposed in the open semi-desert, the Ethiopians inflicted up to 40 per cent casualties on the two Somali brigades involved, and forced them into a hasty withdrawal. Despite this setback, the Somalis regrouped and continued their advance on Jijjiga, assaulting this town in early September in the face of bitter resistance. In the course of the battle for Jijjiga, the CCS lost two additional MiG-21MFs to EtAF F-5Es. In return, the EtAF had its leading F-5E pilot – who had previously scored 4.5 officially confirmed MiG-kills – shot down by Somali ZSU-23-4 Shilkas and captured by the WSLF. Furthermore, in the aftermath of the capture of Jijjiga, the Somalis advanced

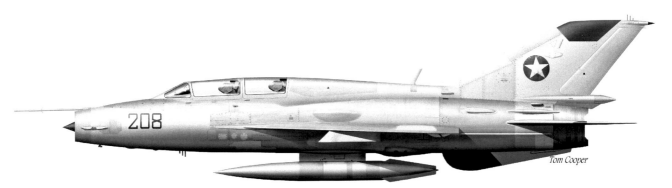

A reconstruction of one of three MiG-21UMs delivered to Somalia in 1974. These aircraft appear to have lacked their forward-view mirror above the rear cockpit and were otherwise left in bare metal overall. Roundels were applied in only two positions on the fin.

A Somali MiG-21MF with one of the lowest known serial numbers, 224 was found abandoned in Mogadishu in 1992. It was camouflaged in one of the simplest variants of the standard pattern applied at the Znamya Truda Works before delivery, and had its serial number applied in blue on the forward fuselage, as usual for all CCS MiG 21s.

The camouflage pattern of MiG-21MF serial number 226 differed only slightly to that of 224, indicating that both were likely painted by the same painter at the Znamya Truda Works. During the Ogaden War, CCS MiG-21MFs were almost exclusively deployed as interceptors, armed with up to four R-3S AAMs.

on the Karamara Pass, destroying the crucial Ethiopian AN/TPS-43D radar station that provided the EtAF with excellent coverage of the entire northern Ogaden. The EtAF subsequently put Somali Army units under such pressure that by late September 1977 these began to suffer from a critical lack of supplies, spares and ammunition. Despite this, the battle for air superiority was effectively over.

Thanks to the superiority of their air force, which continued delivering devastating blows on the Somali Army, the Ethiopians halted the enemy advance on Harrer in October, and by early November 1977 the situation of the Somali military in Ogaden had become critical. Unable to forward sufficient supplies to units on the front lines, unable to obtain any significant reinforcements in terms of heavy equipment, and nervous about the situation on the battlefield, and also over reports of negotiations for arms deliveries between Ethiopia and the USSR, the government in Mogadishu made a major mistake in cancelling its cooperation with Moscow and expelling all Soviet advisors.

Enraged, Moscow rushed to punish Somalia through providing a massive volume of aid to Ethiopia instead. Starting on 13 November 1977, the Soviets opened an air bridge to Addis Ababa, in the course of which they began delivering a batch of MiG-21MFs, together with other equipment, worth almost USD2 billion. Additionally, a Cuban-manned MiG-15UTI/MiG-17F squadron was redeployed from Yemen, while the Soviets provided several MiG-21Rs.

The last group of Ethiopian pilots scheduled to be sent for training in the US was given a crash conversion course on the MiG-17, during which the type was confirmed as unsuitable for EtAF requirements. As a result, although flown by Cubans during the counteroffensive in Ogaden in winter and spring 1978, the entire fleet was subsequently stored and never flown again. Cuban and Russian sources indicate that MiG-21Rs were operational by late December 1977, flying dozens of reconnaissance sorties over enemy positions before the Ethiopians launched their major counteroffensive on 22 January 1978. Ethiopia denies this, however, insisting that its pilots flew all such sorties. Similarly, Ethiopia insists that only Cubans flew MiG-21MFs, since the EtAF insisted on obtaining the more advanced MiG-21bis. The Soviets eventually agreed to provide this variant and the first examples of the MiG-21bis had arrived in Debre Zeit by the end of November 1977. The MiG-21bis were accompanied by several MiG-21UMs and a group of Soviet instructors drawn from the 160th and 927th Fighter Aviation Regiments, normally based at Byeroza. This group of Soviet instructors remained in Ethiopia until July 1978.

The Ethiopian offensive of 22 January 1978 began with a major EtAF raid on Hargheisa air base in Somalia, undertaken by three sections of MiG-21s, with top cover provided by four F-5Es. Although no CCS aircraft were hit on the ground, the raid caused considerable damage to local installations and a nearby radar station, and the CCS would never again rise to the challenge of the EtAF even over its own turf. Elsewhere, the Cuban-flown MiG-17Fs and MiG-21MFs concentrated on destroying concentrations of Somali air defence assets in Ogaden, in the process of which they lost at least one MiG-17 and two MiG-21s. EtAF MiG-21bis – together with remaining F-5s and Canberras – provided CAS to ground troops and also continued a highly successful campaign against Somali Army supply columns and depots. Over 500 combat sorties were flown by the end of the month, causing heavy casualties in terms of men and material.

MiG-21MF serial number 248 was painted in the most widespread variant of the standard camouflage patterns applied at the Znamya Truda Works, with so-called 'horns' of dark olive green, spread in a symmetrical fashion vertically up the fuselage and horizontally along the upper surfaces of the wing. Only small patches of the same colour were applied elsewhere on the wings.

Serial number 252 was camouflaged in nearly the same style. The aircraft is shown in the heaviest configuration deployed during the Ogaden War, carrying three 400-litre (106-US gal) drop tanks (one under the centreline and one under each outboard underwing pylon), and only two R-3S AAMs.

On 1 February 1978, Ethiopian and Cuban ground forces launched an attack on Dire Dawa, outflanking the major Somali Army position in Ogaden and forcing the Somalis into a hasty retreat towards the Marda Pass and Jijjiga. The latter town became the scene of another major battle, beginning on 15 February, when a two-pronged offensive was launched. This succeeded in punching big gaps in the Somali front lines, despite fierce resistance. The ultimate catastrophe for the Somali forces in Ogaden followed on 5 March, when the Ethiopians initiated another major offensive. EtAF fighter-bombers flew no fewer than 150 combat sorties on the morning of that day alone, inflicting heavy damage. Another 400 sorties were flown in the following three days, after which the Somalis ceased fighting and withdrew towards the border, leaving plenty of equipment behind. Mopping up operations continued in Ogaden into April, but the war was already practically over when the sad remnants of the major Somali Army units pulled behind the border and took up positions around Berbera, in late March.

By mid-March 1978 the EtAF was reinforced through the addition of the first of an eventual 44 MiG-23BNs delivered to Ethiopia before 1980. These arrived together with a group of Ethiopian and Cuban pilots fresh from requalification courses in the USSR, and took part in some post-war skirmishes along the border, in the course of which two examples were shot down.

Meanwhile, the CCS was attempting to regroup and reorganise following the destruction of most of its fighter-bomber units. Although at least two groups of

MiG-21MF 224 was one of the few Somali MiG-21MFs that not only survived the Ogaden War and the top secret joint CCS-USAF exercises in the early 1980s (when Somali MiG-21s were flown by US pilots), but also remained intact to be found by UN troops at Mogadishu IAP in 1992.
(Claudio Tosselli Collection)

additional pilots were sent for training in the USSR, in 1978, and one to China, the CCS never really recovered from the losses it suffered during the Ogaden War. All remaining MiG-21s were withdrawn from service and stored in 1978, even though a few might have been flown during joint exercises with US. In 1981, when Somalia began its cooperation with the US, a small group of pilots from the USAF's then secret 4477th Tactical Evaluation Flight 'Red Eagles' spent several weeks in the country for a joint exercise with the CCS. In the course of their visit the Americans flew a number of air combat training missions together with Somali pilots, these exclusively using the last few remaining MiG-21MFs and MiG-21UMs. As far as is known, this was the last opportunity in which this type was flown in Somalia.

In 1979 Somalia ordered Shenyang F-6 fighters and FT-6 conversion trainers from China. Deliveries began the following year, and the type also saw limited service during a number of border skirmishes with Ethiopia in 1981, and particularly in the subsequent civil war, in the late 1980s. In 1987 one of the CCS squadrons forward-deployed several F-6s to Hargheisa air base, from where its pilots flew some combat sorties against various insurgent groups in northern Somalia.

A small number of MiG-17s – some recovered from airframes non-serviceable since the early 1970s – continued to soldier on with the help of spares acquired from China. However, by the mid-1980s the Chinese-made F-6s, as well as British-made Hunters donated to Somalia from various Arab states (and mainly flown by foreign contract personnel) represented the mainstay of the CCS.

Despite the increasingly chaotic situation created by the civil war, CCS F-6s continued flying combat sorties from Hargheisa until the fall of that air base to the insurgents in June 1988. The remainder of the air force then withdrew to Mogadishu, from where additional sorties were flown until the end of the war. In the course of these, at least two F-6s were claimed as shot down during 1989, one of which was subsequently confirmed by independent sources.

By 1990 the CCS still theoretically operated three fighter squadrons, including two equipped with F-6s. However, serviceability of the remaining aircraft was poor and the relatively few pilots that were left lacked continuation training.

As delivered from China in 1980-81, all Somali F-6Cs and FT-6s were painted in matt white overall, apparently in an attempt to provide at least some protection from the strong African sun. Serial numbers were applied in blue, on the forward fuselage, and roundels were worn in six positions (though with the top arm of the white star not pointing in any particular direction). This was the only non-camouflaged F-6s found at Mogadishu in 1992.

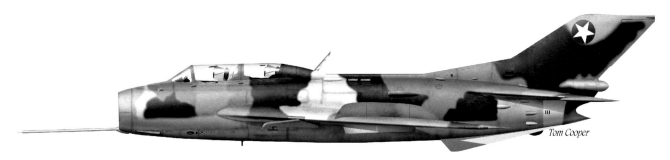

Originally delivered painted in matt white overall, sometime in the mid-1980s most Somali F-6Cs and FT-6s received a crudely applied camouflage pattern consisting of orange, dark green and dark chocolate brown on the upper surfaces, and RLB on the lower surfaces.

This CCS F-6C received a camouflage pattern consisting of no fewer than four colours on the upper surfaces, and RLB on the lower surfaces. Applied under relatively primitive conditions, it tended to wear off quite fast, rendering many of shades – and the borders between them – almost unrecognisable.

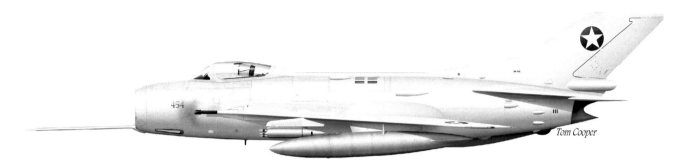

F-6C serial number 454 was one of the most intensively flown aircraft of this type in service with the CCS during the late 1980s. By this time these fighters were primarily used for air-to-ground attacks, and so were often armed with Chinese-made ORO-57K rocket pods, and sometimes also with light bombs.

This F-6C was camouflaged in an interesting mixture of orange, dark green and chocolate brown on the upper surfaces and sides, as well as the RLB on the lower surfaces, though it also had sizeable areas left painted in the original matt white colour. The serial number was applied in black and roundels were worn in six positions.

Serial number 460 was the CCS F-6C with the most intact camouflage pattern when found by UN troops in 1992. The colours applied included orange, dark green and chocolate brown on the upper surfaces, and RLB on the lower surfaces, while roundels were applied in six positions.

The fin of F-6C serial number 456 as found within a maintenance hangar at Mogadishu in 1992. Of interest is the position of the white star on the roundel applied on the fin – almost pointing towards the front of the aircraft. (via Pit Weinert)

In addition to combat losses, the CCS suffered from numerous defections. On 11 July 1988, Capt Ahmed Mohammad Hassan defected to Djibouti flying a fully armed MiG-17. Other aircraft of this type are known to have flown sporadic operational sorties during the civil war that eventually destroyed Somalia, flying as late as 1989. On 15 July 1990 another pilot attempted to defect with his MiG-17 to Yemen. Running out of fuel, he ditched his jet into the Gulf of Aden in the process, but survived to request asylum.[3]

The last flight by any CCS MiG-17 is reported to have occurred on 3 January 1991, when two examples were sighted over Hargheisa.

One of the final missions by a CCS F-6 was undertaken on 26 March 1991, when an example attacked Kismayu airfield, narrowly missing a Boeing 707 airliner with passengers on board. The fighter apparently crashed only minutes later, a few miles away.

The CCS fell apart in April and May 1991, during the final days of the country's existence as an organised state. With most of its former personnel living in exile and all relevant documentation destroyed, only a few of its sad remnants were found strewn around the airfields of Mogadishu and Hargheisa when UN peacekeepers arrived in the country in 1992. Unceremonially pushed aside and largely destroyed in the process, these historic aircraft were all that was left of a once very proud air force.

Starboard side view of F-6C serial number 426 as found at Mogadishu, together with a row of four MiG-21s in the background. (via Pit Weinert)

1   Information based on original Czechoslovak documents, kindly provided by Martin Smisek.

2   Based on ongoing research by Tom Cooper and Solomon Nadew for the forthcoming book *Air War Ogaden*.

3   The CCS pilot in question actually made an emergency landing on the surface of Ghourbet Lake in southwest Djibouti. He was rescued by local fishermen.

Chapter 19

REPUBLIC OF SUDAN

Overview

The Republic of the Sudan, at one time the largest country in Africa and the Arab World, was effectively a British colony during the first half of the 20th century until it gained independence on 1 January 1956.

Foundations for the future Silakh al-Jawwiya as-Sudaniya, or al-Quwwat al-Jawwiyya as-Sudaniyya (Sudanese Air Force – SuAF), were laid as early as 1955, when the first group of 12 Sudanese cadets were sent to study at the Egyptian Air Force Academy at Bilbeis. By the time Sudan was granted independence, each of these pilots had gained around 250 hours of flying experience, and a group of future technicians was nearing the end of technical instruction in Yugoslavia and Ethiopia. This was the cadre around which the SuAF was officially established, in January 1956.

At the time, the Sudanese armed forces were a small, well-disciplined, professional and highly mobile force with the primary task of internal security. As a result, their British instructors tailored the future SuAF to offer transport and COIN support. However, while the British training mission provided all the support required, the SuAF initially had very little actual flying equipment. The first available aircraft were four Gomhouria Mk 2 primary trainers (Bücker Bü 181Ds, licence built in Egypt), donated by Cairo. In 1957 the fleet was reinforced by four Percival Provost T.Mk 53s, intended for use by the SuAF Flying School, which was established in 1958 by the British in

A group of SuAF cadets with their Egyptian instructors at the United Arab Republic Air Force Academy in Bilbeis, in the mid-1960s.
(Tahsin Zaki via David Nicolle)

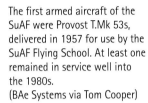

The first armed aircraft of the SuAF were Provost T.Mk 53s, delivered in 1957 for use by the SuAF Flying School. At least one remained in service well into the 1980s.
(BAe Systems via Tom Cooper)

Khartoum. In 1958 a transport unit was established following delivery of a Percival President, a civil version of the Percival Pembroke. Two additional aircraft of the same type were to follow in March 1960, together with the second batch of Provosts. Two months later, a Pembroke C.Mk 54 and two Pembroke C.Mk 55s arrived in Khartoum.

The first Sudanese combat aircraft were four BAC Jet Provost T.Mk 51s and eight Jet Provost T.Mk 52s, delivered in 1962. As early as 26 May of the same year, two Jet Provost T.Mk 51s were lost together with four pilots in a head-on collision during training. Another Jet Provost T.Mk 51 crashed on 13 June 1962, killing the pilot, while a T.Mk 52 was badly damaged in a heavy landing incident in April 1963, forcing Sudan to return the aircraft to the UK for extensive repairs. The fleet was further depleted in 1967, when two Jet Provost T.Mk 52s were handed over to Nigeria, but losses were made good by an order for five Jet Provost T.Mk 55s (in essence, BAC 145s or Strike-master T.Mk 82s) in 1966.

The second half of the 1960s saw considerable reinforcement of the SuAF's transport capacity. In 1964, following the arrival of two C-47s, orders were placed for four Fokker F27M-400s, followed two years later by eight Pilatus PC-6B Turbo Porters.

From 1955 until early 1972, most of southern Sudan was in armed revolt, the local ethnic groups seeking at least autonomy, if not outright secession from the Arab- and Muslim-dominated north. The SuAF was barely involved in the early phases of this conflict and its condition did not significantly alter before 1967, when the situation in the south deteriorated to such a degree that it led to the collapse of the central government. While the first shipments of arms from Czechoslovakia arrived as early as June 1965, the British training mission remained influential for the time being, but the June 1967 Six-Day War alienated Sudan from the UK, and Khartoum increasingly began looking elsewhere for training and equipment. Ever larger groups of students were sent for training to Egypt, Ethiopia and West Germany, and later to Yugoslavia. The British contingent was withdrawn in 1968, and even though all of the Jet Provosts ordered two years earlier were eventually delivered, the UK stopped providing aid.

The Soviets took the place of the British, signing an agreement for delivery of military equipment – including 18 MiG-21 fighters – worth USD96 million. Following a May 1969 military coup, the country turned increasingly towards the Soviet Union and within two years the first of six An-12s and six An-24s had arrived. In 1970, the first SuAF helicopter unit was established, equipped with six Mi-4s and eight Mi-8s.

Moscow's cooperation with Sudan came to a sudden end soon after. Like most Arab governments, Khartoum was not particularly interested in the Soviets spreading their political influence in the country. A coup attempt in July 1971 was instigated by the

Soviets and thwarted with some British support. Soviet advisors were expelled, and China began providing more spares and assistance. In July 1972, Sudan and China signed a contract covering the first batch of Shenyang F-5 jet fighters and two two-seat FT-5s. This was followed by another contract for Shenyang F-6 fighters, signed in June 1973.

Despite the receipt of Chinese armament, by the mid-1970s Khartoum was forced to make some concessions to the south, permitting a degree of self-government. Subsequently, Sudan's reputation in the West recovered sufficiently for the country to request help from West Germany, the UK and the US.

By 1981, when the US began supplying military aid to Sudan, much of the SuAF was grounded. This was soon to change. Cooperation with the US, but also with the UK, and finally Yugoslavia, helped return most of the surviving MiGs, Jet Provosts and Strikemasters to a serviceable condition. A first request for deliveries of Northrop F-5E/F fighter-bombers was turned down by the US, and Sudan then attempted to purchase Dassault Mirage fighter-bombers and Aérospatiale SA.330 Puma helicopters from France instead. Even although the French equipment proved too costly for Sudan, the affair had the desired effect, and in 1976 the US State Department granted supply of Lockheed C-130 Hercules transports to replace the remaining An-12s. Two years later, approval was granted for delivery of F-5E/Fs as well, funded by Saudi Arabia. Thus, by 1981–82, when Sudan found itself in a confrontation with Libya, the SuAF was a force of some 2,000 personnel, flying Soviet-made MiG-21s, Chinese F-5s, US-made F-5Es (the first single-seat Tiger IIs arrived in October 1982, followed by two-seaters in June 1984), and British-made Strikemaster T.Mk 82s and T.Mk 90s.[1]

Despite a period of relative peace and continuous support from abroad, the 1980s eventually saw a slow but steady decline of the entire Sudanese military. The armed forces began to suffer the effects of repeated purges of professional officers and Islamisation, as well as a mutiny by troops from southern Sudan. This led to a new rebellion and riots across the country, prompting another military coup in April 1985. Initially, the military remained in power for only a short period of time. Following general elections in 1986, a new government attempted to find a peaceful solution to end the rebellion in the south. Such intentions and various reforms faced strong opposition from within the armed forces, and the military came back to power in the course of yet another coup in June 1989. This latest coup resulted in the termination of US military assistance and similar cooperation agreements with Yugoslavia. Instead, Khartoum established relations with Iran, and above all with Libya, which had begun providing equipment and assistance from 1988.

During the early 1990s, Khartoum continued to maintain close ties with China, but also introduced a programme of measures including creation of the Popular Defence Forces (PDF), a militia created along the lines of the Iranian Islamic Revolutionary Guards Corps (IRGC). Although intended to supplement the Army's strength in the field, the PDF ended up primarily enforcing 'theological correctness' in the military and maintaining internal security. Considering the poor overall condition of what had since been named the Sudanese People's Armed Forces (SPAF), the PDF's effect on the air force was disastrous. During the fighting against insurgents of the Sudanese People's Liberation Army (SPLA) in the early 1990s, the SuAF suffered such heavy attrition that only a squadron's worth of all combat aircraft and less than a dozen transports were left operational by early 1993.

In the following years the SuAF increasingly became dependent on aid from Iraq. For most of the 1990s, between 30 and 60 Iraqi pilots and technicians served in Sudan, particularly with the air force, and they frequently became involved in combat against the SPLA.

Oil exploration and exploitation had begun in Sudan in the 1960s, but had developed to only a minimal degree by the 1980s. In the 1990s, however, oil began to show its effects. In 1999, following completion of an oil pipeline extending from the southern oilfields through Khartoum to the Red Sea, and with help from Algeria, China, Pakistan, and Russia, Sudan began exporting crude. Increasing oil revenues allowed Khartoum to purchase modern weapons and the SuAF to put an end to its haphazard purchases of second-hand aircraft.

Correspondingly, in recent years, the SuAF has been equipped with ever more modern and effective combat aircraft, including additional MiG and Sukhoi fighters, mainly purchased from Moscow. Cooperation with China has remained intact, and the Chinese have helped with deliveries of equipment for the Safat Aviation Complex, situated at Wadi Sayyidna air base, and now capable of performing maintenance and overhauls of fighter-bombers, helicopters, transports, liaison aircraft, radars and avionics of Soviet/Russian design, as well as training ground personnel. In cooperation with Harbin Dongan Engines, the Safat Complex also became capable of undertaking regular overhauls of Chinese-made fighters and helicopters of Western and Russian origin.

Midway through this rebuilding of the air force and following three years of negotiations, a peace deal was signed with the Sudanese People's Liberation Army (SPLA) in January 2005. Under the terms of the deal, Khartoum ceded roughly half of Sudan's oil wealth to the south, as well as granting nearly complete autonomy, and the right to secede after six years (a corresponding referendum was held in 2011 under UN supervision, and the Republic of South Sudan declared itself independent on 9 July 2011).

However, just as the peace process in the south was making substantial progress, in March 2003 a new insurgency emerged in Darfur, in western Sudan. Here, various parties were accusing the central government of neglecting the region economically. In an attempt to improve their position in Khartoum, local politicians refused to negotiate, instead provoking a major conflagration. Surprised by this development, the government unleashed elements of the PDF, foremost mounted militias, resulting in a brutal war. Despite reaching a relative stalemate by 2004, the conflict not only spilled over into neighbouring Chad, but also ruined the government's reputation and saw it face charges of war crimes, in turn entirely overshadowing the most recent developments within the SuAF.

Deliveries of MiG and Shenyang fighters to Sudan

The first reports concerning Sudan obtaining MiG fighters date from 1967, when Khartoum entered negotiations for their delivery with China. However, Sudan's first experiences with fighter jets of MiG design date back to 1969, when the Soviets delivered the first of 18 MiG-21M single-seat interceptors (with a secondary air-to-ground capability). Over 1,800 Soviet military advisors arrived too, several of them training Sudanese pilots to fly MiG-21s until they were finally expelled in 1971.

Apparently 'only' showing a SuAF Mi-8MT (serial number 506), this well-known photograph taken during Exercise Bright Star '81 also shows a Sudanese FT-5 with the serial number 168, in the background, right.
(US DoD)

Photographed during the same exercise, this was one of the SuAF MiG-21Ms at Wadi Sayyidna air base as it appeared before overhaul at the Zmaj Works in the former Yugoslavia.
(US DoD)

Up to 22 additional MiG-21s and 4 two-seat MiG-21US conversion trainers were delivered by the USSR during the second phase of Sudanese-Soviet friendship, between 1974 and 1977. However, most spare parts for the MiG-21s were lost in the course of a failed coup attempt in October 1976, after which 96 Sudanese officers – including a number of SuAF pilots – were executed. Much of the expertise gained over the time was lost and the condition of the MiG-21s deteriorated to a level whereby the entire fleet had to be overhauled by the Zmaj Works, near Zagreb, then in Yugoslavia, in the early 1980s.

A still from a video showing a row of several SuAF MiG and Shenyang fighters, lined up for display at Wadi Sayyidna AB, in 2010. From the left, it shows MiG-21M 344, an FT-5 with an unreadable serial number (possibly 745), an F-6 (without serial number) and an A-5C.
(via Pit Weinert)

The Chinese began their deliveries by providing 16 Shenyang F-5s (Chinese-made MiG-17Fs) and two-seat FT-5s in 1969. This was followed by the delivery of 12 Shenyang F-6 supersonic fighters and 2 FT-6 two-seat conversion trainers, the first of which arrived in early June 1973. Between 1981 and 1983, 12 additional F-6Cs were delivered – apparently as attrition replacements – and there are reports that another batch of up to 12 F-6Cs was acquired in 1990.

Frequent reports citing deliveries of F-7s from China or Iran cannot be confirmed. However, the flat denial by the Iranian Charge d'Affairs in Khartoum of similar reports concerning Iranian delivery of at least four ex-Iraqi MiG-23BNs and one MiG-23UB – possibly in exchange for the remaining Sudanese F-5E/Fs – in 1992, sounds at least possible.[2]

Furthermore, Sudan received one MiG-21bis when an Ethiopian pilot defected on 6 June 1989. Ever since, this aircraft has been used for technical instruction at Wadi Sayyidna air base.

Meanwhile, newly established ties to Libya resulted in the delivery of at least 12, and perhaps as many as 18 MiG-23MS and MiG-23BN jets from this country in 1988. Libya also operated two MiG-25R reconnaissance fighters on temporary deployment in Sudan around the same period. Roughly half of the MiG-23s were out of service within barely a year, but some might have been overhauled and returned to service more recently.

Left The cooperation between Khartoum and Washington during the early 1980s led to several visits by USAF teams to the SuAF. An American officer is seen here approaching MiG-21M serial number 345 for inspection.
(Tom Cooper Collection)

Right USAF officers inspect MiG-21U serial number 303, probably in 1981. It is very likely that the Americans were also given an opportunity to fly this aircraft.
(Tom Cooper Collection)

The sad remnants of an ex-Libyan MiG-23BN, donated to Sudan in 1988, and subsequently crash-landed and abandoned in the Padak area, sometime in the early 2000s.
(UNEP)

In order to replace worn-out MiG-23s, in 2001 Sudan purchased at least 10, and more likely 12 Nanchang A-5Cs and 2 additional FT-5s or FT-6s. The A-5 was introduced to combat service in December 2001, even although insurgents subsequently often misidentified these aircraft as 'MiG-29s'.[3]

Three SuAF A-5Cs (serial number 403 in the foreground, 407 in the rear, and 402 to the right) at Nyala airfield in March 2006. The type entered service and was deployed in combat during the early stages of the war in Darfur.
(UN)

A scene from Nyala airfield in July 2007, showing two SuAF A-5Cs armed with the Chinese variant of the old Soviet ORO-57K pod containing six 57mm (2.24in) calibre rockets.
(Melting Tarmac Images)

It was only after lengthy negotiations with Moscow and in the course of tensions with Eritrea over that country's support for the SPLA that a contract for at least 10 MiG-29SEhs and a pair of MiG-29UBs was signed during an April 2003 visit to Moscow by the Sudanese defence minister. The first two aircraft arrived at Wadi Sayyidna air base on 29 December 2003, two more on 29 January 2004, and the last two out of at least 12 by July of the same year.[4]

Reports concerning the acquisition of 12 MiG-21s from Ukraine in 2004 have never been confirmed. Instead, based on available serial numbers of SuAF MiG-29s, it now appears that a total of 24 such aircraft were purchased, although it remains unclear whether all have been brought up to MiG-29SEh standard – making them compatible with the modern, Russian-made R-77 medium-range AAM, which is known to be in service with the SuAF – before delivery.

SuAF MiG-29SEh serial number 614, as seen at Wadi Sayyidna in 2009. Of interest are underwing launch rails for R-77 and R-73 air-to-air missiles.
(Yahya Zain al-Abdien)

A pair of SuAF MiG-29s over Khartoum in December 2007. Lead aircraft is MiG-29UB serial 602, and behind it is MiG-29SEh serial number 623.
(Melting Tarmac Images)

In early 2008 the first indications emerged from Belarus that SuAF pilots were undergoing conversion courses on the Su-25, and that a batch of these aircraft was being readied for delivery. Although again misreported as 'MiG-29s', 12 single-seat Su-25s and a pair of two-seat Su-25UBs were delivered to Sudan during summer 2008. Another batch of Su-25s was reported as 'under assembly' following delivery in spring 2010, increasing the total to at least 18 aircraft of this type.

An unidentified SuAF Su-25 in flight, showing at least some details of its relatively simple camouflage pattern as well as the oversized roundels applied on the upper surfaces of the wings.
(via Pit Weinert)

This still from a recently released video indicates that the SuAF has begun training its pilots in nocturnal operations. Seen in the background is Su-25UB serial number 215.
(via Pit Weinert)

Force structure

Contrary to the general structure of the SPAF, which is organised into five military regions that simultaneously function as divisions of the Army, the SuAF's structure is based around squadrons with specialised functions, most of which are based at Wadi Sayyidna air base.[5] Exact designations of specific air force units are uncertain, and it is possible that the known designations (see below for details) are actually 'replacements', assigned to Sudanese squadrons by foreign intelligence services. The only confirmed unit identity is that of the SuAF Flying School.

Originally based at what later became Khartoum IAP, the Flying School moved to Wadi Sayyidna in the late 1960s, and then to a new air base established on the old Port Sudan airfield in 2001. In the course of this transition, the Flying School was apparently expanded to two units, one responsible for basic training and equipped with Chinese-made Nanchang CJ-6 trainers, and the other for jet-fighter training, equipped with FT-5s and Hongdu K-8E Karakorums.[6]

Most SuAF squadrons that operate fighter jets are supervised by the Air Defence Command, which also includes two brigades equipped with SA-2 SAMs, with responsibility for the air defence of Khartoum and Port Sudan. In addition to these two major air bases, during the 1980s and particularly during the war in southern Sudan in the 1990s, SuAF fighter jets are also known to have operated from el-Ubayyid, Damazin, Malakal and Juba. More recently, el-Fasher, el-Geneina and Nyala have been developed into forward air bases in Darfur. Construction of a new airfield in Kadugli was never completed, but during the early 2000s, several other airstrips have received runways hardened enough to support operations by MiG fighters, including Tini and el-Geneina in the west, as well as Wau in the south.

Table 33: Reported SuAF order of battle, mid-1980s until today

Unit	Base	Equipment
No. 1 Interception Squadron	Wadi Sayyidna	F-6 and FT-6 in 1980s; currently MiG-29
No. 2 Interception Squadron	Wadi Sayyidna	MiG-21M and MiG-21US in 1980s; currently MiG-29
No. 1 COIN Squadron	Wadi Sayyidna	Jet Provost and Strikemaster in 1980s; currently A-5C
No. 2 Fighter-Bomber Squadron	Wadi Sayyidna	F-5E/F in 1980s; MiG-23 in 1990s; currently Su-25
No. 1 Transport Squadron	Khartoum IAP	C-130 in 1980s; currently An-26
No. 3 Transport Squadron	Khartoum IAP	F27 and DHC-5D in 1970s and 1980s; later An-26; currently An-72
No. 1 Attack Helicopter Squadron	Khartoum IAP	Former Libyan Mi-25; later Mi-24
No. 1 Helicopter Squadron	Khartoum IAP	Mi-8 and Mi-17; also Bo.105 and IAR-330 in 1980s
Flying School	Port Sudan	Currently CJ-6 and FT-5
	Wadi Sayyidna	Currently K-8E

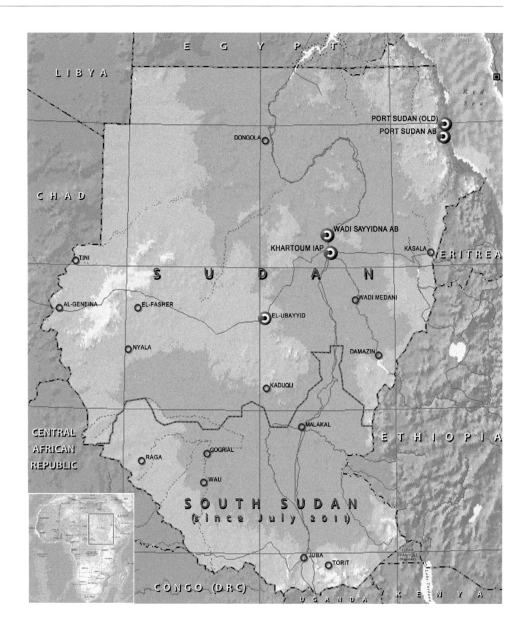

Map of Sudan

National markings

The original Sudanese national insignia included blue, yellow and green colours, and corresponding roundels and fin flashes were worn by SuAF aircraft until 1969. The pan-Arabic flag (red, white and black) was then introduced as a replacement, complete with a green triangle segment.

During the late 1960s a tradition was introduced under which roundels were applied on the forward fuselage of SuAF combat aircraft, and this tradition is very much apparent even on the latest acquisitions, including A-5Cs and MiG-29s. Roundels are also applied in four positions on the wings, and fin flashes are worn on the fins. Su-25s are the first SuAF fighter jets not to wear any roundels on the fuselage, but they retain roundels on the upper and lower surfaces of both wings.

Camouflage colours and serial numbers

During the 1960s and 1970s most SuAF aircraft were left in the colours in which they were delivered. In the case of Sudanese Shenyang F-5s and MiG-21s, this meant that all were left in 'bare metal' overall. The situation changed few years after the introduction to service of the F-6. These aircraft arrived painted white overall, and the wreckage of two F-6Cs found at Juba in early 2005 shows that at least some of them were left as such throughout their service in Sudan. However, other aircraft seen at different opportunities appear to have received a camouflage pattern consisting of beige, dark brown and dark green during the late 1980s.

Libyan MiG-23s were delivered to Sudan still wearing the standardised pattern for this type as exported to Middle Eastern and African countries, consisting of sand (approximately FS13523), dark earth (FS20095) and green (FS30098) on the upper surfaces and sides, and light blue-grey (FS35622) on the lower surfaces. If any of the Iraqi MiG-23s evacuated to the Islamic Republic of Iran in February 1990 were indeed delivered to Sudan, they almost certainly wore the same camouflage pattern as the former Libyan examples.[7]

Surviving SuAF FT-5s in service with the Flying School at Port Sudan have been seen wearing a camouflage pattern consisting of sand, brown and green on the upper surfaces, with light blue undersides. Sadly, more precise details of this pattern remain unknown.

Similarly, A-5Cs operated by Sudan were delivered wearing a standardised camouflage pattern for export aircraft of this type, consisting of yellow sand, dark brown and dark green on the upper surfaces, and light blue lower surfaces. A similar camouflage pattern has since been sighted on at least one F-6C as well, although it is unclear if this was applied fleet-wide.

MiG-29SEhs were delivered wearing a unique pattern of sand, dark earth and olive drab upper surfaces, with undersides in two shades of light grey-blue.

Sudanese Su-25s are camouflaged in yellow sand and dark brown only on the upper surfaces, with a slightly darker shade of RLB on the undersides.

In terms of serial numbers, the first Provosts delivered to the SuAF in 1962 wore numbers applied in both Arabic and Persian numerals on the rear fuselage, and this tradition was continued on Jet Provosts and Strikemasters.

It is known that Shenyang F-5s originally had their serial numbers applied in Persian numerals on the forward fuselage, and in Arabic numerals on the rear fuselage, in both cases in black. The MiG-21 introduced the practice of double application of serial numbers – in Arabic and Persian numerals – on both the forward and the rear fuselage, and this was subsequently continued on all F-6s and A-5Cs received from China.

MiG-29s only received black serial numbers in Arabic numerals on the forward fuselage and fins. This practice was repeated on Su-25s obtained from Belarus in 2008, although their serial numbers are applied much larger.

Curiously enough, Libyan MiG-23s acquired in 1989 received only poorly applied Sudanese national markings, most of which washed out quite swiftly, and retained their original serial numbers. The same was the case with the two Libyan Arab Air Force MiG-25Rs temporarily deployed in Sudan at the same time.

Table 34: Serial numbers of SuAF MiG, Shenyang and Sukhoi fighters, 1969–2009[8]

Aircraft type	Serial number	c/n	Remarks
FT-5	158		Delivered from China, 1969; last seen Wadi Sayyidna, mid-1980s
F-5	160		Delivered from China, 1969
F-5	161		Delivered from China, 1969
F-5	163		Delivered from China, 1969
F-5	164		Delivered from China, 1969
FT-5	168		Delivered from China, 1969
F-5	170		Delivered from China, 1969
FT-5	180		Delivered from China, 1969
FT-5	181		Delivered from China, 1969
FT-5	182		Delivered from China, 1969
FT-5	183		Delivered from China, 1969
FT-5	184		Delivered from China, 1969
FT-5	186		Delivered from China, 1969
FT-5	187		Delivered from China, 1969
FT-5	188		Delivered from China, 1969
FT-5	190		Delivered from China, 1969
Su-25	201		Delivered from Belarus, 2008; last seen el-Ubayyid AB, July 2010
Su-25UB	202		Delivered from Belarus, 2008; last seen el-Obeid, 2009
Su-25	203		Delivered from Belarus, 2008; last seen el-Ubayyid AB, July 2010
Su-25	204		Delivered from Belarus, 2008; last seen el-Fasher, 2009
Su-25	205		Delivered from Belarus, 2008
Su-25	206		Delivered from Belarus, 2008; last seen el-Fasher, 2009
Su-25	207		Delivered from Belarus, 2008
Su-25	208		Delivered from Belarus, 2008; last seen 2009
Su-25	209		Delivered from Belarus, 2008
Su-25	210		Delivered from Belarus, 2008; last seen el-Ubayyid AB, July 2010
Su-25	211		Delivered from Belarus, 2008; last seen Juba, 2010
Su-25	212		Delivered from Belarus, 2008; last seen Wadi Sayyidna AB, 2010
Su-25	213		Delivered from Belarus, 2009
Su-25	214		Delivered from Belarus, 2009
Su-25UB	215		Delivered from Belarus, 2010
Su-25UB	217		Delivered from Belarus, April 2010
MiG-21US	300		Delivered from USSR, 1969; last seen at Zmaj Works, 1980
MiG-21M	301		Delivered from USSR, 1969; last seen at Wadi Sayyidna, 1986
MiG-21US	303		Delivered from USSR, 1969; last seen at Wadi Sayyidna, 1979
MiG-21M	304	7607404	Delivered from USSR, 1969; w/o at an unknown date
MiG-21M	309	7607409	Delivered from USSR, 1969; w/o at an unknown date
MiG-21M	312	7607412	Delivered from USSR, 1969; dumped at Kassala
MiG-21M	315	7607415	Delivered from USSR, 1969; w/o at an unknown date
MiG-21M	331		Delivered from USSR, 1974; last seen at Khartoum IAP, early 1990s
MiG-21M	341	7607401	Delivered from USSR, 1974
MiG-21M	342	7607402	Delivered from USSR, 1974
MiG-21M	343	7607403	Delivered from USSR, 1974

MiG-21M	344	7607405	Delivered from USSR, 1974; last seen at Wadi Sayyidna AB, 2010, used for technical instruction
MiG-21M	345	7607406	Delivered from USSR, 1974; last seen 1982
MiG-21M	346	7607407	Delivered from USSR, 1974
MiG-21M	347	7607408	Delivered from USSR, 1974
MiG-21M	348	7607410	Delivered from USSR, 1974
MiG-21M	349	7607411	Delivered from USSR, 1974
MiG-21M	350	7607413	Delivered from USSR, 1974
MiG-21M	351	7607414	Delivered from USSR, 1974
MiG-21M	352	7607416	Delivered from USSR, 1974
MiG-21M	353	7607417	Delivered from USSR, 1974
MiG-21M	354	7607418	Delivered from USSR, 1974
MiG-21M	378		Delivered from USSR, 1974
MiG-21M	399		Delivered from USSR, 1974
MiG-21bis	1130		Former EtAF aircraft flown in on 6 June 1989; used for technical instruction at Wadi Sayyidna
A-5C	401		Delivered from China, 2001
A-5C	402		Delivered from China, 2001; last seen in March 2007, Nyala (engines removed)
A-5C	403		Delivered from China, 2001; last seen in March 2007, Nyala
A-5C	404		Delivered from China, 2001
A-5C	405		Delivered from China, 2001
A-5C	406		Delivered from China, 2001
A-5C	407		Delivered from China, 2001; last seen in March 2007, Nyala
A-5C	408		Delivered from China, 2001; derelict at Juba, May 2007
A-5C	409		Delivered from China, 2001; last seen 2009
A-5C	410		Delivered from China, 2001; last seen in March 2007, Nyala
MiG-29SEh	601		Delivered from Russia, 2004
MiG-29UB	602		Delivered from Russia, 2004; last seen in December 2007, Khartoum
MiG-29SEh	606		Delivered from Russia, 2004; last seen in December 2007, Khartoum
MiG-29SEh	614		Delivered from Russia, 2004; last seen at Wadi Sayyidna, 2010
MiG-29SEh	623		Delivered from Russia, 2004; last seen in December 2007, Khartoum
MiG-29SEh	624		Delivered from Russia, 2004; last seen in December 2007, Khartoum
F-6	701		Delivered from China, 1980
F-6	702		Delivered from China, 1980
F-6	703		Delivered from China, 1980
F-6	704		Delivered from China, 1980
F-6	705		Delivered from China, 1980
F-6	706		Delivered from China, 1980
F-6	707		Delivered from China, 1980
F-6	708		Delivered from China, 1980
F-6	709		Delivered from China, 1980
F-6	710		Delivered from China, 1980
F-6	711		Delivered from China, 1980
F-6	712		Delivered from China, 1980
FT-6	713		Delivered from China, 1980

FT-6	714	Delivered from China, 1980
F-6C		Delivered from China, early 1990s; derelict at Juba, early 2005
FT-5	745	Delivered from China, early 1980s; last seen at Wadi Sayyidna, 2010, in non-operational condition
F-6C	748	Delivered from China, early 1990s; derelict at Juba, early 2005
F-6C	764	Delivered from China, early 1980s
MiG-23MS	06916	Delivered from Libya, 1988; wreckage at Juba, 1989
MiG-23MS	06918	Delivered from Libya, 1988; w/o at an unknown date
MiG-23MS	09055	Delivered from Libya, 1988; last at Wadi Sayyidna, 2010, in non-operational condition

A batch of FT-5s delivered from China in 1969 represented some of the first MiGs to enter service with the SuAF. These aircraft were initially left in 'bare metal' overall, and wore serial numbers applied in Persian numerals on the forward fuselage, and serial numbers in Arabic numerals on the rear fuselage. It remains unknown if any roundels were applied on the wings.

The second batch of FT-5s, probably delivered together with the first batch of F-6s, in around 1983, were painted in white overall and received a full set of serial numbers as well as larger set of roundels and fin flashes.

MiG and Shenyang fighter operations in the Republic of Sudan, 1969–1972

Almost nothing is known about the possible participation of the SuAF in the First Sudan Civil War – at least not before a group of well-placed Sudanese Army officers, sometimes referred to as the 'Young Officers', overthrew the civilian government in Khartoum in a bloodless coup on 25 May 1969.[9] The group was headed by the officer in command of the Khartoum garrison, Col Jafaar an-Nimeiry. The coup took place when all 14 of the most senior officers in the armed forces were out of the country, either on official or private visits. The new military leaders established a Revolutionary Council, suspended the constitution, abolished the Supreme Council and the National Assembly, proclaimed the establishment of the 'Democratic Republic of the Sudan', imposed censorship on all newspapers except for two under their control, and announced comprehensive reforms aiming at modernising the entire country.

The new government in Khartoum had numerous and powerful enemies, particularly within the military, and came to power at a time in which the military was involved in fighting an insurgency in the southern half of the country. This campaign aimed to put down the Land Freedom Army, better known as Anya-Nya (AN), which had been active since 1955.

During July, August and December 1969 several plots to overthrow the new government were exposed, resulting in a weakening of Sudan's contacts with the West. With widespread unrest around the country and additional coups and counter-coups – some of which resulted in fighting in the streets of Omdurman during early 1970 – the air force was preoccupied with other issues, and the the first Shenyang F-5s and MiG-21s to be operated by the SuAF entered service only very slowly. Nevertheless, SuAF MiG-21s are usually said to have flown their first combat sortie even before their operating unit was declared operational, namely on 20 December 1969, when three fighters are reported to have bombed the town of Nyerol, in Upper Nile Province, then held by Anya-Nya insurgents.

The second opportunity for the SuAF 'MiGs' to enter combat followed only a few months later. After fleeing the country following their unsuccessful uprising, the members of the Ansar sect launched an uprising on Aba Island and attempted to assassinate President Nimeiry. The group subsequently reported that between 27-30 March 1970 they came under attack by up to '25 MiGs', in addition to at least two Army brigades and some armour. According to the same sources, because the SuAF had no pilots to fly such aircraft at the time, the Sudanese MiGs were flown by Egyptian and Soviet pilots, who used rockets in their attacks.[10] However, it is perfectly possible that the 'MiGs' in question were actually some of the Jet Provosts that remained in service with the SuAF.

Indeed, despite the presence of several dozen Egyptian and no fewer than 1,800 Soviet military personnel in Sudan, both Egypt and the Soviet Union later denied any involvement. The Egyptian assistance mainly concentrated on the development of the SuAF's organisation and infrastructure at three main bases – Wadi Sayyidna, Juba and Port Sudan. Considering the shaky relationship between the new government and Cairo at the time, any Egyptian involvement is somewhat doubtful. Still, when another coup attempt prompted the government to return the battalion of Sudanese troops serving in the Suez Canal back to Khartoum, on 22 July 1970, this had to be flown back in Libyan transport aircraft.

Crest of SuAF

Patch of Khartoum AB
Several details applied below the 'Hawk of Sallahuddin', cannot be seen clearly on the few available photographs and are missing in this reconstruction.

Aided by the continuous presence of Chinese advisors, Shenyang F-5s became operational early in 1970, followed by the MiG-21 unit, which was officially declared operational in February of the same year. These two types subsequently formed the backbone of the SuAF combat component, together with No. 1 COIN Squadron that flew Jet Provost T.Mk 51/52s, Jet Provost T.Mk 55/Strikemaster T.Mk 82s and Strikemaster T.Mk 90s. However, the condition of the MiG-21 fleet gradually deteriorated following the severing of relations with Moscow in the light of rumours concerning Soviet involvement in the aforementioned coup attempt.

Due to widespread unrest and the series of military coup attempts – both of which resulted in a series of purges affecting hundreds of Sudanese military officers – as of early 1971 the SuAF still numbered only around 450 personnel. This number increased to more than 700 by the time the Soviet advisors were expelled from the country, but the training of new personnel remained quite problematic due to the lack of modern training aids and collective training, as well as the Sudanese refusal to accept Soviet attempts at imposing their military doctrine and to intermix politics with training.[11]

Another problem was the relatively slow pace at which new Sudanese pilots were trained in the USSR. Pilot training on the MiG-21 usually lasted no less than two years and the trainees first had to acquire a working knowledge of Russian, which resulted in considerable time lags. Irrespective of their previous experience, even the more experienced SuAF pilots were subsequently put through the standard training courses, including a year at the Flight School at Primorsko Atharsk air base, during which they flew around 100 hours on Yakovlev Yak-18As. It was only during the second year that they would convert to MiG-15UTI jet trainers, flying around 100 hours on these, before continuing with another 100 hours on MiG-17s and MiG-21s. Such a relatively slow pace of training – as well as the considerable quantities of political training that the Sudanese had to sit through – was considered by most of participants to be a waste of time and an irrelevance.

Nevertheless, foreigners that witnessed the SuAF at work in the early 1970s usually described high standards of morale and discipline. Therefore, during the early 1970s, the SuAF came increasingly into action against AN insurgents in the south of the

The last from a batch of five Jet Provost T.Mk 55/Strikemaster T.Mk. 82s ordered in 1966 and delivered in March 1969. These served with the SuAF as advanced trainers and light strike aircraft. Given the generally poor recognition skills of local observers, it is likely that some of their operations were misreported as those of the 'MiGs'. Note the old Sudanese national insignia in blue, yellow and green.

country, usually deploying pairs of MiG-21s to strafe and launch rockets in support of Army columns that frequently cooperated with helicopters. The rotorcraft were used to lift troops forward into battle, or to suddenly surround enemy strongpoints.

Persistent rumours that many of the aircraft were flown by Egyptian and Soviet pilots mainly dervied from AN sources and remain unconfirmed to this day. Both Cairo and Moscow consistently deny that any of their personnel were involved in operations in the south. This was characteristic for this little known, shadowy and hidden war, where unreliable 'official' communiqués, vague rumours and many allegations from officials of both involved parties were often the only 'truths' that reached the media.

Meanwhile, it is likely that some Egyptian or Soviet advice was behind some operations, including that launched against an AN HQ near Morta, in Equatoria State, in September 1970. This was first attacked by truck-borne infantry, before the Army battalion involved was ambushed and suffered some losses. Reinforced to brigade strength through additional units, this force was then ferried to Bori by helicopters, and on 24 September advanced on Morta under the cover of artillery fire and supported by one Antonov and three MiG-21s, the latter deploying bombs and unguided rockets in the process. With the Army attack repulsed again, the SuAF came back in force on the next day, deploying additional MiGs to rocket the insurgent positions. The third and fourth assaults on Morta, launched on 25 and 26 September 1970, respectively, were again resisted. Instead of fading away into the forest after nominal resistance, the Anya-Nya fought back fiercely.

This necessitated a new plan of attack. Once again, troops were lifted by helicopters, but this time they deployed into an advantageous position on high ground, which they would not have been able to reach on foot, and which was actually behind the rough AN front line. Simultaneously – and for the next few days – the insurgents came under successive aerial strikes by SuAF MiG-21s, forward deployed at Juba. Following extensive preparations, on 1 October the Army assaulted the Anya-Nya lines from the rear, finally forcing the survivors to abandon their positions and disperse. During this operation the SuAF is reported to have suffered the loss of one MiG-21 that crashed near Juba and another MiG-21 reportedly shot down, together with one Mi-8 helicopter.[12]

Egyptian and Soviet advice enabled the SuAF to launch a sizeable aerial offensive against insurgent camps and bases in early 1971. In the course of these operations up to 25 fighter jets reportedly hit the same target in quick succession – often in cooperation with the crews of An-12 transports, which were deployed for reconnaissance purposes. Such attacks often led to allegations that the government was bombing civilian targets. The Anya-Nya claimed that 800 people had been killed by SuAF attacks in November 1970 alone. In another instance, in February 1971 it was alleged that a bombing raid on an Anya-Nya base near Morta, on the border with Uganda, caused 1,000 civilian casualties. In response, the government insisted that there was no practice of random bombing, and that aerial action was only taken against clearly identified AN camps.

Despite managing to secure itself in power, Numairy's government found itself internationally isolated as well as unable to win the war against the AN, which now enjoyed significant support from Israel. The latter established military training missions for southern Sudanese insurgents in Ethiopia, Uganda and Zaire. Three mercenary groups also operated in support of the insurgents, including a one-aircraft charter company, Southern Airmotive, which dropped supplies en route to Uganda. Since some airfields

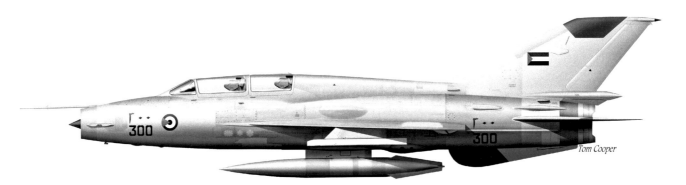

MiG-21US serial number 300 was probably one of the first aircraft of this type to enter service with the SuAF, in the 1969-1970 period. The aircraft remained operational into the early 1990s, all the time left in 'bare metal' overall and wearing the same set of markings.

Seen in these markings and configuration at Wadi Sayyidna around 1985, MiG-21M serial number 301 was one of around two dozen Sudanese MiGs overhauled in the former Yugoslavia in the early 1980s.

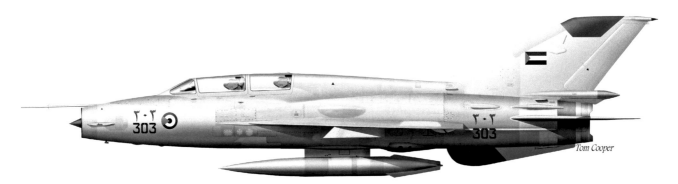

This MiG-21US was last seen in these colours and markings following overhaul at the Zmaj Works near Zagreb, Yugoslavia, in the early 1980s.

in Ethiopia were repeatedly used to supply the rebels, these were on several occasions hit by SuAF MiG-21s.[13]

Following lengthy negotiations that began in May 1971 and continued through February 1972, the government finally gave concessions to the insurgents, enabling a degree of self-government in the states of southern Sudan. The settlement was agreed through a series of compromises, including establishment of a unified government for the southern states to represent the interests of the local population in Khartoum, integration of 12,000 AN dissidents into the military, and tolerance of different regions and cultures.

The last known occasion on which SuAF MiG-21s appeared in public during this period occurred on 20 September 1972, when two examples intercepted a formation of C-130 transports of the Libyan Arab Air Force (LAAF) under way with 399 troops to Uganda. The MiGs forced the Hercules to land at Khartoum IAP. Due to good relations between Khartoum and Tripoli, the Libyans were permitted to take off and fly back home via Cairo several hours later. However, once airborne, all five transports continued their voyage to Entebbe, regardless.

MiG and Shenyang fighter operations in the Republic of Sudan, 1972–1983

Following the ceasefire there were hopes that peace would enable economic recovery to take place. However, recovery was slow, and southerners were wary that some costly development schemes – primarily the Jonglei Canal project, which aimed to cut through the Sudd, a huge swampy area of the southern Nile basin – would endanger their farming and herding economy. Other domestic and international difficulties continued as well, exacerbated by the deepening economic crisis, which was in turn aggravated by the terrible droughts of the early 1970s. Therefore tensions continued between north and south, as well as with Ethiopia.

Eventually, the economic situation forced the government to make overtures to the West, and Khartoum re-established relations with the UK, resulting in joint exercises with the British Army in 1975. In turn, an RAF contingent was stationed in Khartoum to help return the Jet Provosts to operational condition (it is possible that around this time some RAF pilots were seconded to the SuAF to fly them, too). The US followed the British pattern, sending a small military delegation, which also 'inspected' all surviving SuAF MiGs. Connections to Washington resulted in permission for the sale of six C-130Hs to Sudan, although the first Sudanese request for deliveries of F-5E Tiger II fighters was turned down by the US administration.

By the early 1980s Sudan had become involved in the conflict between the US and Libya, which initially erupted over the Libyan claim for the entire Gulf of Sirte as its territorial waters, and subsequently expanded through Libyan support for a number of international terrorist organisations, plots for the assassination of the US president, and the Libyan invasion of Chad. On a direct order from the US administration, the CIA began providing support to insurgents in northern Chad from bases in Egypt and particularly Sudan. In response, beginning in late August 1981, Libya launched a number of air strikes against insurgent camps in western Sudan, primarily in el-Geneina, Kulbus, Tandatu and Asognam. The frequency of such attacks increased over time,

MiG-21M serial number 331 as noted at Khartoum IAP in the late 1980s. The type was originally purchased with the primary task of serving as an interceptor, and was armed with R-3S missiles for this purpose.

This Sudanese MiG-21M saw a long and probably distinguished career with the SuAF, being flown in the wars against the Anya-Nya, during exercises with the USAF in the early 1980s, and during the early stages of the war with the SPLA. This aircraft is still extant and was last seen – still wearing these markings and insignia – stored at the Safat Aviation Complex at Wadi Sayyidna in 2010.

In addition to interception duties, SuAF MiG-21Ms saw extensive service during the war against the southern Sudanese insurgency in the late 1980s and 1990s. Reportedly, the type was normally armed with UB-16-57 rocket pods.

and on 16 September 1981 a Libyan SF.260WL Warrior light strike aircraft was shot down near el-Geneina, and its pilot killed. In revenge, the LAAF despatched a Tupolev Tu-22 bomber to attack the State Radio station in Omdurman. This attack, flown a few days later, resulted in three FAB-500 bombs missing their target, but destroying several houses, killing and injuring at least 20 civilians. Only a few days later, the Egyptian President Anwar el-Sadat was assassinated in Cairo. Uncertain about the future of Egypt and Sudan, US President Ronald Reagan immediately authorised extensive shipments of arms and equipment to both countries, as well as a deployment of two Boeing E-3A Sentry AWACS to Cairo West air base in Egypt. In November 1981, the US and Egypt staged their first joint exercise, Bright Star '81, in the course of which the US Air Force deployed assets including Boeing B-52 Stratofortress strategic bombers to Egypt.

These developments, combined with the continued LAAF offensive against US- (and French-) supported insurgents in northern Chad, eventually prompted the administration in Washington to launch Operation Early Call. The plan for this operation envisaged a mock coup in Khartoum, after which the supposed perpetrators would call upon the LAAF for help. Once the Libyan fighters reacted, the two USAF E-3As stationed in Egypt were to vector Egyptian and Sudanese interceptors to shoot them down, while aircraft from the carrier USS *John F. Kennedy* (CV-67) would aid in the protection of Egyptian airspace. However, Operation Early Call was revealed by the US media and had to be called off while various American units were in the process of deploying to Egypt.[14]

Another problem with Operation Early Call was the sad state of the SuAF in the early 1980s, as well as increasing tensions between Sudan and Ethiopia, and the fact that by this time the government in Khartoum was facing a new insurgency in the south. Direct cooperation with the US enabled Sudan to request deliveries of US-made F-5E/F fighter-bombers, order its first batch of Shenyang F-6s from China, and purchase new shipments of spares for Jet Provosts and Strikemasters in the UK.

Furthermore, the government reached an agreement with Yugoslavia under which all surviving MiG-21s would be overhauled at the Zmaj Works in Nova Gorica, near Zagreb. In the course of this work, Yugoslavia also trained a number of SuAF technicians in the maintenance of the MiGs, finding the Sudanese fast learning and eager to work. Interestingly, it was only upon redelivery of the first batch of overhauled MiGs that the government in Khartoum concluded it could not pay for all the work undertaken by Zmaj. Nevertheless, the factory received at least a payment for all the components used during the overhaul, and all the aircraft were redelivered by 1986.[15]

It was because of this deal that the US advisors to the SuAF observed a dramatic decrease in the number of MiG-21s available during the early 1980s. They reported 16 MiG-21Ms and 2 MiG-21US as operational in 1979; 14 MiG-21Ms and 3 MiG-21US as operational in 1980; 11 MiG-21Ms and 3 MiG-21US in 1981; and (in the last available US report), only 9 MiG-21Ms and 2 MiG-21US as operational in 1984.[16]

With Sudan receiving its F-6s from China in 1982, followed by US-built F-5E/Fs in 1982 and 1984, Wadi Sayyidna air base became the scene of an unusual situation during the mid-1980s. From 05.00 until 14.00, the airfield was used for training SuAF F-6 pilots, supported by Chinese instructors. In the afternoon, US instructors would train Sudanese pilots on the F-5E/Fs. In between, Yugoslavian instructors would support the training of SuAF MiG-21 pilots and ground personnel, while a group of British advisors

Very little is known about the service history of FT-6s in Sudan, but it is known that at least two were delivered and operated by the SuAF, and that they were pained in white overall during their active careers. This example was last seen while undergoing overhauls at the Safat Aviation Complex in early 2008.

Together with another, unidentified example, this F-6C was found dumped near the northern end of the taxiway of Juba airfield in early 2008, after the Sudanese military abandoned that installation. The application of the standard set of markings and insignia is obvious, but it remains unknown if any roundels were applied on either the upper or lower surfaces of the wing.

Sometime during the late 1980s SuAF F-6s received their first coat of camouflage colours, about which very little is known. Some survivors recently overhauled by the Safat Aviation Complex received this camouflage pattern, quite similar to that of SuAF A-5Cs. The insert shows a reconstruction of the top view of the same aircraft.

and technicians supervised the overhaul of surviving Strikemasters and the training of their crews. Flight operations had to be supported by several translators, one for each of the languages used by the foreign advisors. The advisors lived in Khartoum and travelled to Wadi Sayyidna and back every day for their work, and maintained very good relations between each other. Except for the crash of one F-5E barely two weeks after delivery, in 1984, all training missions were completed without incident, and most advisors left Sudan by 1986, by which time the Chinese had trained 12 Sudanese F-6 pilots and over 100 ground personnel.

MiG and Shenyang fighter operations in the Republic of Sudan, 1983–2003

In early 1983 the Second Sudanese Civil War broke out, when elements of the SPAF – consisting of ethnic groups from southern Sudan – mutinied against the government's decision to move them into northern garrisons. The mutiny was uncoordinated and followed a pattern whereupon once a certain unit protested, a wholesale desertion of its troops to the bush would follow. Over time, some of the mutineers began establishing new insurgency organisations, including the Libyan-financed Southern Sudanese Liberation Front (SSLF), and then the SPLA, which captured and held sizeable areas of southern Sudan as early as 1984, inflicting heavy losses upon the SPAF in the process.

At least one ironic episode occurred early on in the fighting, when the pilot of a SuAF F-6 under way from Khartoum to Juba became disorientated and was forced to land at the tiny dirt strip in Boma, deep within the area controlled by insurgents. With the help of several South Africans who happened to be in the area, over the next two weeks he managed to find fuel, and then extend the strip just long enough to allow take-off. Miraculously, the insurgents found the site of this drama only three days after the F-6 took off for Juba.

By 1985 the SPLA was organised into five battalions and was operating anti-aircraft weapons, including MANPADS, which it claimed to have used to shoot down two SuAF MiG-21s. Exactly how the SuAF operated its fighters in COIN operations during this period remains unclear, but there appears to be no evidence of a well-developed COIN doctrine. When over 3,500 SPLA fighters moved against the city and SuAF air base of Juba, in Bahr al-Jabal State in southern Sudan, in February 1985, Sudanese fighter jets were not even reported as being active. Thus, even though it was prevented from occupying Juba, the SPLA was free to put under siege or occupy other important towns in the area, including Boma and Yirol. As the insurgents gained strength in early 1985, President Nimeiry was ousted in a bloodless military coup led by his defence minister, on 6 April of the same year, and the plotters subsequently handed over control to a civilian government.

Following the fall of Nimeiry, the SPLA exploited the situation to launch an offensive in the Adok area, capturing several smaller garrisons in the process. Having established a strong position in the Federal State of Upper Nile in November 1986, the insurgents successfully stopped a drive by five SPAF battalions from Makal towards Anatyer, and then routed this force during a series of engagements in the Nasir-Akobo-Pachala area. The SPLA even published a warning that it would shot down any aircraft – including civilian airliners – flying over the areas it controlled, since the

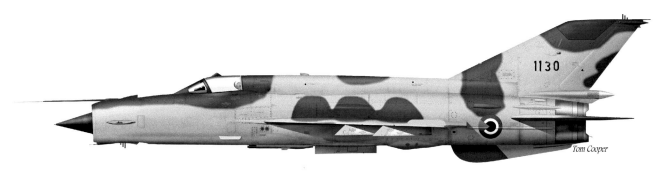

This Ethiopian MiG-21bis was flown to Sudan by a defecting Ethiopian pilot on 6 June 1989. The aircraft appears not to have entered active service with the SuAF, but has ever since been used for technical instruction at Wadi Sayyidna.

In 1988, Libya donated between 12 and 18 MiG-23s to the SuAF – together with a contingent of pilots that helped convert Sudanese to this type, and who probably also flew some combat sorties. Attrition was heavy and no fewer than six aircraft were lost in combat and to training accidents within two years of their arrival. The wreckage of this example was found by UN workers in southern Sudan in 2007.

Another positively identified SuAF MiG-23MS was last seen in 2010, stored at Wadi Sayyidna, still wearing its original LAAF serial number, as well as national markings washed out to a degree where the original insignia was also to be seen.

government made extensive use of transports to move troops around the country. This threat was made good on 16 August 1986, when a Fokker F27 was shot down with the loss of 57 passengers and crew while en route from Malakal to Khartoum.

Both sides spent most of 1987 in reorganisation and stockpiling supplies. The SPLA ended the year organised into 12 regular battalions with a total of 12,000 fighters. The SuAF had meanwhile been reinforced through the arrival of the first Libyan MiG-23s, which were rushed into service – reportedly flown by Libyan pilots – in December 1987. At the same time the SPLA launched Operation Bright Star and simultaneously put Juba, Wau, Torit, Malakal, Bentiu, Uweyl, Rumbek, Gogrial, Nasser, Akubu, Yei, Bor Maridi, Mundri and other towns under siege. The SuAF was deployed in intensive attacks, flying up to 30 combat sorties a day – many of these based on intelligence collected by two MiG-25RBs detached from No. 1035 Squadron LAAF, and forward deployed to Khartoum IAP in 1988. Flown by Libyan pilots only, the two MiG-25s usually conducted two sorties a week.

It remains unclear how heavily the SPLA was hit by the SuAF during this period, but it is quite obvious that the SuAF began suffering heavily from the effects of insurgent-operated MANPADS, as well as accidents. Indeed, one former Libyan MiG-23 was confirmed as crashing following an attack on insurgent positions in Kurmuk, around 500km (311 miles) south of Khartoum, on 18 December 1987. Another was shot down – and its Libyan pilot captured – on 13 December 1988. In addition to combat losses, there were also a number of accidents, and by the end of 1988 only six MiG-23s were reported as still operational. The SPLA also claimed one F-6, two de Havilland Canada DHC-5D Buffalos, two C-130s, one An-24 and another F27, as well as at least one Mi-8 helicopter as shot down during the same period of time. Nevertheless, SuAF fighter-bombers continued to pursue the SPLA into Uganda as well, bombing towns such as Moyo, on 15 November 1989, in addition to Yirol and Wau in southern Sudan.

Although not managing to capture any major garrisons, by the end of Operation Bright Star, the insurgents controlled most of southern Sudan, and the situation led to the overthrow of the government by a group of military officers heavily influenced by radical Islamist ideas, and calling themselves the National Salvation Revolutionary Command Council (NRSCC).

During the following two years, the NRSCC subjected the SPAF to considerable reorganisation. By this time the SPAF was essentially a light infantry force, supported by specialised elements, but it was to become a massive mechanised army, supported by various local militias – established and armed by the government – operating under the aegis of the PDF. This new army was to be put to its first test in the course of a major offensive launched in autumn 1991, coincidentally taking place at the same time as a split occurred within SPLA forces holding the Upper Nile. One of the factions left a sizeable SPAF contingent to attack from Juba via Bor and Kapoeta towards Torit, the SPLA's main stronghold, which was captured in the process, despite insurgent claims of downing at least two F-6s and several helicopters. The loss of Torit was a heavy blow, and the insurgents needed two years to recover, leaving the SPAF and SuAF in the position to acquire additional and more modern weapons, as well as to train further personnel.

During the years of war in south Sudan and Darfur, there has been some debate in the Western media as to who is actually flying SuAF aircraft and what types of aircraft are deployed. It is meanwhile almost certain that since the late 1960s the SuAF has

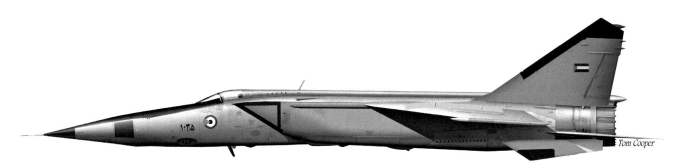

Tom Cooper

In addition to donating a sizeable batch of MiG-23s to Sudan, the LAAF also operated two MiG-25RB reconnaissance-bombers in 1988 and 1989, reportedly from Khartoum IAP. Both jets wore Sudanese markings, while the serial number of the only known example was based on that of the Libyan unit from which it was detached: No. 1035 Squadron, based at al-Jufra/Hun air base.

always had enough of its own pilots, particularly due to the availability of training facilities. However, the standards of flying can at best be described as 'varying', mainly due to the lack of realistic training and training aids, but also due to frequent shortages of spare parts. Nevertheless, there is no doubt that significant contingents of foreign pilots have served with the SuAF over the years. When Libya donated MiG-23s and Mi-25s to Sudan in 1988, these arrived together with a group of up to 100 LAAF personnel. During 1992 several Iraqi Air Force (IrAF) pilots arrived in Sudan for the first time, following a visit by a high-level delegation from Baghdad. A group of around 15 pilots – mostly from IrAF ground-attack units and with previous experience on MiG-21s and MiG-23s – followed the call for a tour in Sudan on the assumption that they would train SuAF pilots to fly MiG-21s, but eventually found that their hosts expected them to do much more.

The Iraqis found the SuAF almost in a state of disarray, lacking discipline and even the most basic ideas about deploying their aircraft efficiently in combat. Only four operational MiG-21s were available. Although attached to the SuAF as advisors, before long the IrAF pilots ended up flying combat sorties themselves –although not before modifying the Sudanese MiGs, and several Shenyangs, through the addition of GPS receivers connected to the navigational platforms. Thanks to very attractive payment, most of the IrAF pilots eventually remained in Sudan for the next two years, even although every six months they would receive a month's leave, usually spent in Iraq.[17]

Reports concerning the arrival of advisors from the Islamic Republic of Iran Air Force (IRIAF) around the same time cannot be confirmed, even although the IRGC deployed a number of advisors that worked with the SPAF.

The presence of combat-hardened IrAF veterans was insufficient to change the situation on the ground, particularly since the Sudanese government failed to mount follow-up operations that could have destroyed the SPLA when it was going through the most serious crisis of its existence. Instead, 1993 ended with Malakal and Juba again under siege.

The war intensified again in March and April 1996, with a SPAF offensive along the Yuba-Yei road, stopped and then repulsed by a SPLA counteroffensive, during which the insurgents claimed additional SuAF MiGs and helicopters destroyed. In February 1997 the SPLA launched its first offensive supported by several MBTs captured in previous fighting with the Sudanese Army. The offensive captured Yei, and the SuAF responded with a massive aerial bombardment. It was around this time that Sudan began deploying ever-larger numbers of Antonov transports for bombing purposes; the term 'Antonov bomber' was soon in colloquial use around the country and abroad (for details on military and civilian transport aircraft deployed by the SuAF and various associated civilian airlines in Sudan during the early 2000s, see Appendix 2).

During early 1998, drought led to famine in southern Sudan, particularly along the border with Uganda. This time the government in Khartoum exploited the situation, banning all flights into the area by transport aircraft chartered by foreign aid agencies, before the 1st Division SPAF launched a major offensive. Together with a series of bombardments flown by Antonovs chartered by the SuAF, this attack caused a humanitarian catastrophe and up to 100,000 deaths. The SuAF is known to have lost two MiG-21s during this campaign: one shot down by Ugandan troops near Bibia in late January, and another by the SPLA near al-Jablain, 80km (50 miles) east of Juba, on 25 October.

During the subsequent years of war in Sudan, the deployment of Antonovs for bombing purposes became ever more widespread, until they became an essential element of SuAF COIN doctrine. Able to carry massive quantities of bombs (and also 'home-made' explosive devices, resembling empty fuel drums filled with explosive) and in possession of long endurance and equipment that included a bombsight, An-26s in particular were highly appreciated by the Sudanese. Proceeded by several reconnaissance flights at high level in order to establish SPLA AAA positions, this doctrine envisaged initial strikes by SuAF fighter-bombers to soften up defences, followed by the Antonovs, which sometimes operated from medium or even low level, in the face of the MANPADS threat. In the wake of the fighter-bombers and Antonovs, SuAF Mi-24s would sometimes hit remaining sites from which resistance was offered. Strangely enough, no examples are known of such attacks being followed by heliborne commando assaults. More often than not, operations of this kind were launched against villages or towns already surrounded by SPAF ground forces.

Additionally, An-26s would frequently fly surprise attacks against settlements that the insurgents considered to be outside the range of the SuAF. More than 259 such raids were flown between January 1997 and December 2000 (including 69 in 1999 and 132 in 2000), leaving severe destruction and several hundred victims in their wake.[18] A classic example of such attacks was the that flown by two Antonovs against Kauda in February 2000. One of the bombers hit the local airstrip but the other bombed the Holy Cross School, killing 19 students and a teacher. On 14 March 2000, the Episcopal Church and the nearby school of 1,000 children in Nimule were repeatedly hit by MiG-23s and Antonovs, killing one and injuring eleven others. Two subsequent strikes completed the destruction of both objectives.

On 20 November 2000, Yei was hit by 14 bombs dropped by one Antonov, killing 18 and injuring more than 50. The heaviest attack of this period was flown on 24 November, when a Catholic school in Panllit, in the Bahr al-Ghazal State, was hit while most of the 700 students were attending classes. The two bombers involved made three passes each, dropping a total of 14 cluster and GP bombs, two of which exploded inside the classrooms. The number of victims in this attack was in excess of 30. Yei was hit again only two days later, simultaneously with Ikotos – a major base for several aid agencies – some 280km (174 miles) east of Juba and 150km (93 miles) west of Lokichogio. In both cases, the bombs hit the centre of the town, killing and injuring dozens. Another attack occurred on 1 April 2001, only hours after a transport aircraft carrying the Sudanese deputy defence minister and 13 other high-ranking officers

Taken at Nyala airfield in July 2007, these two photographs show two unidentified SuAF A-5Cs and three Mi-35s, providing evidence that Sudan continued ignoring UN Resolution 1591 of 2005, which explicitly forbids deployment of heavy weapons to Darfur. (Melting Tarmac Images)

crashed during take-off from Adaril. The sole An-26 bombed the airstrip near Kauda, used by several humanitarian agencies, and which at the time was hosting a ceremony to thank a group of Italians for their support. The 14 bombs dropped fell astray but still killed one and injured two persons.

However, the Antonov bombers proved useless against the SPLA, which by the end of the year found itself in control of the towns of Dendro, Koro-Yara, Adsi, Dim-Saad, and Kilo, in the Blue Nile State.

In December 2001 the first SuAF A-5Cs reportedly deployed to al-Ubayyid air base, in North Kordofan Province. The type was foremost used to replace worn out, ex-Libyan MiG-23s, but also the few remaining Strikemasters, only a few of which were left operational by this time. Nevertheless, all three types became involved in a series of battles that raged through southern Sudan from January until April 2002, deploying large numbers of napalm bombs. These battles were initiated by a SPAF offensive in the Bahr al-Ghazal State, which had been easily repelled by the SPLA. The insurgents subsequently forced the Army to fall back in disorder towards the north, evacuating even the capital of Blue Nile State, Damazeen, and the town of Raga in the process. This defeat came so swiftly that the SuAF was completely unable to participate in the fighting.

Once again, the government's response was the 'Antonov bombers'. Although Khartoum announced a halt to all attacks on the south on 24 May 2001, only two days later the town of Awada was hit heavily. The number of towns and villages bombed by the SuAF further increased before the Sudanese foreign minister explained in June that the SuAF was, *'resuming strikes in order to defend the country in the face of continued aggression'*. It is perfectly possible that Khartoum felt compelled to such measures, since by the time the SPLA had put Wau under siege and successively destroyed several Army columns attempting to approach that town. However, the results of the SuAF attacks had tragic consequences for many civilians. Throughout the summer, the Antonov bombers and MiGs successively hit one hospital and aid agency base after another, even though most of these were marked with red crosses. The International Rescue Committee and Save the Children UK recorded no fewer than 33 separate bombing attacks, with more than 250 bombs dropped in July 2001 alone. When the bombing of their bases continued with the same intensity into August, the UN took the unprecedented action of grounding all its flights into southern Sudan.

Eventually, the government came under severe pressure to stop its aerial offensive. Freed from the air-to-ground mission, the SuAF then concentrated on intercepting

transport aircraft hauling aid provided by foreign relief agencies, many of which were under way over southern Sudan on an almost daily basis.

The UN had two C-130s chartered especially for the purpose of flying 'food-bombing' missions deep over Sudan, foremost on behalf of the UN World Food Programme. Other private air freighters served various aid agencies. Most of the aircraft were flown by freelance pilots, contracted directly by these agencies, but there were some that served under the auspices of the Operation Life-Line-Sudan. The main base for most of such flights was Lokichogio, the second largest town in southern Sudan held by the SPLA. Theoretically, all relief supplies were only dropped in areas agreed with Khartoum, but in typical 'daredevil' fashion pilots often displayed little regard for territorial integrity and sovereignty, in particularly if the claimant was the government in Khartoum. For many of the fliers involved, all that counted was whether the SPLA authorised the flight. Knowing that flying early in the morning meant that the chance of being intercepted by the SuAF was next to minimal, and that its fighter-bombers and Antonovs usually attacked only in the afternoons, they continued taking their chances, despite all the threats and declarations from the Sudanese capital. In their favour, some of the SPLA teams at airstrips such as Yei, Chukkudum, Laboone and elsewhere proved capable of unloading even a C-130 within only 15 minutes. In order to curb such flights, the SuAF set up a radar site equipped with a system manufactured by Alenia-Marconi in Juba, and another in el-Ubayyid. Both air bases saw frequent deployments by pairs of A-5Cs and F-6Cs, and the latter type in particular made several intercept attempts. Overall, however, neither type ever proved successful in catching any foreign transport aircraft within Sudanese airspace.

The government's aerial offensive against the south reached its peak on 20 February 2002, when two Mi-35s attacked the food supply centre of the World Food Programme in the village of Bieh, in the western Upper Nile State. The attack came as some 4,000 civilians lined up for rations, and thus saw the two helicopter gunships firing unguided rockets and machine-guns into a mass of women, children and aid workers. Seventeen civilians were killed and over 100 injured.

The attack on Bieh led to an immediate reaction from the US. The US administration recalled its envoy and ceased its mediation between the government and the SPLA. Fearing the SPLA would intensify attacks on the oil-exporting industry, and knowing the US was supportive of the insurgents' cause, Khartoum finally stopped all further attacks and agreed to a ceasefire. This led eventually to a settlement of the conflict through the Machakos Agreement, signed in Kenya on 15 October 2002. Under the agreement, 10 states in southern Sudan were granted the right to secede, following the appropriate results of a referendum. Held in early 2011, this referendum ended with 98.83 per cent of the electorate opting for secession, and resulted in the decision that this part of the country would secede from the rest of the Sudan. This duly occurred on 9 July 2011, South Sudan declaring its independence, with the new capital in Juba.

402 403
ε◊٢ ε◊٢

A batch of at least 10, more likely 12, A-5Cs was delivered to Sudan sometimes between the late 2001 and early 2003. These aircraft wear a camouflage pattern consisting of tan, dark green and chocolate brown on top surfaces and dark RLB on the lower surfaces. Drop tanks are usually painted white overall. Insert shows the fashion in which serial numbers were applied on examples with serial numbers 402 and 403: nearly every Sudanese A-5C has its serial numbers applied in different fashion.

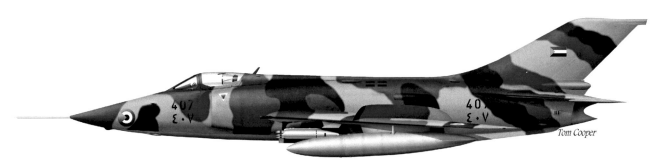

SuAF A-5Cs are usually seen armed with the Chinese-variant of the old Soviet-made ORO-57K rocket pods. A few of the aircraft have meanwhile been observed carrying drop tanks finished in 'bare metal' overall, probably replacements for those jettisoned in combat.

The SuAF's A-5C operating unit is probably the so-called No. 2 Fighter-Bomber Squadron. The unit known to applying serial numbers in an entirely different fashion on each of its aircraft: it seems that no two aircraft received their Arabic numerals in the same size, style and position. Notable are four hardpoints under the fuselage, the outsides of which are painted in camouflage colours, the insides in dark RLB. Weapons used by these A-5Cs include: the Chinese-made variant of the ORO-57K pod, 250kg GP bombs, 350kg napalm tanks and Chinese variants of the Soviet-made FAB-250M54 bombs.

MiG, Shenyang and Sukhoi fighter operations in the Republic of Sudan, 2003–2011

In early 2003 a new war erupted in western Sudan. Here, various militias, colloquially known as 'Janjaweed', had become active under PDF auspices in the mid-1980s. Local tribes were prompted to establish their own militias, including the Darfur Liberation Front (DLF), later expanded into the Sudan Liberation Army (SLA), and the Justice and Equality Movement (JEM). Carefully monitoring the situation in southern Sudan, the leaders of the DLF/SLA and JEM demanded their share of oil income and power from Khartoum. When early negotiations failed, the SLA launched its first attacks against Sudanese security installations in February 2003, taking the badly under-strength 6th Division SPAF by surprise, and capturing significant quantities of arms and ammunition in the process.

Already overextended due to the situation in southern Sudan, the government offered renewed negotiations on several occasions. Instead, in a scene reminiscent of many operations during the wars in Chad since the late 1980s, on 25 April 2003, a column of 33 Toyota pickups equipped with heavy machine-guns attacked el-Fasher airfield. Achieving complete surprise, SLA fighters killed 75 Sudanese Army and Air Force personnel, destroyed three Mi-17s, one Mi-24 and two Antonov transports, and captured large quantities of arms and equipment. Bolstered by this success, the SLA launched additional attacks against SPAF units in the following days and weeks, causing heavy casualties to the garrison in Kutum, some 75km (47 miles) north of el-Fasher. On 29 April, the insurgents even captured the Army commander of the area, while in late May they ambushed and largely destroyed an entire battalion of the 6th Division.

Surprised by the outbreak of violence, and in no condition to respond with regular troops, the government reacted through the activation of PDF militias. It was only in mid-May 2003 that a mechanised brigade of the 3rd Division SPAF was airlifted to el-Fasher, from where it launched an attempt to relieve the besieged garrison in Kutum. This unit ran into a series of ambushes and suffered losses as well. After airlifting additional units of the 3rd Division to el-Fasher with the help of its own and chartered military transport aircraft, the SPAF launched a new advance towards Kutum, but the town fell on 1 August 2003 and in return became the target for a series of strikes flown by SuAF fighter jets.

With only 5,000 troops left in well-organised and trained units in all of Darfur, and with most of the Army in the process of re-equipping and refitting following the fighting with the SPLA and the signing of an agreement for military cooperation with Russia, in April 2002, the government eventually decided to unleash the PDF militias and the SuAF upon the insurgents. Such efforts were well coordinated by late August 2003 and resulted in the next humanitarian catastrophe.

Without participation by regular, well-trained troops, the situation spiralled completely out of control, since the members of the Janjaweed militias proved increasingly interested in ethnic cleansing entire landscapes, and looting, and less willing to fight the JEM and SLA. Operating in groups of 50 to 100 mounted fighters out of camps around el-Fasher in the east and Nyala in the south, they began attacking villages of the ethnic Fur, killing men and raping women, kidnapping children and stealing cattle and sheep. They forced most of the local population out of their villages, burned these down and destroyed water wells, schools and even hospitals. Villages that proved out

of reach of the PDF were then put on the targeting lists of A-5Cs and Antonov bombers, as well as helicopter gunships.

A typical pattern of operations that developed around this time was described by a number of eyewitnesses after the attack on Jidad village on 28 June 2003. The Janjaweed firstly surrounded the area, cutting off all routes out of Jidad. Two hours later, the village was hit by one Antonov, followed by two Mi-35s. The 'Antonov bomber' dropped around two dozen bombs into the centre of Jidad and helicopters saturated the area with unguided rockets. Subsequently, the militia launched its assault. Within two hours, the village was completely destroyed: 35 people were killed and survivors were left to flee in the direction of the border with Chad.

By late summer 2003, the PDF campaign against the local population had reached areas settled by ethnic Massalit and Zaghawas in South Darfur. It was here that the Janjaweed encountered stronger insurgent formations for the first time – and suffered a series of setbacks. The situation eventually prompted the SPAF to intervene through the deployment of one of its mechanised brigades. This caused heavy losses to the SLA, prompting the leaders of this organisation to demand a ceasefire in September 2003. This time, Khartoum ignored offers for negotiations and reinforced its efforts through the deployment of additional Army units in North Darfur State. During October 2003, a series of massive attacks hit nearly every village in the Kornoy area. SuAF operations here followed a different pattern to those observed in South Darfur. Since many of the villages included insurgent camps, the initial blow was always delivered by A-5Cs in order to soften up the opposition. An-26s then delivered the major blow, and were always followed by helicopter gunships. Finally, mounted militia – sometimes supported by regular SPAF units – rode into the target zone. These tactics have since been only slightly adapted, in so far as the operations sometimes include SPAF units that seal off all land and telecommunications links into the combat zone.

On 28 August 2003 the SuAF's attempts to intercept some of the transport aircraft delivering relief supplies in Darfur were successful for the first time. On this occasion, an unknown aircraft entering Sudanese airspace from Kenya was claimed shot down over northern Darfur, near the border with Chad. Subsequent reports indicated that the aircraft was actually destroyed on the ground, while unloading its cargo.[19]

Overall, by the end of 2003, the Army and forces loyal to the government had launched three large-scale campaigns in Darfur. According to the available reports, mainly from sources associated with the UN, these resulted in the over 2,300 villages destroyed and over 30,000 civilians killed, as well as more than 200,000 Sudanese refugees crossing the border into Chad.[20] Similarly, whether the government's campaigns in Darfur purposely and explicitly targeted civilians remains a matter of some controversy. Although massive civilian suffering is indisputable, there is little doubt that these offensives hit the JEM and SLA insurgents as well. Indeed, these forces were hit heavily, forcing most of them to flee beyond the border to Chad. In pursuit of these insurgents, by early 2004 the PDF's militias began launching cross-border raids up to 200km (124 miles) deep into the neighbouring country.

Satisfied with the results of its military efforts, on 9 February 2004 the government in Khartoum declared an end to the conflict in Darfur. The conflict continued, however, although at a much reduced scale, and fighting stagnated through most of 2004 and 2005, during a series of UN-sponsored meetings between the government and the insurgent leaders. In the course of these meetings the first cracks began to appear

The primary armament of the MiG-29SEh consists of up to four R-77 medium-range air-to-air missiles, one of which can be seen on this video still from a video taken in 2010.
(via Pit Weinert)

Although principally operated as an interceptor, the SuAF MiG-29SEh packs a formidable air-to-ground punch. As this video still from a 2010 exhibition shows, the fighter can carry B-8M rocket pods as well as MBDZ multiple-ejector racks for up to two 250kg (551lb) bombs. Notable are also the underwing rails for (from the back): R-27, R-77 and R-73 AAMs.
(via Pit Weinert)

within the JEM and SLA, resulting in the separation of several factions from both organisations. Some of these groups signed ceasefires with Khartoum, and even sided with the government, while others refused and continued to fight. This not only made the war even more complex, but also caused fighting between various factions, and another flood of refugees into Chad.

In 2008 the conflict in Darfur became internationalised. In early May 2008, apparently in response to a similar raid launched by Chadian insurgents supported by the government in Khartoum against N'Djamena, JEM insurgents supported by the Chadian government launched a high-speed raid mounted on Toyota pickups from Darfur via North Kordofan against the Sudanese capital.[21] Rapidly advancing towards Khartoum, on 9 May the raiders attacked Wadi Sayyidna air base. Although repulsed, they shot down a SuAF MiG-29 flown by a Russian pilot while this was taking off to counterattack them. The pilot managed to eject from his aircraft at very low level, but his parachute failed to open in time and he was killed.[22]

Following their failure at Wadi Sayyidna, the JEM raiding party regrouped and attempted to continue its advance into Khartoum via Omdurman. Already warned of its approach, however, the SPAF stepped up security, deployed mechanised troops along all entry points to Omdurman, and killed or captured most of around 500 raiders in a pitched battle through the streets of the town on 10 May.[23]

The JEM raid on Khartoum put Sudan on a collision course with Chad, and ever since, the conflict in Darfur has increasingly turned into an intra-Zaghawa Tribe war. Members of the same tribe –but from different clans and different sides of the Chadian-Sudanese border – began fighting against other, usually with the support of either the Chadian or Sudanese militaries.

On 15 and 16 May 2008, Chadian combat aircraft – including newly delivered Su-25s – and attack helicopters launched three strikes against insurgents that were attempting to concentrate on the border for a new attack on N'Djamena. Some of these

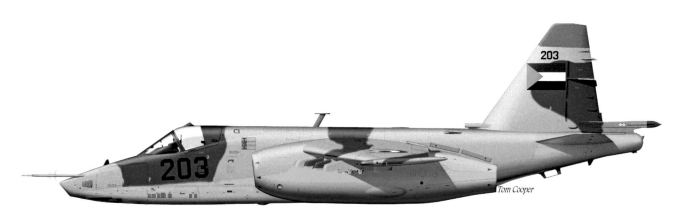

Although expected for some time, the appearance of the Su-25 in Sudan in 2008 surprised many observers and was originally misreported as 'deliveries of MiG-21s from Ukraine', or 'MiG-29s from Russia'. All Sudanese Su-25 wear the same camouflage pattern, consisting of yellow sand and dark earth on the upper surfaces and sides, and dark RLB on the lower surfaces. Large serial numbers are applied below the cockpit and are repeated at the top of the fin.

SuAF Su-25s usually carry armament comprising a pair of B-8M rocket pods (containing 20 rockets of 80mm/3.15in calibre). The aircraft also frequently appear to carry launch rails for R-60MK air-to-air missiles.

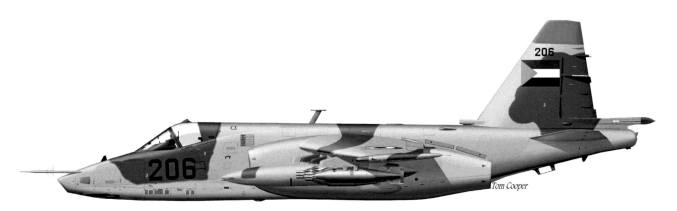

Other weapons noticed to date on SuAF Su-25s comprise UB-32-57 rocket pods (for 32 rockets of 57mm/2.24in calibre) and RBK-250 cluster bombs, as shown on this example.

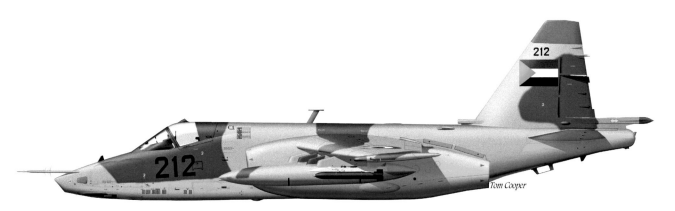

Row of Sudanese Su-25s at el-Ubayyid AB, in summer 2011. At the time, the type was involved in combat operations over the Abyei area, disputed between the government in Khartoum and the newly-independent government of the Southern Sudan. (Melting Tarmac Images)

This Su-25 appears to have suffered some kind of combat damage during the fighting over the Abyei area, in June 2011, or an in-flight fire due to hydraulic problem, and made an emergency landing at el-Ubayyid AB. (Melting Tarmac Images)

strikes hit camps near Jebal Sindo, in the el-Genina area, 60km (37 miles) inside Sudan, and Chadian authorities subsequently claimed to have destroyed seven groups of insurgents.[24] Following an exchange of diplomatic protests, and despite an explanation by the government in N'Djamena that its operations inside Sudan were over, on 19 May 2008, Sudan declared such Chadian attacks to be an 'act of war' and threatened to destroy the Chadian forces concentrated on the border.

During the following weeks, the SPAF exploited the situation to deploy additional troops in Darfur and launch a number of attacks on the JEM and SLA, some of which continued through July, August and September 2008. It was in the course of one of the offensives against the SLA bases in North Darfur that the insurgents claimed the downing of a SuAF unmanned aerial vehicle, on 28 August 2008. By this time, all such operations were characterised by the increasing deployment of A-5Cs, Su-25s and An-26s, as well as helicopter gunships from airfields in el-Fasher and Nyala, which have since had their runways extended and reinforced so as to enable operations by Ilyushin Il-76 transports. This period of the war in Darfur ended with a ceasefire, agreed between all belligerents in November 2008, and the deployment of UN peacekeepers in western Sudan.

In fact, by this time the situation had reached something of an 'enforced stalemate': under pressure from outside powers, particularly the US and UK, the government in Khartoum stopped attacking insurgents in Darfur. Nevertheless, despite a UN embargo and an agreement not to deploy heavy weapons or undertake offensive operations in that state, the SPAF continued to maintain at least one motorised brigade in the area, while the SuAF continued to deploy combat aircraft and helicopters on local airfields. In turn, large parts of the SLA sided with the government – much to the dislike of the JEM.

The already flimsy ceasefire was broken by the JEM in mid-January 2009, when its insurgents assaulted the town of Muhajaria, in the west of South Darfur, and held by a faction of the SLA that respected the ceasefire agreement with the government. Taken by surprise and without major Army units in the area, Khartoum ordered the two SuAF A-5Cs and two An-26s forward deployed in Nyala into action. These flew a number of

Another weapon deployed by several SuAF Su-25 in 2009 and 2010 is the S-24B unguided rocket, of 240mm (9.45in) calibre. These are usually carried on weapons stations numbers 2 and 10.

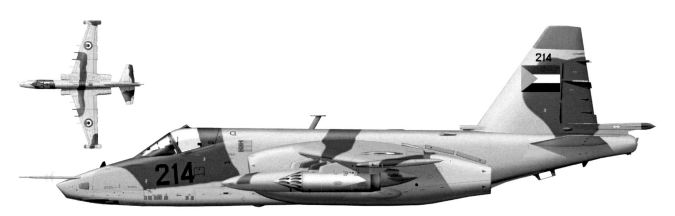

None of the Sudanese Su-25s observed in service to date seems to have been over-painted since arrival, which means that their camouflage colours can be used as a sort of 'fingerprint' to allow their identification in photographs.

Whether single- or two-seaters, most SuAF Su-25s have received chaff and flare dispensers attached to the upper surfaces of the rear of the engine nacelles. This Su-25UB is one of the latest deliveried: it arrived at Wadi Sayyidna in April 2011.

strikes against the JEM insurgents in and around Muhajaria, on 13 and 14 January 2009. After additional A-5Cs and Antonovs were re-deployed to air bases in Darfur, this aerial offensive was widened, and by 20 January 2009, the SuAF also hit several villages in the area – including Aadona, Abdu Damiat, Abu Dangal, Aweer, Hajara, Hilat Idda, Shahddad (together with the nearby refugee camp), Shangli Tobye, Shiairia, Sinait and Zalat. These caused some losses to the insurgents, but also prompted another wave of refugees to flee across the border to Chad. The attacks by the SuAF – which in several causes pursued the insurgent groups well beyond the border – were joined by a two-pronged advance by an Army brigade from el-Fasher towards Muhajaria. These actions, combined with pressure from the UN, eventually forced the JEM to evacuate the area, despite vows to fight fiercely and hold the town, and this was subsequently put under the control of the UN peacekeepers.

The SPAF offensive against the JEM ended in March 2009, by which time the attention of the government had been distracted by an Israeli air strike against a convoy of trucks under way north of Port Sudan in the direction of Egypt. This convoy was reportedly carrying arms for the Gaza Strip. At the same time, Maj Gen Omar Bashir, President of Sudan, was indicted by the International Criminal Court (ICC) for genocide, crimes against humanity, and war crimes.[25]

The second withdrawal of the JEM into Chad actually served to bolster this organisation. The insurgents remained capable of freely crossing the border from Chad into Sudan and then withdrawing back as necessary. Furthermore, the JEM obtained improved access to the refugee camps inside Chad, meanwhile harbouring more than 500,000 refugees from Darfur, where they could recruit additional fighters. The organisation thus grew to around 35,000 fighters under weapons. This was illustrated in mid-May 2009, when – despite negotiations between the government and the JEM – two insurgent units crossed the border and one attacked a SLA post in Umm Baru as well as a SPAF garrison in Kornoy, some 50km (31 miles) northwest of el-Fasher, to declare a 'liberated zone'. When the insurgents lined up their technicals in front of Kornoy, the local Army soldiers simply turned and ran, leaving most of their armament and equipment behind.

Once again, the SuAF reacted first, flying several strikes – possibly involving Su-25s – on 11 and 13 May. The number of attacks increased over the following days and weeks, prompting fierce accusations and complaints from the insurgents. However, before the SPAF managed to airlift any mechanised units into the area, the JEM remained in possession of Kornoy, since its highly mobile columns proved easily capable of avoiding bombardments by the 'Antonov bombers' of the SuAF. However, once the SPAF mechanised units reached Umm Baru, the town was retaken relatively easily, and when the JEM attempted to counterattack, on 25 May, it was beaten back with the loss of 43 insurgents (in exchange for 20 soldiers KIA and 31 WIA).[26]

During the following week the SuAF intensified its aerial campaign, bombing not only the insurgents in Kornoy, but also their camps and columns in the Furawiya area (240km/149 miles north of el-Geneina). Although claiming that only civilian objects were hit and that they did not suffer any losses, once again the insurgents were forced back over the border into Chad, on 28 May.[27] Contrary to earlier practices, the Sudanese did not stop this time. Two days later, three formations of two Su-25s attacked for the first time the JEM insurgents in their camps near Goz Beida, around 70km (43 miles) inside Chad.

SuAF MiG-29SEh serial number 623 low over Khartoum in late December 2007, showing details of the colours applied on the lower surfaces and sides. The type is now the pride of the Sudanese Air Force.
(Melting Tarmac Images)

Following another period of ceasefires and negotiations – including renewed assurances from the government that the war in Darfur was over – the situation flared up once again in late November 2009. In response to one of its border patrols driving over a mine planted by the insurgents, the Chadian military launched a major operation inside Sudan. This time Armée de l'Air Tchadienne (AAT) Su-25s bombed insurgent camps in advance of an attack by ground forces. The Sudanese reacted with the deployment of SPAF units and claimed to have ambushed the Chadian column, causing over 100 casualties.[28]

Indirectly, this clash led to an escalation between part of the SLA and the SPAF, and in mid-January 2010 this turned into a firefight near Gulu. In response to this, SuAF aircraft rocketed and bombed insurgent camps in the Jebel Moon and Jebel Marra areas, as well as around the market town of Deribat. This time, the SuAF's Su-25s appear to have attacked first, targeting insurgent vehicles and fixed anti-aircraft positions with unguided rockets before their camps would be hit by bombs rolled from rear loading ramps of the Antonovs. The SLA immediately accused the government that such raids had killed at least 170 civilians, but Khartoum denied any involvement by the SPAF and in turn accused the insurgents of fighting between each other and attacking civilians. However, on 9 March the truth came to light when the government suddenly announced that it had wrested control of the strategically positioned Jebel Marra from the SLA.

As Khartoum subsequently explained, the SPAF launched a major offensive against the JEM, hitting most of its larger camps. When the JEM units fled the area, they met head-on with the SLA in several areas, and were then hit by the SuAF again. Eventually, remnants of several units from both insurgent organisations attempted to withdraw towards Malha, in the farthest northern part of North Darfur State, but suffered a series of defeats in the process, leaving at least 400 KIA and captured fighters behind them. Khartoum subsequently felt it was in a strong enough position to declare the JEM 'defeated'.[29]

The service life of this A-5C ended when it overshot the runway at Juba, sometime in 2006. With all useful spares removed, the hulk was left to rust, and was found in this condition in May 2007. The rebels claimed at least three other A-5Cs as shot down by that date, though they usually identified them as 'MiG-29s'.
(Melting Tarmac Images)

The insurgents remained active, nevertheless, though mainly through raids against various SPAF posts. One of these attacks prompted the Army to launch yet another offensive in the Jebal Moon and Jebel Marra areas, in January 2010.

Ever since, it appears that the insurgents have been unable to maintain control over any areas of significant size within Darfur, and are limited to ever smaller operations, most of which effectively amount to armed robberies of the local population.

Exactly to what degree the SuAF was influential in the eventual success of the government remains unclear. Considering historical experiences regarding aerial

A row of four SuAF Su-25s (headed by serial number 201) at el-Fasher in 2008. This highly effective and survivable ground-attack aircraft may well have proven its worth during more recent stages of the war in Darfur.
(Louis Charbonneau)

dominance over an enemy armed force exposed in the desert, as well as the fact that in recent years Sudan obtained at least 18 Su-25s, it is perfectly possible that the Sudanese Air Force proved decisive in this conflict. The Su-25 is a twin-engined ground-attack aircraft with excellent range and load-carrying capability.

Most SuAF examples have been seen armed 'only' with B-8M pods for unguided rockets of 80mm (3.15in) calibre. Such weapons proved more effective against non-armoured vehicles and light infantry operating in the open expanses of the desert, compared to general-purpose bombs.

On the other hand, the JEM insurgents in particular have repeatedly claimed to have shot down 'MiG-29s' in the course of their operations. Theoretically, this is not impossible. However, the SuAF is not known to have deployed its MiG-29s on any of the airfields in Darfur, and the type lacks the range to operate over this area when launched from el-Ubayyid or Wadi Sayyidna. Instead, the SuAF is known to have deployed its brand-new Su-25s – in addition to the nearly 'omni-present' A-5Cs and attack helicopters – in Darfur on a number of occasions. The cockpit and engine nacelles of the Su-25 are protected by titanium armour and the aircraft is renowned for its ability to survive heavy damage, and neither the JEM nor the SLA appear to have managed to obtain any modern MANPADS capable of tackling such a threat. On the contrary, their major anti-aircraft weapon remains the 23mm ZU-23 automatic cannon, usually mounted on technicals. Although still some of most effective weapons of their kind, and very useful for ground warfare as fought in Darfur, without proper training of their gunners, the ZU-23 is of only limited effectiveness against such jets as the Su-25.

At the time of writing, the war in Darfur continued at a low scale despite massive international pressure upon the Sudanese government, largely a result of atrocities that are claimed to have killed over 300,000 and displaced up to 3 million. Exactly to what degree the government alone is to blame for this remains unclear: press communiqués from both the government and insurgents have so far not proven particularly reliable. On the contrary, the JEM in particular has proven very keen to blame the government for 'attacks on civilians' whenever one of its camps inside Darfur is hit.

It is therefore hardly surprising that countless negotiation attempts – some sponsored by the UN and the OAU, others by the Arab League – and practically every single ceasefire agreement have proven to be not worth the paper on which they were inked.

Little positive can be said about the deployment of an extremely expensive yet largely futile 36,000-strong peacekeeping contingent of the UN, mainly drawn from African armies. To date, this has usually proven barely capable of monitoring the

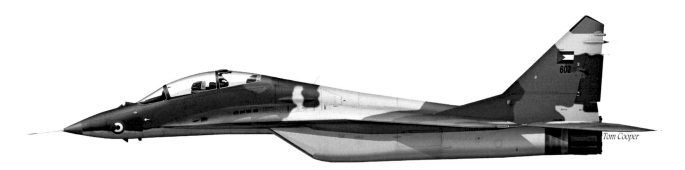

The only MiG-29UB two-seat conversion trainer identified in service with the SuAF to date, serial number 602 appears to be flown very intensively, and has been sighted in public on a number of occasions.

One of the major differences in regards the colours applied on Sudanese MiG-29SEhs is that some examples have an 'anti-glare panel' in matt black in front of the cockpit, while others do not. Another characteristic is that although developed as interceptors and never noted as deployed in combat in Darfur, they are often seen carrying launch rails for S-24B unguided rockets, as shown here.

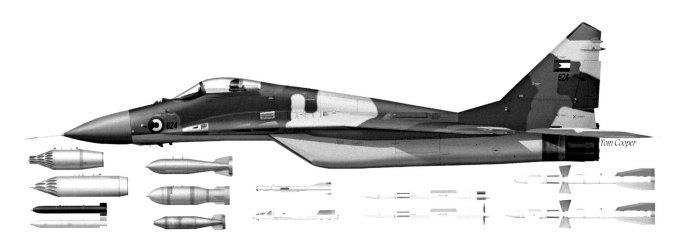

624 is the highest serial number known to be applied on any Sudanese MiG-29. The fighter is shown together with weapons known to have been delivered to the SuAF to date, including (from left to right): UB-32-57 and B-8M rocket pods and S-24B unguided rockets; FAB-250M-62, ODAB-500 and RBK-250 bombs; R-60MK and R-73E short-range air-to-air missiles; R-77 medium-range air-to-air missiles (the upper example shown with its fins in the folded position, the lower example with its fins in the deplpyed position), and R-27T (IR-homing) and R-27R (radar-guided) medium-range air-to-air missiles.

fighting going on around its bases, and a number of its contingents have been fired upon, or even robbed.

A UN-imposed arms embargo against Sudan is largely ignored by China as well as by Russia (which continues to deliver heavy weapons and provide assistance via Belarus). Similarly, in spite of UN Resolution 1951, which prohibits the deployment of heavy weapons in Darfur, the SuAF continues to operate A-5Cs, Su-25s and helicopter gunships from local airfields on a regular basis. Similarly, Sudanese aircraft and transports chartered from various foreign companies are still frequently seen delivering heavy weapons, arms and supplies to the airfields in el-Fasher, el-Geneina and Nyala.

Whether a political solution to this conflict might eventually be found must therefore be considered highly dubious.

Safat Aviation Complex (SAC): a domestic maintenance solution

One of the major problems the SuAF encountered while operating its MiG and Shenyang fighters in the 1970s and 1980s was the issue of maintenance. Above all, frequent breakdowns in relations with the USSR had negative effects upon Sudan's ability to obtain spare parts. This not only had negative effects upon the training of pilots and ground personnel, but several times almost put an end to operations by the air force's MiGs. Furthermore, the Soviets did not provide single spare parts, but entire subassemblies, so that even minor repairs required the removal of an entire subassembly from the aircraft. Similarly, the short time between major overhauls of equipment purchased from China meant that the aircraft had to be transported to that country for periodic maintenance, in turn leaving them out of service for extended periods of time. After 30 years of operations under these conditions, the government finally found a solution in founding the Safat Aviation Complex (SAC) works at Wadi Sayyidna air base.

Established within the framework of the Military Industrial Complex (MIC) of Sudan, with the aim of providing the Sudanese armed forces with the equipment and spares necessary to perform their duties, the SAC came into being with extensive Chinese support in 2004, and was inaugurated in 2005. This company of around 700 full-time employees, qualified engineers and technicians now operates 50 specialised workshops within 14 hangars.

SAC is composed of several departments, including: Fighters, Helicopters, Transport Aircraft, Light Aircraft, Radars and Training. Since 2006, all of these are approved to conduct at least periodic maintenance on nearly all types of combat and transport aircraft, as well as helicopters, in service with the SuAF and other branches of the Sudanese military and security forces. Some of the departments have since been declared capable of undertaking works related to the prolongation of airframe life expectancy, as well as the production of spare parts and materials, and special tools. For example, the Fighter Maintenance and Overhaul Department is capable of undertaking periodic maintenance on types including the FT-5, F-6, FT-6, MiG-21M, MiG-29, and A-5C, and of manufacturing most spare parts for these.

Recently, SAC has been expanded through the addition of an Aircraft Development and Manufacturing Department. This has so far designed, assembled and flight-tested prototypes of two types of light aircraft, the Safat 1 and Safat 3 (the latter is actually a locally assembled UTVA-75 primary trainer), and one new light helicopter type (Safat 2).

This still from a video shows the details of the upper-surface camouflage applied on an overhauled F-6C, in 2010. It seems to be based on the camouflage applied on SuAF A-5Cs, and is not directly related to the pattern and colours originally applied on Sudanese F-6s in the late 1980s. (via Pit Weinert)

The rear fuselage section of F-6C serial number 764 undergoing overhaul at the SAC in 2010. Visible are details of the original camouflage pattern – consisting of beige, dark brown and dark green – applied on the F-6 during the late 1980s. (via Pit Weinert)

MiG, Shenyang and Sukhoi fighter operations in the Republic of Sudan, 2011

Pending the declaration of independence by South Sudan on 9 July 2011, a major new confrontation between the SPAF and the SPLA flared up over the Abyei region, in South Kordofan. This area is claimed by which both South Sudan and the government in Khartoum. The first clashes between the SPAF and the SPLA were reported in May 2008, and resulted in the large-scale destruction of the town of Abyei. The two parties subsequently agreed to bring the issue to the Permanent Court of Arbitration, in the Hague, and to hold a separate referendum on whether the local population wished to join the Republic of Sudan or South Sudan. This referendum never took place.

On 19 May 2011 the SPLA attacked a convoy of SPAF troops moving in the Abyei area, reportedly killing 70 officers and soldiers. Three days later, the Sudanese Army deployed two mechanised brigades to assault the town and four nearby villages, including Todach and Tagalei. This operation was supported by intensive attacks by SuAF fighter-bombers launched from el-Ubayyid, together with 'Antonov bombers', which reportedly also hit the positions held by the 9th Division SPLA in Pariang County, as well as those of South Sudanese irregulars in Kadugli. In the course of additional air strikes that, according to the South – 'caused a displacement of 75,000 civilians and hit nine areas in South Kordofan' – on 10 June 2011, the South claimed to have shot down two SuAF aircraft, including an 'Antonov bomber' near Kalkul and a 'MiG' in the Kauda area.[30]

Only three days later, the Republic of Sudan and South Sudan agreed 'in principle' to demilitarise the Abyei region and to allow an Ethiopian peacekeeping force to enter the area. However, the SuAF campaign of bombing the SPLA and South Sudanese irregulars continued into mid-June 2011. Among the targets were several airstrips in Southern Kordofan, some of which were in use by UN peacekeepers, including Kauda, hit on 14 June.[31]

As of mid-2011, the SuAF was regularly rotating two or three Su-25s or A-5Cs to el-Fasher in Darfur. Similar deployments, together with the presence of MiG-29s, have been reported at el-Ubayyid. However, because the latter airfield is nearly 400km (249 miles) away from the Abyei crisis area, it is more likely that the SuAF deployed some of its fighter jets – the involvement of which was reported repeatedly throughout May and June 2011 – at the much closer airfield in Kadugli.

A fine study of the camouflage applied on three SuAF MiG-29s that were put through paces by their pilots during celebrations marking the 60th anniversary of Sudanese independence, on 1 January 2008. (Melting Tarmac Images)

152

Table 35: Confirmed and reported attrition of Sudanese combat aircraft and helicopters, 1969–2011[32]

Date	Aircraft	Serial number	Pilot/crew	Remarks
September 1971	MiG-21M			Crashed 4km (2.5 miles) from Juba under unknown circumstances
September 1971	MiG-21US		2 crewmembers KIA, reportedly 'Russians'	Claimed shot down by AN during engagement in Morta area
September 1971	Mi-8MT			Claimed shot down by AN during engagement in Morta area
November 1983	Mi-8MT			w/o under unknown circumstances
1984	MiG-21M			Claimed shot down by SPLA
1984	MiG-21M			Claimed shot down by SPLA
23 June 1984	F-5F	82-0004		Crashed during training mission from Wadi Sayyidna AB
14 April 1985	DHC-5D	833	4 crewmembers KIA	Shot down by SPLA during engagement in Akobo area
16 April 1985	F27	ST-DAY	70 crew and passengers killed	Operated by Sudan Airways, shot down by SPLA SA-7 en route from Malakal to Khartoum
4 April 1986	DHC-5D	800	Seven out of 14 crew and passengers KIA	Shot down by SPLA during engagement in Bor area
11 May 1987	C-130H		5 crewmembers reported KIA	Claimed shot down by SPLA SA-7
18 December 1987	MiG-23			Former LAAF aircraft; shot down by SPLA during engagement in Kurmuk area
Early 1988	MiG-23			Former LAAF aircraft; shot down by SPLA during Operation Bright Star
Early 1988	MiG-23			Former LAAF aircraft; crashed during Operation Bright Star
Early 1988	MiG-23			Former LAAF aircraft; crashed during Operation Bright Star
Early 1988	MiG-23			Former LAAF aircraft; crashed during Operation Bright Star
Early 1988	F-5E			Claimed shot down by SPLA during Operation Bright Star
Early 1988	F-5E			Claimed shot down by SPLA during Operation Bright Star
Early 1988	F-5E			Claimed shot down by SPLA during Operation Bright Star
Early 1988	DHC-5D			Claimed shot down by SPLA during Operation Bright Star
Early 1988	DHC-5D			Claimed shot down by SPLA during Operation Bright Star
Early 1988	F-6			Claimed shot down by SPLA during Operation Bright Star
Early 1988	Mi-8MT			Claimed shot down by SPLA during Operation Bright Star
13 December 1988	MiG-23		Pilot POW	Former LAAF aircraft; shot down by SPLA SA-7 in Kajo Kaji area
9 January 1990	An-24TV			Claimed shot down by SPLA SA-7 during engagement in Kajo Kaji area
8 February 1990	C-130H			Claimed shot down by SPLA SA-7 while under way from Harare to Maridi
18 July 1992	Unknown helicopter			Claimed shot down by SPLA during engagement in Torit area
20 July 1992	MiG-21M			Claimed shot down by SPLA during engagement in Torit area
20 July 1992	MiG-21M			Claimed to have crashed in Torit area during engagement with SPLA
20 July 1992	Bell 205		5 crew and passengers reported KIA	Claimed shot down by SPLA during engagement in Torit area
1 August 1995	FT-5		Crew KIA	Crashed on training sortie
26 February 1996	C-130H		91 crew and passengers killed	Shot down by SPLA during engagement in Jabal Awliya area, killing all on board
19 March 1996	MiG-21			Claimed shot down by SPLA SA-14
20 March 1996	An-24TV			Claimed shot down by SPLA SA-14 during engagement in Kuli Papa area
10 April 1996	Bell 205			Claimed shot down by SPLA during engagement in Kit area
July 1996	MiG-21 or MiG-23			w/o under unknown circumstances
30 December 1996	Unknown helicopter		Crew of 3 reportedly KIA	Claimed shot down by Eritrean Army

19 March 1997	MiG-21			Shot down by SPLA SA-14 during engagement at Mile 435 on Juba-Yei road
20 March 1997	An-24TV		4 crewmembers KIA	Claimed shot down by SPLA SA-14 during engagement in Kuli Papa; aircraft crashed while attempting to land in Juba
10 April 1997	Unknown helicopter			Claimed shot down by LRA during SPAF attack on LRA HQ in Aruu; actually hit by SPLA SA-14
18 May 1997	Unknown helicopter			Claimed shot down by SPLA during engagement in Chali el-Fil area
17 May 1997	Unknown helicopter			Claimed shot down by SPLA during engagement in Jebel Musa area
17 May 1997	Unknown helicopter		Crew survived and escaped from the crash site	Shot down by SPLA during engagement in Jebel Musa area
9 December 1997	MiG-21		Pilot KIA	Shot down by SPLA during engagement in Bibia-Nimule area, on Nile River
1997	An-26-100	7711	Crew fate unknown	Hit by SPLA and emergency-landed in Gogrial, w/o
12 February 1998	An-26 or An-32		26 crewmembers and passengers killed	Skidded off runway during take-off at 'Nasser AB' and plunged into Sobat River, killing Vice-President Zubair Mohammed Saleh
22 October 1998	MiG-23			Claimed shot down by SPLA during engagement near al-Jablain, 64km (46 miles) east of Juba; loss confirmed by Khartoum
3 June 1999	An-32			Reportedly crashed 80km (50 miles) east of Khartoum
2 April 2001	An-26		14 crewmembers and passengers killed	Crashed on take-off at Adaril, killing Deputy Defence Minister Col Ibrahim Shamsul-Din
13 July 2001	Mi-35		Crew of 2 KIA	Claimed shot down by SPLA during engagement in Wehda area, but reportedly crashed due to mechanical failure
11 September 2002	Unknown fighter			Claimed shot down by SPLA
24 December 2002	Unknown fighter			Claimed shot down by SPLA
9 March 2003	Unknown helicopter			Claimed shot down by DLR during engagement in Tura area
8 April 2003	Mi-17		Crew and passengers survived	Shot down by DLF during engagement in Tura area
25 April 2003	An-12B	700	None	Destroyed while parked at el-Fasher airfield during attack by SLA
25 April 2003	An-12B		None	Destroyed while parked at el-Fasher airfield during attack by SLA
25 April 2003	Mi-17		None	Destroyed while parked at el-Fasher airfield during attack by SLA
25 April 2003	Mi-17		None	Destroyed while parked at el-Fasher airfield during attack by SLA
25 April 2003	Mi-17		None	Destroyed while parked at el-Fasher airfield during attack by SLA
25 April 2003	Mi-35		None	Destroyed while parked at el-Fasher airfield during attack by SLA
25 April 2003	Mi-35		None	Destroyed while parked at el-Fasher airfield during attack by SLA
17 July 2003	Mi-35	923		w/o under unknown circumstances
24 September 2003	An-12	ST-SAR	4 Russian, Armenian and Uzbek crewmembers and 1 Sudanese official KIA	c/n 402102; operated by Sarit Airlines; burst info flames while on approach to Wau
29 October 2003	Mi-17		20 crewmembers and passengers KIA	Crashed while evacuating officers injured in car accident
3 November 2003	An-12BP	EK-11997		c/n 6344407; operated by Sarit Airlines; crashed in el-Geneina, circumstances unknown
17 November 2003	An-12	ST-SAA		c/n 5342905; operated by Sarit Airlines; crashed in Wau, circumstances unknown
11 May 2004	An-12	ST-SIG		c/n 1400101; operated by el-Magal Aviation Services; crashed near Dalang, circumstances unknown

7 June 2004	An-26B	ST-ARO		Crashed in el-Geneina, circumstances unknown
26 June 2004	An-12	SI-SAI		c/n 5343502; operated by Sarit Airlines; crashed in Wau due to bird collision
5 October 2004	An-12	ST-SAD		Operated by Sarit Airlines; crashed in Khartoum, circumstances unknown
19 October 2004	An-12	ST-SAF		Operated by Sarit Airlines; crashed near Heglig, circumstances unknown
25 July 2005	Mi-17		19 crewmembers and passengers KIA	Crashed in bad weather near Nyala
11 February 2006	An-26		7 crew and 20 passengers killed	Burst tyre on landing in Aweil, then crashed into building
14 February 2006	Mi-24		Capt Muawiya Zubeir POW	Shot down by JEM or SLA AAA during engagement in Shiairia area
7 August 2006	An-26	ST-ZZZ		Operated by SuAF as 'Antonov bomber'; claimed shot down by JEM, confirmed as crashed in el-Fasher
November 2006	An-??			Shot down by JEM during engagement in eastern Chad
22 December 2006	helicopter			Claimed shot down by SLM during engagement in Kutum area
22 December 2006	helicopter			Claimed shot down by SLM during engagement in Kutum area
2006	A-5C	408?		Overshoot the runway in Juba and w/o under unknown circumstances
2007	MiG-23MS	06916		w/o under unknown circumstances
January 2007	Mi-35			Claimed shot down by SLM during engagement in el-Fasher area
24 February 2007	An-12BP	ST-ADE		c/n 01400106; operated by Sarit; crashed near el-Geneina
2007	An-26	ST-APO		c/n 12792678011005; seen wrecked in Wau, April 2007
28 April 2007	Mi-35		Pilot Muawya Hussein Mohammed POW, 2 crewmembers KIA	Shot down by SLA during engagement in Umrai area
8 July 2007	'MiG-29'			Claimed shot down by JEM during engagement in Wad Ginja
8 July 2007	'MiG-29'			Claimed shot down by JEM during engagement in Wad Ginja
7 August 2007	'MiG-29'[33]		Pilot ejected; fate unknown	Claimed shot down by JEM during engagement in Adila area
1 September 2007	Unknown helicopter			Claimed shot down by JEM during engagement in Haskanita area
9 September 2007	Mi-35	908		Claimed shot down by JEM during engagement in Haskanita area
9 September 2007	Unknown helicopter			Claimed shot down by JEM during engagement in Haskanita area
3 October 2007	'MiG-29'			Claimed shot down by JEM during engagement in Adila area, wreckage reportedly located 4.5km (2.8 miles) south of Adila
8 November 2007	An-12		Crew fate unknown	Operated by Juba Air; made emergency landing in Khartoum, crashed into three MBTs and caught fire
27 December 2007	An-26			Claimed shot down by JEM, but hit by Chadian Army ground fire during engagement in Jebel Moun area; crashed near Nyala
5 January 2008	An-26			Claimed as shot down by JEM during engagement in Geneina area
20 January 2008	'MiG-29'			Claimed shot down by JEM during engagement in Jebel Moun area
19 February 2008	Unknown helicopter			Claimed shot down by SLA during engagement in Jebel Moun area
25 February 2008	Unknown helicopter			Claimed shot down by JEM during engagement in Kondifay area, 15km (9.3 miles) north of el-Geneina; loss confirmed by SuAF but technical malfunction cited as cause
10 May 2008	'MiG-29'		Russian pilot KIA	Shot down by JEM during engagement in Wadi Sayyidna area, pilot killed when parachute failed to deploy
30 June 2008	Il-76TD	ST-WTB	4 crewmembers KIA	c/n 1003499994; crashed on take-off from Khartoum IAP while under way to Darfur

28 August 2008	Al-Quds UAV[34]		Claimed shot down by SLA in Jebel Marra area; loss confirmed by government
15 October 2008	Unknown helicopter		Claimed shot down by JEM
8 November 2010	'MiG-29'		Claimed shot down by JEM during engagement in Majrur area
December 2010	FT-5 or K-8E	2 crewmembers ejected	Crashed during night-time training mission over Red Sea
13 April 2011	Mi-35	1 crewmember KIA	Crashed during take-off from Khartoum IAP
18 April 2011	Mi-17	5 crewmembers KIA	Crashed due to technical problems 3km (1.9 miles) from el-Fasher
10 June 2011	'Antonov'		Claimed shot down by SPLM in Kalkul area
10 June 2011	'MiG'[35]		Claimed shot down by SPLM in Kauda area

1   Sudan received a total of 10 F-5Es and 2 F-5Fs from the USA. One of F-5Fs crashed barely a week after delivery, in 1984; two were claimed shot down in combat with the SPLA, in 1985, and at least three in period 1988–1989. Although the fleet was reinforced by the defection of two Ethiopian F-5E pilots to Sudan, in May 1991, one F-5F (82-0005) was sold to Jordan a few years later (where it serves with No.17 Squadron Royal Jordanian Air Force), probably indicating the lack of interest to continue flying the type on the part of the SuAF. It is likely that the remaining F-5Es were subsequently exchanged for spares and other kind of support from the Islamic Republic of Iran. The BAC Strikemaster T.Mk 90s were delivered in two batches of two – in November and December 1983, respectively.

2   Corresponding reports were published repeatedly by the Sudanese media, foremost by various newspapers in Khartoum, and not by the SPLA or any other insurgent organisation, as might be expected.

3   Sudan has introduced its fleet of MiG-29 fighter-jets into the civil war in the South, *World Tribune*, 9 July 2002 – citing anonymous US officials who stated that 12 MiG-29 have been seen while deployed at el-Ubayid AB and flying combat sorties in southern Sudan.

4   Sudan taking delivery of the last of 12 MiGs, *VOA*, 22 July 2004

5   SPAF Regional Commands and Divisions as of 2001 were as follows:
    Southern Command, 1st Division, HQ in Juba (later withdrawn to the north, and probably integrated into the Khartoum Command)
    Eastern Command, 2nd Division, HQ in Khashm al-Qirbah
    Central Command, 3rd Division, HQ in al-Ubayyid (Kordofan)
    Western Command, 6th Division, HQ in el-Fasher
    Khartoum Command, 7th Division, HQ in ash-Sharjah, near Khartoum

6   The Nanchang CJ-6 is a further development of the Nanchang CJ-5, which in turn is a copy of the Soviet Yak-18 basic trainer. In addition to Sudan, the CJ-6 serves also as a basic trainer in Tanzania.

7   Notably, the Islamic Republic of Iran Air Force began applying new camouflage patterns only on some of ex-Iraqi aircraft that entered its service – primarily on Sukhoi Su-24s – and then only after 1994, i.e. after the time-frame in which deliveries of ex-Iraqi aircraft by Iran to Sudan was reported. This means that even if the Iranians ever delivered any such aircraft to Sudan, these were certainly left in their original colours, as flown in Iraq.

8   Based on Brent, *African Air Forces*, pp17-23, with additional details extracted from media reports and various other publications.

9   Jafaar Numeiry was a graduate of the Sudanese Army Military College and Staff College, as well as of the General Staff College course at Fort Leavenworth, in the USA, O'Ballance, *The Secret War in the Sudan*, p104

10 Ibid. pp106–107; note that these 'MiGs' likely included Jet Provosts delivered to Sudan by the UK, in the late 1960s.

11 The Southerners persistently alleged the Sudanese military of indiscipline, but independent observers repeatedly confirmed that discipline was good and the officers had full control over their men. See O'Ballance, *The Secret War in the Sudan*, pp119–121 and 177.

12 It was following the second of the above-mentioned MiG-21 losses that the AN claimed, ' …the two of the dead were identified as Russians by dental evidence' (see O'Ballance, *The Secret War in the Sudan*, p122). In what fashion could the insurgents obtain original dental records of any of Soviet instructors in Sudan at the time, in order to compare these with any of the bodies they might have found, remains unknown.

13 Flintham, *Air Wars and Aircraft*, p151.

14 Stanik, *El Dorado Canyon*, pp74-78.

15 Sudanese MiG-21s were delivered to the Zmaj Works on board SuAF C-130Hs. This was also the case with SuAF Mi-8s, overhauled in Yugoslavia around the same time. Meanwhile, Zmaj was also overhauling Libyan MiG-21bis and Egyptian MiG-21MFs. On one occasion the fin of an Egyptian MiG-21MF was misplaced and delivered to Sudan together with a SuAF MiG-21M, while the fin of the Sudanese MiG-21M was delivered to Egypt. Other than this glitch, swiftly corrected by Yugoslav technicians, all the works were completed to complete customer satisfaction, although the Soviets were not the least pleased by this arrangement.

16 Interviews with former USAF FTD officer, provided on condition of anonymity, 2001-03.

17 Brig Gen Ahmad Sadik (IrAF, ret), interview, March 2006.

18 The actual number of such attacks flown by the Sudanese should actually be significantly higher, then most of them targeted remote areas along the border to Uganda.

19 'Rebel Plane Downed by Sudan Came From Kenya', AFP, 1 September 2003.

20 Mortality figures for the war in Darfur differ strongly, depending on the source. Sudanese authorities claim a death toll of roughly 19,500 civilians, while various non-governmental organisations claim as many as 400,000 victims, see 'Old Dogs, New Tricks', *al-Ahram Weekly*, 6 December 2006 and 'Tallying Darfur Terror: Guesswork with a Cause', International Herald Tribune, 11 May 2005. The World Health Organization estimated there had been 70,000 deaths in Darfur within an 18-month period since the beginning of the conflict – 'but', mostly due to starvation and disease – while a more recent British Parliamentary Report estimated that over 300,000 people have died; see 'How Many Have Died in Darfur?', BBC, 16 February 2005, 'Darfur Death Toll May Be 300,000, Say UK Lawmakers', Reuters, 30 March 2005 and 'The Genocide in Darfur Isn't What it Seems', Christian Science Monitor, 19 August 2009.

21 President Idriss Déby Itno of Chad is a member of the Bidayat, a tribe closely related to the Zaghawas, which nowadays lives on both sides of the Chad-Sudan border, but originates from the Sudan. The Sudanese Zaghawa are one of main tribes fighting the Khartoum regime. Déby gained power in December 1990, with help of the government in Khtaroum, and in the course of a major raid by Toyota pickups against the Chadian capital, N'Djamena, launched from Darfur – in Sudan. At first, Déby refused to help his fellow tribesmen on the other side of the border and even tried to help the government in Khartoum. However, after facing outright military revolt from within 'his' Zaghawa tribe – who made up the core group of the Chadian armed forces – he faced the choice of either switching sides or being overthrown. Evetually, Déby found himself supporting the JEM, in turn angering the Khartoum government, which then started to recruit disaffected elements from Chad – primarily former aides of the government in N'Djamena.

22 'Russia says fighter pilot shot down in Sudan was an ex-military officer', *Ekho Moskvy/Interfax*, 30-31 May, 2008

23 According to the local media, the SPAF captured up to 300 insurgents in the course of this battle. 82 of these were subsequently put to trial, found guilty of terrorism and illegal possession of weapons, some also for an attempt to overthrow the government, and sentenced to death; see 'Eleven Darfur Rebels Sentenced to Death', *AFP*, 22 April 2009.

24 'Chad readies Forces to Strike Rebels in Sudan', *Reuters*, 19 May, 2008.

25 IAF Airstrike in Sudan Hit Convoy of Weapons Destined For Gaza, *Haaretz*, 26 March, 2009; according to US State Department documents subsequently released by the WikiLeaks, the Government in Khartoum was startled by this attack and wondered for weeks about its possible backgrounds. Firstly, the Sudanese Air Force completely failed to at least detect the attackers, nor proved capable of responding to it, and then could also not find out who attacked the truck column in question. Initially, Khartoum assumed that the bombing was carried out by the US, because only days before the US officials approached them about information related to weapons shipment from Iran to Gaza through Sudan – which Khartoum denied.

26 Sudan Says it Repelled Rebel Attack in Darfur, *AP*, 24 May, 2009, containing statements by Brig Gen Osman Mohammed al-Aghbash & In Remote North Darfur, An Upsurge in Clashes between Rebels and Government Forces, *Christian Science Monitor*, 26 May, 2009

27 Sudan Army Base Attack Kills 63, *BBC*, 26 May, 2009; Rebels Say They Evacuated Darfur Towns to Protect Civilians, *Reuters*, 29 May, 2009 and Sudan Aircraft Bomb Settlement near Chad, *Reuters*, 2 June 2009

28 Chad Uses Air Support to Fight Rebels, *Reuters*, 15 December, 2009

29 Bashir says Sudanese Army militarily defeats JEM in Darfur, *Xinhua*, 21 July, 2010

30 'Two North Sudan Army Planes Downed', *PressTV*, 13 June 2011.

31 'Sudan Air Attacks Causing 'Huge Suffering'', al-Jazeera (English Service), 14 June 2011.

32 The reason this list includes not only the SuAF MiG and Shenyang fighters is that the reporting about the losses of the SuAF by all belligerents of Sudanese civil wars is frequently dubious in regards of aircraft identification. Furthermore, there are next to no publications summarizing the combat deployment of the Sudanese Air Force in the last 50 years, and the authors therefore decided to provide the best possible coverage of this topic. The list is based on all available sources, including various printed periodicals, books, TV and other media reports, the internet, as well as several first-hand sources. It should not be considered 'complete', and only the entries marked in bold can be considered as confirmed (by photographic evidence or independent reports).

33 Starting with this claim and until today, JEM insurgents tend to claim any SuAF fighters they report as 'shot down' to have been a MiG-29. Although the SuAF MiG-29s are well-armed for air-to-ground operations, they have not been observed as deployed on any of three major airfields in Darfur so far, while A-5Cs were sighted at el-Fasher and Nyala on a number of occasions since 2003, and Su-25s several times since 2009. Because of this, it is most likely that nearly all of 'MiG-29's claimed as shot down by the rebels during engagements in Darfur were A-5Cs (sole exception should be the Russian-flown MiG-29 shot down by the JEM in the course of engagement in Wadi Sayyidna area, north of Khartoum, on 10 May 2008).

34 In September 2008, the Military Industry Corporation of Sudan (which includes the Safat Complex at Wadi Sayyidna AB), reported its capability to manufacture 'unmanned surveillance planes', colloquially known as the UAVs (for unmanned aerial vehicles). None of related reports ever included the designation of the UAV-type in question, but the photographs released at that and subsequent opportunities showed a vehicle not only 'closely resembling' the Iraqi el-Qods type, manufactured in the late 1990s, but also painted in exactly the same fashion. Given that the Safat Complex has recently assembled and rebuilt a number of aircraft Sudan clandestinely obtained from abroad (such like at least one UTVA-75 basic trainer, built in the former Yugoslavia until 1991, and rolled out as 'Safat-3', in 2010), but also considering the tight cooperation between the IrAF and the SuAF in the 1990s, it is very likely that this 'new' Sudanese UAV is actually the Iraqi al-Qods manufactured and assembled in Sudan.

35 In the official SPLA release mentioning this claim, the second SuAF aircraft claimed as shot down on 10 June 2011 was named 'MiG Joint-3'. What type should that means remains unknown, but it is known that the SuAF had A-5Cs and Su-25s deployed at el-Ubayyid AB (in North Kordofan, and approximately 200km from the reported engagement area) during the spring of 2011.

Chapter 20

UNITED REPUBLIC OF TANZANIA

Overview[1]

The United Republic of Tanzania came into being on 26 April 1964, when the states of Tanganyika (British-administered until 1961) and Zanzibar (a former British colony, which gained independence in 1963, and which was ruled by an Arab Sultan for a year) were united.

The basis of the Tanzanian military – the Jeshi la Wananchi la Tanzania (JWTZ – Tanzania People's Defence Force) – was formed around the British-organised and run Tanganyika Rifles. This unit mutinied over pay, promotions and the removal of British officers in 1964, however, and was subsequently disbanded, despite the government's understanding of the reasons for the mutiny. Subsequently, a new military was established consisting of new recruits.

A small transport and liaison air arm, named Usafirashaji wa Anga (Air Wing) was established within the JWTZ Air Defence Command in early 1965, when 10 Tanzanian students were sent to West Germany for pilot training. West Germany intended to provide extensive assistance to the JWTZ, including deliveries of P.149Ds, Do 27 and Do 28s, as well as Noratlas transports. However, within a few weeks, all such plans had to be abandoned amid differences between the West German and Tanzanian governments over the presence of an East German ambassador in Dar es-Salaam, as well as due to West German involvement in deliveries of aircraft to Portugal, then involved in fighting insurgents in neighbouring Mozambique. Correspondingly, only eight disassembled Focke-Wulf-built P.149Ds arrived at Dar es-Salaam, where they remained stored for a lengthy period of time.

Canada, keen to gain a foothold in Tanzania since 1963, took the place of West Germany and in 1965 launched a project worth USD10.5 million with the aim of bolstering the JWTZ. The future air arm would include one or two squadrons of combat aircraft to counter Portuguese and Rhodesian forces. Canada initially provided 80 instructors from the Royal Canadian Air Force (RCAF), these arriving in January 1966 with the intention of establishing the necessary infrastructure. Simultaneously, 24 Tanzanians travelled to Canada to receive training as pilots and ground personnel. A number of de Havilland Canada DHC-3 Otter and DHC-4 Caribou transports were readied to be used by the Tanzanians in Canada, as well as for delivery to the JWTZ. Once in Dar es-Salaam, the Canadians assembled the P.149Ds delivered from West Germany, and launched a local training programme for Tanzanians. Thus, by May 1967, the JWTZ operated eight DHC-3s, three DHC-4s, and eight P.149Ds, and by the end of the year possessed a small cadre of well-trained pilots and ground personnel.

Cooperation with Canada came to an end in 1968, when the Tanzanian government decided to establish close ties with China instead.

China had established a relationship with Tanzania by 1964, and provided substantial aid grants in the following years. Among other projects, the Chinese completely built, equipped and staffed a police college at Moshi, and over 13,000 Chinese workers helped construct the 2,000km (1,243-mile) Tanzania-Zambia railroad, from Kapiri Mposhi to Dar es-Salaam. In 1970, a sizeable contingent of Chinese military advisors arrived with the intention of constructing a major air base near Ngerengere, then some 140km (87 miles) outside Dar es-Salaam, as well as preparing the JWTZ with an introduction to jet fighters.

During the same year, 170 Tanzanian military personnel travelled to China to be trained as pilots and ground personnel. Limited connections to Canada remained intact, however, and in 1970 Tanzania ordered eight additional DHC-4s, all of which were delivered the following year, by which time the JWTZ started selling some of its older DHC-3s. Using Canada as an intermediary, in 1971 the US delivered four Piper PA-28-140 Cherokees to reinforce the fleet of tired P.149D basic trainers.

The JWTZ underwent major expansion following the short war with Uganda in 1971, when China and the Soviet Union swiftly delivered significant quantities of MiG fighters and a battalion of SA-3 SAMs, plus associated ground support equipment including radars. Acquisition of no fewer than 34 jet fighters from China – followed by MiG-21s from the USSR – led to a number of problems associated with maintenance and training, and the JWTZ spent most of the mid-1970s attempting to remedy these. It was only in late 1977 and early 1978 that the Tanzanian military found the time and resources for further new acquisitions. During this period, acquisition concentrated foremost on helicopters and additional transport aircraft, which proved of great value during the major war with Uganda. This conflict erupted in October 1978 and culminated with a Tanzanian invasion of Uganda, and the capture of Kampala in April 1979. The cost of this war and subsequent occupation of Uganda, which lasted until 1982, was massive, and losses could only partially be replaced using captured equipment. Correspondingly, in the late 1970s and through most of the 1980s, Tanzania was forced to sell many of its transport aircraft, while keeping a watchful eye towards the south, where a new war was raging in Mozambique.

Until the mid-1990s, the JWTZ was essentially paralysed by a lack of funding, and kept only a handful of light liaison and transport aircraft in an operational condition.

Major revitalisation projects were launched only in recent years, again with some Chinese assistance, but also through the acquisition of light aircraft and helicopters from the West, followed by several medium transports. During 2009 and 2010, it

This photograph came into being in 2005, but shows one of the JWTZ's FT-5s in its original livery – 'bare metal' overall, with a large black serial number on the forward fuselage. The reason for the lack of national markings remains unknown, but is possibly related to the overhaul though which this aircraft was put through in 2004.
(P. P. via Tom Cooper)

became obvious that the JWTZ had begun training new pilots (or retraining available pilots), and that a number of older aircraft were undergoing local overhauls. Finally, in late 2010, it became known that the air force had received brand-new Chengdu F-7 fighters, equipped to a very high standard.

Deliveries of MiG, Shenyang and Chengdu fighters to the United Republic of Tanzania

As the United Republic of Tanzania came into being, the government envisaged the establishment of at least one jet fighter squadron. Following the establishment and gradual development of the JWTZ through the 1960s, and the construction of Ngerengere air base with Chinese aid in 1971, the air force was finally considered ready for an appropriate acquisition. In late June 1973, the first of an eventual 12 Shenyang F-6s arrived from China, followed by up to 22 Shenyang FT-5 two-seat conversion trainers. One year later, the first of an eventual 14 MiG-21MFs and 2 MiG-21UMs arrived from the USSR.

During the war with Uganda in 1979, Tanzania reportedly captured several intact Ugandan Army Air Force (UAAF) MiG-21s (for details see below and Chapter 21: Republic of Uganda). The Tanzanians attempted to fly at least three of these to Mwanza, but available reports indicate that two crashed under way, their pilots barely managing to eject.

Reports concerning deliveries of Chengdu F-7s from China in the 1980s were obviously incorrect. Instead, Tanzania received 12 F-6Cs and up to 4 FT-6s. Various reports of deliveries of between two and five second-hand F-7 fighters from the Islamic Republic of Iran are also erroneous.

During the period 2006-08, reports and photographs appeared indicating that the JWTZ had begun the process of locally overhauling a number of FT-5s, FT-6s and F-6s, as well as training their pilots. In the course of 2009 and 2010, unconfirmed reports emerged concerning possible deliveries of F-7s or MiG-21s from China or an East European source, re-deliveries of overhauled MiG-21s, or operations by a small number of MiG-21-type aircraft from Kilimanjaro airport. Similarly, Russia has attempted to generate interest in MiG-29s, but this offer was turned down by Tanzania for financial reasons.

The first firm evidence of similar developments appeared in late 2010, when the first photographs of at least two different FT-7s and one F-7 appeared. While the precise numbers of newly delivered aircraft remain unknown, it is now certain that the JWTZ operates several examples of this type equipped to a relatively high standard. This is in addition to three FT-5s (one example crashed in 2010, see below for details), one FT-6 and at least three F-6s.

The appearance of JWTZ MiG-21MFs remains very much a mystery to this day. Details seen in this series of photographs taken on 10 October 1985 at Mwanza, and showing seven MiG-21MFs and two MiG-21UMs, indicate that all the aircraft were painted in 'air superiority grey' overall, and had four-digit serial numbers applied on their forward fuselages. (P. P. via Greg Swart)

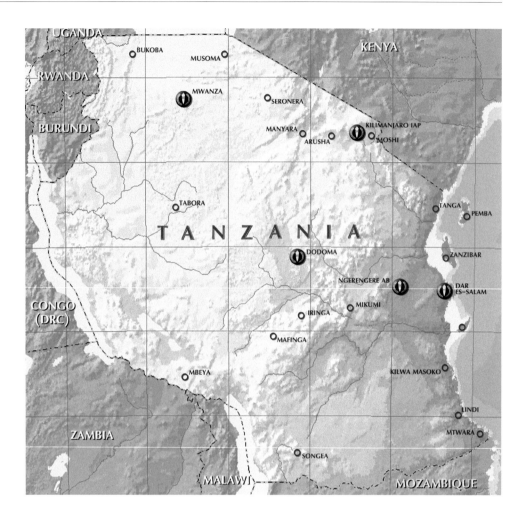

Map of Tanzania

Force structure

The Air Wing of the JWTZ is organised into Kikosi cha Jeshi (KJ – Brigades), three of which are known to exist: 601 KJ is controlling all the aircraft and helicopters; 602 KJ is probably a technical unit; and 603 KJ operates all air defence equipment.

Ngerengere is the main base for an unknown unit flying fighter aircraft, known only as 'Squadron 601'; another brigade operates trainers, while all transport aircraft and helicopters are based at Dar-es-Salaam. Mwanza air base was officially closed in the early 2000s and no longer houses any military installations, even though there is still some military presence at the airfield, which is also 'home' to at least 10 MiG-21s (stored since 1993). Thirteen F-6 and FT-6s, as well as a number of FT-5s and CJ-6s have been stored at Ngerengere since the 1990s.

Recently delivered F-7s wear 'TAFC' titles on their forward fuselages, standing for 'Tanzania Air Force Command'. The same is applied on the lower surfaces of both FT-7s sighted to date, indicating that the JWTZ has developed a new structure, dedicated to the defence of Tanzanian airspace.

Taken more recently, this photograph reveals additional details of two of the JWTZ's MiG-21s, including what looks like the 'Torch and Laurel Wreath' applied as a fin flash on the MiG-21MF to the left, and parts of the camouflage pattern on the MiG-21UM to the right. (P. P. via Tom Cooper)

National markings

When the United Republic of Tanzania was created from Tanganyika and Zanzibar in 1964, elements of the flags of both preceding countries were combined to form the national flag. This consists of green, yellow and blue fields, with a black diagonal stripe. The flag device was applied on the fins of most JWTZ aircraft in the 1960s, and probably also on the fins of F-6s in the 1970s. Whether any national markings were ever applied on the upper or lower wing surfaces remains unknown.

JWTZ MiG-21s apparently either received the national flag or a stylised 'Torch and Laurel Wreath' as a form of national insignia on their fins.

FT-5s and F-6s returned to service in recent years did not initially wear any kind of national markings, but in 2008 the JWTZ crest was applied on the fins of most overhauled F-6s. The same crest is also applied on recently delivered F-7s.

It appears that none of Tanzania's combat aircraft have ever worn any form of roundel, and that these are applied on trainers, transports and helicopters only.

Camouflage colours and serial numbers

Very little reliable information is available as regards the colours and serial numbers of FT-5s and F-6s as originally delivered to Tanzania. However, reports of the JWTZ acquiring 'JJ-2s' (supposedly Chinese-built MiG-15UTIs) and marking these with a running zebra insignia, as well as applying serial numbers similar to those worn by USAF aircraft, are almost certainly untrue.

FT-5s sighted in recent years initially appeared in 'natural metal' overall, perhaps indicating that the JWTZ operated them in such a livery in the 1980s as well. However, all four examples returned to service in recent years were subsequently painted in matt white overall. Interestingly, most of them have no paint applied on their airbrakes on the rear fuselage.

It is possible that at least the first batch of F-6s delivered to Tanzania was originally painted in white overall, and camouflaged in sand, brick red and dark green on the upper surfaces and sides, and RLB on the lower surfaces, sometime after their delivery.

Overhauled in 2004-2005, these three FT-5s (from left to right: 9121, 9120 and 9118) have been painted in matt white overall (except for their airbrakes) and are now used for training new pilots.
(P. P. via Tom Cooper)

Nowadays, the F-6s wear a camouflage pattern consisting of sand, dark olive green and chocolate brown on the upper surfaces, with dark RLB on the lower surfaces. Serial numbers are applied in large digits on the forward fuselage, and the title 'JWTZ' is applied in black on the rear fuselage.

Even less is known about Tanzania's MiG-21MFs and MiG-21UMs. They appear to have been painted in overall 'air superiority grey' during their service, in common with the MiG-21s later delivered to Madagascar. Four-digit serial numbers, probably in the range 92xx upwards, were applied in black or dark grey on the forward fuselage.

Taken in late 2004 at Dar-es-Salaam IAP, after this aircraft went through local upgrade, this photograph reveals the details of the original camouflage pattern applied on JWTZ F-6s. The only marking that is still visible is the title 'JWTZ' applied on the rear fuselage.
(P. P. via Tom Cooper)

Following their overhaul and the training of new pilots and maintenence crews, JWTZ F-6s are now painted in sand, dark green and chocolate brown on the upper surfaces, with light blue lower surfaces. Notable is the serial number 9205 on the forward fuselage and the new national insignia on the fin.
(via Pit Weinert)

'JWTZ' titles were probably worn on the rear fuselage. Available photographic evidence indicates that it is possible – although by no means confirmed – that the MiG-21s wore their full military registrations, for example 'JW-9221', on the fin, directly below the fin flash.

Recently delivered F-7s appear to wear a camouflage pattern of dark grey overall. (Reports of them wearing a camouflage pattern consisting of two shades of grey, apparently similar to that of F-7s operated by the Pakistani Air Force, cannot presently be confirmed.) The F-7s have 'TAFC' titles applied on the forward fuselage and appear to wear their serial numbers – prefixed by 'JW' (short for 'military') – on the rear fuselage.

The FT-7 two-seat conversion trainers are camouflaged in dark sand or beige, green and dark chocolate brown on the upper surfaces, with a light-blue shade similar to RLB on the lower surfaces. They wear large 'TAFC' titles on the lower surfaces of both wings, and their full serial numbers – prefixed by 'JW' – are worn on the forward fuselage.

Both variants appear to have the JWTZ crest applied on the fin as national insignia. Construction numbers are applied in black on the cockpit rails, and all maintenance stencils are applied in dark red or dark blue, in English language.

Table 36: Known serial numbers of JWTZ fighters, 1973–2009[2]

Aircraft type	Serial number	c/n	Remarks
FT-5	9101		Delivered in 1973 from China
FT-5	9102		Delivered in 1973 from China; active as of 2004
FT-5	9103		Delivered in 1973 from China
FT-5	9104		Delivered in 1973 from China
FT-5	9105		Delivered in 1973 from China
FT-5	9106		Delivered in 1973 from China
FT-5	9107		Delivered in 1973 from China
FT-5	9108		Delivered in 1973 from China
FT-5	9109		Delivered in 1973 from China
FT-5	9110		Delivered in 1973 from China
FT-5	9111		Delivered in 1973 from China
FT-5	9112		Delivered in 1973 from China
FT-5	9113		Delivered in 1973 from China
FT-5	9114		Delivered in 1973 from China
FT-5	9115		Delivered in 1973 from China
FT-5	9116		Delivered in 1973 from China
FT-5	9117		Delivered in 1973 from China
FT-5	9118		Delivered in 1973 from China; active as of 2004
FT-5	9119		Delivered in 1973 from China; w/o in accident 29 June 2010
FT-5	9120		Delivered in 1973 from China; active as of 2004
FT-5	9121		Delivered in 1973 from China; active as of 2004
FT-6C	9122		Delivered in 1982 from China
FT-6C	9123		Delivered in 1982 from China
FT-6C	9124		Delivered in 1982 from China; active as of 2009

FT-7	9125		Delivered in 2010 from China; active as of 2011
FT-7	9126		Delivered in 2010 from China; active as of 2011
MiG-21UM	91??		Delivered in 1974 from USSR; stored at Mwanza since 1993
MiG-21UM	91??		Delivered in 1974 from USSR; stored at Mwanza since 1993
MiG-21UM	91??		Delivered in 1974 from USSR; stored at Mwanza since 1993
MiG-21UM	91??		Delivered in 1974 from USSR
MiG-21MF	92??		Delivered in 1974 from USSR; stored at Mwanza since 1993
MiG-21MF	92??		Delivered in 1974 from USSR; stored at Mwanza since 1993
MiG-21MF	92??		Delivered in 1974 from USSR; stored at Mwanza since 1993
MiG-21MF	92??		Delivered in 1974 from USSR; stored at Mwanza since 1993
MiG-21MF	92??		Delivered in 1974 from USSR; stored at Mwanza since 1993
MiG-21MF	92??		Delivered in 1974 from USSR; stored at Mwanza since 1993
MiG-21MF	92??		Delivered in 1974 from USSR
MiG-21MF	92??		Delivered in 1974 from USSR
MiG-21MF	92??		Delivered in 1974 from USSR
MiG-21MF	92??		Delivered in 1974 from USSR
MiG-21MF	92??		Delivered in 1974 from USSR
MiG-21MF	92??		Delivered in 1974 from USSR
F-6	9201		Delivered in 1973 from China
F-6	9202		Delivered in 1973 from China
F-6	9203		Delivered in 1973 from China; active as of 2009
F-6	9204		Delivered in 1973 from China; active as of 2009
F-6	9205		Delivered in 1973 from China; active as of 2009
F-6	9206		Delivered in 1973 from China
F-6	9207		Delivered in 1973 from China
F-6	9208		Delivered in 1973 from China
F-6	9209		Delivered in 1973 from China
F-6	9210		Delivered in 1973 from China
F-6	9211		Delivered in 1973 from China; active as of 2009
F-6	9212		Delivered in 1973 from China
F-6C	9226?		Delivered in 1982 from China
F-6C	9227		Delivered in 1982 from China
F-6C	9228		Delivered in 1982 from China
F-6C	9229		Delivered in 1982 from China
F-6C	9230		Delivered in 1982 from China
F-6C	9231		Delivered in 1982 from China
F-6C	9232		Delivered in 1982 from China
F-6C	9233		Delivered in 1982 from China
F-6C	9234		Delivered in 1982 from China
F-6C	9235		Delivered in 1982 from China
F-6C	9236		Delivered in 1982 from China; active as of 2009
F-7G	9242	1140	Delivered in 2010 from China; active as of 2011

MiG and Shenyang fighter operations in the United Republic of Tanzania, 1973–1980[4]

The decision of the government in Dar es-Salaam to equip the JWTZ was intimately related to tensions with Uganda, and several border incidents that occurred in the early 1970s. These tensions began to increase again from 1976, prompting China to increase the aid furnished to Dar es-Salaam once again, foremost through the deployment of additional advisors to the JWTZ. Chinese advisors working in Tanzania encountered several problems with the military discipline of the locals. For example, while Chinese officers, pilots and ground personnel spent most of their service time within their bases, most JWTZ personnel would leave their base at noon to go home for lunch. At the end of the working day, most officers would leave the base to go to work in different functions outside the military. Only JWTZ pilots – in particular the 11 Tanzanians trained to fly F-6s at the time – spent most of their time at Ngerengere air base. Although all stationed at Ngerengere, the Chinese and Soviet advisors that supported Tanzanian fighter units in 1976 and 1977 were strictly segregated.

A memorial to the JWTZ pilot shot down and killed by 'friendly' AAA while attempting to land at Mwanza.
(via Pit Weinert)

The situation changed once the JWTZ decided to deploy a detachment of the F-6 unit to Mwanza airfield, sometime in 1976. Constructed directly on the shores of Lake Victoria, Mwanza was thus only 150km (93 miles) away from the border with Uganda, and 280km (174 miles) from Entebbe air base. The deployment of this unit almost ended in an early catastrophe. While the F-6s were approaching Mwanza from the direction of Ngerengere, local AAA units opened fire at them and shot one fighter down, killing its pilot, Ayekuwa Akiirusha. Short of fuel and unable to divert to another airfield, the other pilot braved the heavy defensive fire. Although the jet crashed after running out of fuel, some 50km (31 miles) away, the pilot ejected safely. A subsequent investigation revealed that there had been a grievous mistake within the chain of command, and nobody had informed locally based units of the decision to deploy F-6s to Mwanza. As a result, AAA gunners misidentified the F-6s as Ugandan MiGs about to attack the airfield and opened fire.

As of 1978, the JWTZ was still in the process of training the personnel for its jet fighter force when relations between Tanzania and Uganda led to another war. In September 1978, in the light of intelligence that Tanzania was about to launch an invasion of Uganda, the top military commanders in Entebbe ordered a preventive attack into Tanzania. UAAF MiG-17s and MiG-21s flew a series of raids against various targets in the Bukoba area, causing damage that left dozens of civilians dead and caused a flow of refugees towards the south.[5]

Following these raids, on 28 September 1978 two Ugandan Army units of around 2,000 – including the Suicide Reconnaissance Regiment – crossed the border to Tanzania at four different places and advanced into the Kagera Salient. This latter was part of the Tanzanian territory north of the Kagera River that the government in Kampala had previously claimed for Uganda.

The Tanzania People's Defence Force (TPDF) had two major units deployed in the area at the time, including the 208th Brigade, based at a camp in Katoro, a village near the strategically important Kyaka bridge, and the 206th Brigade, camped further away in the west. Although reinforced by armed Ugandan dissidents based in several camps in the Kyaka area, and several JWTZ teams equipped with SA-7 MANPADS, these forces were taken completely by surprise and fled the area.

African MiGs | Volume 2

Not all Ugandan MiGs claimed shot down during the first phase of the war with Tanzania in autumn 1978 were MiG-17s: this wreckage is mute witness to the loss of a MiG-21MF. Sadly, the date and place of this loss remain unknown. (via Martin Smisek)

The government in Dar es-Salaam became aware of the fact that the Ugandan invasion presented it with a perfect opportunity to hit back in force and launch a counter-invasion of Uganda, thus solving its problems with Kampala once and for all. However, an operation of this kind could not be launched without sufficient preparation, particularly since at the time TPDF forces in the area were barely able to stop the Ugandan advance. In order to buy the time required for mobilising its military and deploying it into the combat zone, in early October 1978 Tanzania supported an unsuccessful assassination attempt against the Ugandan president. In response, on 10 October 1978, Uganda declared war on Tanzania. However, the Ugandan Army proved unable to carry the fighting deeper into Tanzania. On the contrary, in the course of the pursuit of the assassins, several smaller units mutinied and defected to Tanzania, where later, in January 1979, most of their troops joined up with thousands of other dissidents to establish the Uganda National Liberation Army (UNLA).

Meanwhile, a major drama was developing on the battlefield. Emboldened by his success at Kyaka, the Ugandan commander reported to Entebbe that the Tanzanians were advancing into Uganda and requested permission to continue his own advance 'in return'. Falling for the lie, his superiors granted their permission and the Ugandan Army regiments continued attacking, facing very little resistance until 1 October, when they reached the Taka bridge on Kyaka River, thus effectively sealing off the entire Kagera salient.

By this time, both air forces were active flying CAPs over their airfields, but while the Tanzanians seldom crossed the border, the UAAF MiGs continued flying strikes into Tanzania. On 1 October 1978 the government in Dar es-Salaam again claimed to have shot down three Ugandan jet fighters over its territory, and the government in Kampala admitted having lost one. The fighter in question was a MiG-17 flown by Maj Omita. The pilot managed to eject safely and was able to escape towards the rapidly advancing Ugandan units. Despite this loss, the Ugandan government then extended its claim, noting that its jets had 'routed a Tanzanian air attack headed for major Ugandan cities' – almost certainly an exaggeration.[6]

Amid Ugandan announcements concerning annexation of the Kagera Salient, however, the Ugandan advance stalled: the two regiments could not capture the Taka bridge and could also not advance due to the lack of equipment for amphibious operations. In contrast, the Tanzanians constructed their own pontoon bridge and on 3 November 1978 launched a counterattack that hit heavily the exposed flank of the Ugandan Army units – meanwhile busy celebrating their victory, looting and gang raping the local population. Their commanders immediately requested air support, calling the UAAF to hit the Tanzanian pontoon bridge. The UAAF reacted as expected, but its MiG-17 pilots encountered heavy ground fire and not only missed their target, but – according to Tanzanian claims – lost two fighters shot down by SA-7s.

Although the JWTZ is not known to have flown any kind of air raids into Uganda before April 1979, by this time the media in Kampala was full of claims that UAAF jets had 'routed' one Tanzanian attack heading for major Ugandan cities after the other. In fact, the UAAF expanded its operations over Tanzania, but the same weapons that caused considerable damage in local towns proved less efficient when used against well-protected Tanzanian military units. Even on the ground, where the Ugandans considered themselves vastly superior to their opponents, the Army proved unable to organise and launch a large-scale invasion of Tanzania. Indeed, the Ugandan Army eventually had to withdraw its units out of the Kagera Salient by late November 1978,

even though UAAF MiG-17s and MiG-21s flew several additional raids on targets in the Bukoba area, including the local dirt landing strip, and effectively controlled the skies over the battlefield.

In late November 1978 another raid by two MiG-17s reportedly hit the airfield at Mwanza, even though Tanzania reported that no damage was caused. In turn, at least one of the involved MiG-21s – the aircraft flown by Capt Kiiza – returned to Entebbe badly damaged, hit by an SA-7 in the tail section. Kiiza was subsequently promoted to the rank of major and was appointed CO of the sole UAAF MiG-21 squadron, based at Entebbe.

In December 1978, Tanzania mobilised its Army reserves, closed all the schools in the combat zone, recruited the local population to build underground shelters, and the JWTZ apparently deployed one of its SA-3 SAM systems to protect Mwanza airfield.

By January 1979 the TPDF had mobilised over 60,000 troops and deployed two additional brigades into the combat zone, including the 201st and 207th, while the F-6 squadron deployed to Mwanza was reinforced by the MiG-21 squadron, and both units flew regular CAPs along the border. Some 2,000 UNLA fighters received additional training and formed the Minziro Brigade, which was to operate together with around 20,000 Tanzanian Army troops deployed in the combat zone. Additional units meanwhile underwent intensive training deeper inside Tanzania, including the 205th Brigade, trained in the Kakuuto area.

At the border, the troops of the Ugandan Suicide Reconnaissance Regiment had entrenched themselves in the Mutukula area, but were subjected to continuous artillery, rocket and air attacks. When a formation of UAAF MiG-17s and MiG-21s attempted to intervene with attacks on Tanzanian artillery, they encountered heavy fire from anti-aircraft defences and aborted their only attack. The shelling of the almost isolated Ugandan unit in Mutukula went on for weeks, while at the rear of the Tanzanian positions the TPDF had hauled sufficient supplies for an advance on Entebbe.

On 20 January 1979, 12,000 TPDF troops supported by Chinese-made Type 59 and Type 69 tanks and numerous artillery pieces, including BM-21 multiple rocket launchers, crossed the border in strength, launching a frontal attack from the east to smash the forward Ugandan positions. Instead of reacting to this offensive, the Ugandan government and military leadership preferred to ignore it, failing to send any kind of reinforcement to the embattled unit in Mutukula. The Suicide Regiment finally withdrew towards the north, its troops on the verge of mutiny after weeks under heavy enemy fire.

Despite considerable losses sustained while breaking through the Ugandan front lines, within a few days the involved TPDF forces had advanced on Rakai, and constructed a forward airstrip near Mutukula, enabling JWTZ transports to deliver supplies and fuel direct to the front lines. In the course of the next two weeks, Tanzania occupied the Simba Hills and also the Lukoma airstrip on 13 February, again enabling JWTZ transports to bring in supplies. Two UAAF MiG-21s flew at least one air raid against this airstrip, but without success.

The TPDF then deployed each of its brigades along a different route of advance. The 207th moved out of Kyaka via Kyotera to Masaka, and was then to advance straight on Kampala via Lukaya. The 205th advanced from Bukoba via Kyaka and Kyotera to Masaka, and then marched on Mbende, with the intention of continuing towards Hoima and Masindi to Gulu in northern Uganda. The 206th and Minziro Brigades set off from Nykanysasi, via Mbarara to Kasese, Fort Portal, Hoima, Masindi, Pakwach,

Tom Cooper

FT-5s of the JWTZ appear to have been originally operated in this relatively simple livery: 'bare metal' overall, with only the large black serial number revealing anything of their identity.

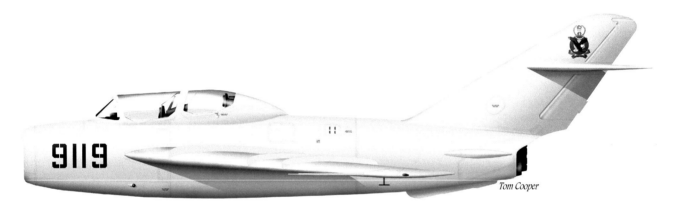

Tom Cooper

Since their overhaul in 2004-05, JWTZ FT-5s have been painted in matt white overall, wear the 'new roundel' on the top of the fin, and display slightly larger serial numbers applied in black on the forward fuselage. No roundels are known to have been applied on the wing surfaces.

Arua and then Kobuko. Finally, following in the wake of the 207th Brigade, the 201st and 208th Brigades advanced from Bukoba via Kyaka, Kyotera and Masaka, on Lukaya, Kampala, Jinja, Tororo, Mbale, Lira and Gulu.

The Tanzanian invasion of Uganda prompted a Libyan intervention, and in mid-February the LAAF launched a major airlift of combat forces to Entebbe. Libya sent 2,500 troops of the Libyan Army, Libyan People's Militia and members of the Islamic Pan-African Legion, supported by T-54 MBTs, APCs, BM-21 MRLs, artillery and plenty of supplies and ammunition. Whether Libya deployed some of its MiG-21s or Mirage 5s in Uganda, as often reported, remains unknown. However, it is confirmed that two LAAF Tu-22 bombers arrived in Nakasangola air base, in northern Uganda, sometime in early March 1979.

Meanwhile, the UAAF was certainly fighting on its own, even though not particularly successfully, since neither the political nor the military leadership of the country took the situation seriously enough. Furthermore, when a large formation of Ugandan MiGs attacked the airstrip in Mutukula on 27 February 1979, three MiG-21s were claimed as shot down by Tanzanian SA-7s. It was likely in the course of these attacks that the UAAF lost two MiG-21 pilots, including Lt Nobert Atiku, who was captured by the Tanzanians after ejecting safely.

The UAAF might have suffered additional losses during the fighting in Tororo, in western Uganda, near the border with Kenya. This fighting erupted in early March 1979, apparently when one of the local Army units mutinied against the government. According to contemporary media reports, the Ugandan Army then rushed reinforcements from Jinja in commandeered civilian transport aircraft and recaptured Tororo with the help of air strikes flown by UAAF jets.[7]

By early March 1979, the 201st, 207th and 208th Brigades of the TPDF had reached Masaka, a major town south of Lukaya, where a 20km (12-mile) causeway stretched northwards over a deepwater swamp, which could be easily defended from the solid ground at its northern terminus. The Tanzanians were held for a few days in this area, while facing elements of the same Suicide Reconnaissance Regiment they had already faced on the border. Subsequently, this Ugandan unit was replaced by Libyan forces, which proved less able to hold the front line.

Although the exact date is unavailable, it was around the time of the battle of Masaka, during the first half of March 1979, that the MiG-21s of the two air forces clashed for the only time in the course of this war. Except for the outcome, additional circumstances of this air battle remain unknown: a Ugandan MiG-21 was hit and crashed near Byesika village, 5km (3.1 miles) from the Masaka-Mubende road, killing its pilot. The successful Tanzanian pilot remains unknown.

On 10 March 1979 the TPDF sent the 201st Brigade to attack Lukaya along the causeway, while deploying the 208th Brigade in a flanking movement around the western edge of the swamp. Unknown to the Tanzanians, on the northern end of the causeway a brigade-sized Libyan force had arrived. Supported by a company of T-55s and APCs each, some Land Rovers with 106mm (4.17in) recoilless rifles and a battery of BM-21s, the Libyans had orders to launch an advance on Masaka. By coincidence, their attack occurred at the same time as that of the 201st Brigade, thus catching the Tanzanians by surprise. Facing BM-21s for the first time, the Tanzanian unit suffered losses and withdrew, and the Libyans took Lukaya in the face of limited resistance. However, instead of pushing forward on Masaka, the Libyans stopped to regroup, in turn enabling the TPDF to regroup and launch a counterattack, as well as to bring back the 208th Brigade into a position northwest of Lukaya. The attack from two directions took the Libyans by surprise and caused the survivors to flee towards the north, leaving behind more than 200 casualties and much equipment.

The catastrophe at Lukaya did not prevent the Libyan government from deploying 2,000 additional troops of the People's Militia to Uganda in the following days. A regular shuttle of LAAF transports operated into Entebbe to deliver these troops and their supplies. However, much of the equipment brought in piled up around the airport since the Ugandans lacked the manpower and transportation means to distribute it. Unsurprisingly, the Tanzanians advanced rapidly on Kampala and put Entebbe air base under siege by the end of March. In a bid to force Dar es-Salaam to call off its invasion, the LAAF and UAAF launched a number of air strikes against Mwanza, even assigning one of the Tu-22s the task of bombing the local fuel depot by night, on 1 April. The bombs missed not only all of their targets but also the entire city, however, and landed in a nearby game reserve, injuring one person and killing a large number of antelope.[8] Similarly, another attack by Tu-22s against one of Tanzanian bases south of the border ended with Libyan bombs landing near Nyarubanga – inside Burundi![9]

By early April the Tanzanians approached Kampala and began to reduce the Ugandan and Libyan units that had taken up positions at key crossroads to the south and west

This photograph shows the large crater near Kassambya, in central Uganda, caused by an unknown weapon – possibly a bomb from a Libyan Tu-22, dropped during an attack towards the end of the Kagera War.
(Associated Press)

The only Tanzanian FT-6 known to be operational at the time of writing was painted white overall, with its serial number on the forward fuselage and service title on the rear fuselage. A roundel is worn in two positions on the fin.

A reconstruction of the camouflage pattern applied on most JWTZ F-6s sometime during the 1980s. Sadly, no other details of markings are known, except that the jet had the title 'JWTZ' applied on the rear fuselage.

The first of the two F-6s returned to service since 2005 wears the serial number 9205 and is camouflaged in sand, dark green and chocolate brown on the upper surfaces, with light blue on the lower surfaces

of the city. In response to attacks by LAAF Tu-22s on Mwanza on 2 April 1979, the JWTZ hit back in force, sending at least four MiG-21s to crater the runway at Entebbe, after which this airfield was temporarily out of service. Tanzanian MiGs also hit fuel depots in Kampala and Jinja on 2 April. However, reports from foreign diplomatic personnel as well as local residents point to no losses sustained by JWTZ MiGs during these operations, while indicating that the bombs they dropped damaged the building of the Libyan Arab Uganda Bank and injured 15 people.[10]

A still from a video showing the smouldering wreckage of LAAF C-130 serial number 116, shot down on take-off from Entebbe IAP by a Tanzanian RPG-7. (via Pit Weinert)

The situation eventually prompted the Ugandan government – which claimed one of the Tanzanian MiGs as 'shot down and crashed into Lake Victoria' – to flee from Kampala to Jinja, in turn leading to a collapse of morale in the Ugandan Army, most of which abandoned its positions as result. After receiving an order to move towards the south and launch a counterattack, elements of the Ugandan Army stationed in Soroti, in northern Uganda, mutinied against the government and established themselves in control. Similarly, Army and Air Force units based in Tororo mutinied and sided with the approaching Ugandan exile insurgents, helping them capture that town.

Beaten, the UAAF decided to attempt an evacuation of some of its remaining operational MiGs from Entebbe to Nakasangola air base, but this effort fell apart in the face of additional Tanzanian attacks.[11] Ali Kiiza, meanwhile advanced in rank to lieutenant colonel, defected, while the CO of the MiG-17 Squadron, Lt Col Andrew Mukooza, was appointed C-in-C of the UAAF and thus withdrawn from flying. The Tanzanians were therefore free to put the Libyan force dug in around Entebbe air base under artillery bombardment, supported by several attacks by JWTZ MiG-21s.

Under pressure from a slow, methodical attack by the 208th Brigade TPDF, as well as a combination of artillery and MiGs, the resistance of the Libyan units at Entebbe eventually collapsed on 6 April 1979. Dramatic scenes occurred as several LAAF C-130s that had just flown at least 600 additional Libyan troops into Uganda managed to take off barely minutes before the main runway fell under TPDF control in the afternoon. The last Hercules was hit by an RPG-7 fired while in the process of rolling, and exploded. Entebbe airfield was completely secured by Tanzanian troops by 8 April, when the Tanzanians also found the burning wreckage of a Uganda Airlines Boeing 707, as well as 12 more or less non-operational or damaged MiGs.

The fall of Entebbe not only ended the Libyan airlift effort, but also led to the surrender of most of the Libyan units in the Kampala area. Although their units were not yet ready for a major assault, and their MiGs were still busy attempting to hit one of the major ammunition depots in the city, the Tanzanians thus decided to rush their advance parties into the Ugandan capital on 9 April 1979.[12] These forces entered Kampala from three sides on 10 April 1979 and in the face of only sporadic and chaotic resistance, although not without leaving a narrow corridor towards Jinja open for the Libyans to flee. This latter escape route was made known to Tripoli by the government in Dar es-Salaam.

With this, the war in Uganda was effectively over, even although TPDF units had to complete an advance from Kampala into other parts of northern Uganda. By the end of April, the Tanzanians had also taken Nakasangola and then Gulu airfields, where the last remaining UAAF MiG-17s and L-29s were captured. The surviving Libyan forces retreated eastwards through Jinja and then overland to Kenya and Ethiopia, from where they were eventually repatriated to Libya. The war thus ended with total defeat for Uganda, which remained under Tanzanian occupation until 1982.

F-6C serial number 9236 is the third aircraft of this type operated by Squadron 601 at the time of writing. Apart from a few minor differences, it wears the same camouflage pattern as 9205 and 9211.

A reconstruction of the first F-7G delivered to Tanzania about which at least something is known. The fighter wears large 'TAFC' titles on either side of the forward fuselage, the construction number on the cockpit rails, and the full serial number including the prefix 'JW' on the rear fuselage. It remains unknown if the camouflage colour consists of only one shade of grey, and the exact appearance of the fin is unknown, but a roundel is probably applied there.

A reconstruction of one of two FT-7s known to be operated by the JWTZ in recent times. Curiously enough, these aircraft look completely different to the only F-7G photographed to date, and wear a three-colour camouflage pattern on the upper surfaces and sides (apparently including beige or even tan and the same light green shade as on Namibian F-7s), with RLB on the lower surfaces. Noteworthy is also the application of the full serial number – including the prefix 'JW' – on the forward fuselage, as well as 'TAFC' titles on the lower surfaces of *both* wings.

MiG and Shenyang fighter operations in the United Republic of Tanzania since 2004

Following the end of the conflict with Uganda, most of the Tanzanian military was demobilised and the majority of the JWTZ's surviving MiGs (some 9-10 examples, including one ex-Ugandan example) were stored at Mwanza air base, while Shenyangs (between 13 and 15 aircraft) met a similar fate at Ngerengere air base. Next to nothing is known about their operations in the following 20 years.

According to official Tanzanian sources, all JWTZ MiG-21s have been stored since 1993, though some local sources indicate that at least a few flights with either that type, or even some F-6s, were undertaken repeatedly until around 2002.

Quite surprisingly, in 2004 the JWTZ decided to return four FT-5s, two F-6s and one FT-6 to service with help of a locally undertaken overhaul. Ever since, these aircraft have been operated from Ngerengere air base.

Pilot training for these 'new' fighters was undertaken with the help of older Tanzanian pilots still serving, and a few Chinese instructors, in the years that followed. However, this was often organised on an ad-hoc basis, the cadets having to 'earn' themselves the privilege to fly in addition to ground instruction. Furthermore, despite its overhaul in 2004-05, the sole FT-6 was apparently unserviceable for most of 2006, and reappeared only in early 2007.

All three types have been more regularly flown in recent years, though mainly for display purposes (for example during the military parade in Dar-es-Salaam on 9 December 2010), or during local elections when there have been tensions between the political parties on the mainland and those on several islands off the coast of Tanzania.[13]

'Squadron 601' – the sole JWTZ fighter jet unit, operating all the FT-5s, F-6s and FT-6s – is known to have re-deployed to Kilimanjaro IAP for exercises at least once, in September 2007, and probably again in September 2009.

According to reports from Tanzania, in 2010 the first female JWTZ pilot, Rose Katila, underwent training on jet fighters, and likely joined the unit presently working up on F-7s and FT-7s.

The presence of Chinese advisers and technicians during the presentation of the F-7s to the President of Tanzania, at Dar-es-Salam air base on 11 March 2011, indicated that the unit slated to operate this type – probably the same 'Squadron 601' that previously flew other fighter jets – was still in the process of training and formation.

The intensified aerial operations of the JWTZ resulted in several accidents. One of the most serious occurred on 29 June 2010, when FT-5 serial number 9119 crashed into a passenger bus while attempting to make an emergency landing on a straight stretch of the Sagera Road, killing the crew of two. (P. P. via Tom Cooper)

The second F-6 overhauled and returned to service with the JWTZ in recent years wears the serial number 9211. The fighter was painted in almost exactly the same camouflage pattern as F-6 serial number 9205. (Ben Wilhelmi via Pit Weinert)

The sole FT-6 still active with the JWTZ is serial number 9124. The jet was overhauled in 2004-2005, was apparently unserviceable in 2006, and was then returned to service a year later, painted in matt white overall and wearing its full markings.
(Ben Wilhelmi via Pit Weinert)

The JWTZ is known to have received at least these two FT-7s from China, sometime in 2010. These are now operated from Ngerengere – with some help from Chinese advisers, as the training of their pilots and maintenance crews continues.
(via Chuck Canyon)

1 Largely based on Wulf Petermann, 'Die Flieger des Julius Nyerere', *Fliegerrevue Extra*, Vol. 26/September 2009 (in turn, that article was based on interviews with one of the Chinese advisors involved in Tanzania in the 1970s, as well as CIA documentation released in response to a FOIA inquiry). Additional sources included Pollack, *Arabs at War*, and the blog by Idi Amin Awongo Alemi Dada, the son of the then President of Uganda, as of 2009 available at: http://www.idiamindada.com/A_Daring_Rescue.html

2 Based on Wulf Petermann, 'Die Flieger des Julius Nyerere', *Fliegerrevue Extra*, Vol. 26/September 2009.

3 Designation 'F-7G' is usually named as such in various Tanzanian publications.

4 Parts of this sub-chapter related to the war between Uganda and Tanzania in 1978-1979 are largely based on Rwehururu, *The Cross of the Gun*, but expanded through additional contemprorary report from the media as well as first-hand sources.

5 *Ocala Star Banner*, 31 October 1978.

6 *Milwaukee Sentinel*, 1 November 1978.

7 *Toledo Blade*, 3 March 1979 and *The Bulletin*, 3 March 1979.

8 *St Petersburg Times*, 31 March 1979.

9 Yoweri Museveni, 'The Qaddafi I know', *Foreign Policy*, 24 March, 2011.

10 *Free-Lance Star*, 3 April 1979.

11 *Sunday Star*, News Section, 2 April 1979 and *The Age*, 3 April 1979.

12 'Tanzania Mounts Massive Attack on Ugandan Capital', *The Prescot Courier*, 9 April 1979.

13 First-hand reports, provided on condition of anonymity, indicated also deployments of the JWTZ's sole operational SA-6 site near the Dar-es-Salaam IAP at the same opportunity. This was taken out of storage, overhauled and returned to service in 2005. The two SA-3 sites constructed near the same airport in the 1980s are both non-operational since at least ten years.

Chapter 21

REPUBLIC OF UGANDA

Overview[1]

The former British protectorate of Uganda was granted independence on 9 October 1962. The original cadre of the Ugandan armed forces was formed from the former King's African Rifles, the British colonial army in East Africa, and most officers were British. The situation changed in January 1964, when the British were requested to leave following mutinies by several military units, these demanding nationalisation of the officer corps and better pay, among others. During the next few years, Israeli military assistance became extensive and influential in the establishment of the Police Air Wing, followed closely by the Ugandan Army Air Force (UAAF) in 1964. The first three Ugandan pilots were trained in Israel, and – after the Congolese Air Force aircraft flew several strikes against targets inside Uganda – Israel also sold the UAAF its first combat aircraft, including Fouga CM.170 Magisters and C-47s.

With continuous Israeli aid, the UAAF developed into a strong, well-balanced and well-trained air force during the second half of the 1960s. The UAAF was equipped with aircraft made in the US, Italy, the Soviet Union and Czechoslovakia, including a total of 16 Piper PA-18 Super Cubs and Piper PA-23-250 Aztecs, 4 P.149s, between 10 and 14 L-29s (pilots and groundcrews for which were trained in Czechoslovakia in 1965–67), 9 CM.170 Magisters, 5 MiG-17Fs, 2 MiG-15UTIs, and 6 C-47s. Aircraft were deployed on air bases at Gulu, Kampala and Entebbe.

During the late 1960s, the military influence in Ugandan politics increased consistently, culminating in the 1971 coup, after which the Israeli military mission was expelled. During a visit to Moscow by a Ugandan delegation in 1972, a large order was placed for MiG-21s, tanks, APCs, AAA pieces and assorted weapons. Most of this equipment was delivered between 1973 and 1975, when Soviet advisors were expelled from the country amid disagreement over the situation in Angola. The government in Kampala subsequently began antagonising both Western powers and Israel, while simultaneously finding itself facing a major insurgency at home, this resulting in widespread destruction and thousands of victims.

Under indirect US threats and in the face of an Israeli intervention that resulted in the destruction of a sizeable part of the UAAF in 1976, the government re-approached the USSR and also established close ties to Libya, where a number of additional Ugandan pilots were sent for training. Air force strength numbered around 1,000 personnel at this time, operating up to 65 aircraft and helicopters. However, in 1978 Uganda provoked a war with Tanzania that resulted in the collapse of its military and the almost complete destruction of the UAAF.

Over time, MiG fighters operated by Uganda are known to have worn a host of different roundels. These are shown in chronological order, beginning with the earliest example, applied on MiG-15UTIs in 1965, and completed by variants sighted more recently.

During the early 1980s, a new military was established with some US and British assistance. The Uganda People's Defence Force (UPDF) was based on the former insurgent group, the National Resistance Army. From the mid-1980s, the UPDF accepted many Rwandan refugees and members of the Rwanda Patriotic Front, which established itself in power in Kigali after the terrible civil war of the mid-1990s. During the mid-1990s, Uganda joined Rwanda in its efforts to overthrow the Zairian government in favour of rebels from the east of that country. When the new government of the renamed Democratic Republic of the Congo requested Uganda to withdraw its troops, the government in Kampala again sided with Rwanda in launching an invasion of the DRC, resulting in the Second Congo War. Although eventually pulling out its troops by spring 2003, the Ugandan government continues to support insurgent groups in the DRC, and in late 2008 launched an intervention in the northeast of that country, aimed at neutralising one of its own insurgent groups.

The foundation of the modern-day air force was laid in the late 1980s, when the UPDF began work to establish its Air Wing (UPDF/AW). Nominally still under direct army control, the UPDF/AW initially numbered barely 100 officers and NCOs and operated only a handful of aircraft, including three Swiss-made FFA AS.202-18A1 Bravos, five SF.260Ws and one Saab MFI-17 Supporter. Sometime around 1987, Libya donated three L-39 jet trainers to Uganda, but these were left inside one of the hangars at Entebbe and were never made operational.

The helicopter force experienced a significant expansion during the following years. Helicopters proved highly effective in the course of COIN operations, and were also operated in strength by the Police. Originally, the backbone of the new Ugandan helicopter force was a fleet of two Bell 206 Jet Rangers and three Bell 412s, donated by Libya, as well as three Agusta-Bell AB.206s and six AB.412s purchased from Italy. However, except for two examples lost in accidents, all the Model 412s were in storage by the mid-1990s, and were later sold. Nevertheless, in 1996, Uganda ordered four Mi-8MTV-2s from the Mil factory in Kazan.[2] By 1998, when two Mi-172 Salon helicopters were acquired, the number of Mi-8s had increased to eight, and at least six additional Mi-8MTV-5s were to follow. Meanwhile, Uganda acquired three Mi-24s from Belarus, via the Consolidated Sales Corporation Company, at the grossly inflated price of USD13 million. These arrived late in 1998 and became subject of a major scandal once it became apparent that they had not been refurbished before delivery, as specified by the contract. Nevertheless, the C-in-C UPDF/AW recommended their purchase.[3]

The three Mi-24s were all returned to Belarus, and replaced by four overhauled and upgraded Mi-24s, capable of night-time operations. The fleet was reinforced through the purchase of three additional Mi-24s, delivered in 2003, and the number of helicopters acquired from Russia continued to increase in the last decade. Initially, the UPD/AW purchased enough Mi-17MTV-5s to replace all the Mi-8MTV-2s acquired in the 1990s, and in 2011 another batch of Mi-17MTV-5s was added to increase the fleet, now heavily involved in fighting against the insurgents of the Lord's Resistance Army (LRA).[4]

By 2005 it was apparent that the government's unilateralist approach in the pursuit of insurgents deep inside neighbouring states had resulted in the isolation of the entire nation. As a result there followed a general reorganisation of the doctrine of Ugandan national defence and the entire UPDF. In the course of this reorganisation, the UPDF/AW was re-organized as the Uganda People's Defence Air Force (UPDAF).

A rare photograph of three Ugandan MiG-17Fs (and two C-47s) at the military side of Entebbe airport, in the late 1960s. All three MiGs wore a camouflage pattern applied in colours as used by the Israeli Defence Force/Air Force at the time.
(Albert Grandolini Collection)

Thereafter, Uganda reached an understanding with the government of the DRC concerning joint military deployments along the common border, and in August 2005 a separate command for the Air Force was established. Correspondingly, in late 2008, Uganda Air Force (UAF) MiG-21s conducted deployments within the DRC during operations in pursuit of Ugandan and Congolese insurgents. In 2011 similar 'external' operations were undertaken within the Central African Republic and Sudan.

Deliveries of MiG fighters to the Republic of Uganda

In July 1965, Kampala and Moscow signed a treaty that granted the supply of five MiG-17Fs and two MiG-15UTIs, military maintenance facilities, spare parts, communication equipment and weapons to the UAAF. Also included was the training of 250 Ugandan personnel, including 20 pilots and 50 technicians that would receive instruction in the USSR. Ten other pilots and 22 technical officers received basic training Czechoslovakia. In support of this project, the Soviet Union deployed at least 25 Soviet instructors to Uganda. These arrived in 1966, together with the first MiGs, and apparently worked at least parallel to Israeli instructors, deployed in Uganda since September 1964 within the frame of the Operation Nail, with the aim of training UAAF pilots and Army paratroopers.

In July 1972, Uganda signed the next contract with Moscow, ordering between 16 and 18 MiG-21MFs and at least 3 MiG-21UMs, together with a sizeable supply of spare parts, 850 bombs and several thousands of unguided rockets, nine radar sets required to support operations of manned interceptors, and other military equipment. All of this materiel was delivered to the UAAF during 1975. Additional MiG-17s were also ordered and delivered within this deal, but Uganda never received MiG-21Fs or MiG-21F-13s, as frequently reported in the past.

At least four MiG-17s and seven MiG-21s were destroyed on the ground during the Israeli intervention at Entebbe, in 1976. The USSR delivered seven new MiG-21MFs as replacements but these were all destroyed or captured during the war with Tanzania, in 1978-1979. Thirty additional Ugandan pilots were sent to the Soviet Union for conversion training in 1978 but following Uganda's military defeat by Tanzania in April 1979, most of these pilots found refugee in Libya, where they were integrated into the LAAF, together with several other pilots that managed to escape the Tanzanian advance.[5]

A poor but nevertheless highly interesting photograph of an Ugandan MiG-21MF airborne over Entebbe, in the mid-1970s. The fighter had its airbrakes deployed in order to slow down prior to landing.
(Tom Cooper Collection)

In 1998, Uganda purchased six ex-Polish Air Force MiG-21bis and one MiG-21UM through the Israeli company Silver Shadow. An additional MiG-21UM was obtained via the Georgian TAM company and, more recently, at least one - through probably more – former Algerian Air Force MiG-21bis was acquired from Ukraine, then despite at least three major incidents, six aircraft remain in service.

In April 2010, reports concerning Uganda ordering a number of Su-30 fighter-bombers, published in the Russian media, were initially denied by the government in Kampala, which insisted that the UPDAF instead reported that a decision was taken to send its six MiG-21s to Russia for overhaul. Nevertheless, in December of the same year, the Government signed a contract ordering six Su-30MK2s, support equipment, weapons and training for pilots and ground personnel, worth $744 million. Although not sanctioned by the Ugandan Parliament, this order was confirmed by the government, in May 2011, and subsequently the Parliament granted permission for an initial payment of $466 million.

The first two Su-30MK2s were delivered to Entebbe air base on board a Volga-Dnepr Antonov An-124 transport aircraft on 6 July 2011. Following assembly and all the necessary ground-testing, the first of these two aircraft undertook its initial post-delivery test flight on the afternoon of 12 July.

Force structure

The original UAAF established its first two jet squadrons in 1968, one flying L-29s and Magisters, the other MiG-17s. Both units were stationed at Entebbe AB, but also operated from Nakasangola AB, in northern Uganda, the latter base being constructed by Israel in the mid-1960s. Some pilots assigned to these two units underwent advanced courses in the UK in the early 1970s.

Following the delivery of MiG-21s, a new squadron equipped with this type was established and nicknamed 'Sungura'. This unit moved to Gulu AB in 1976, before returning to Entebbe during the war with Tanzania. The Sungura Squadron remained operational until the collapse of the Ugandan military in the face of the Tanzanian invasion in April 1979. The last CO of the unit was Lt Col Ali Kiiza.

Due to combat attrition, the MiG-17 Squadron was rendered largely inoperational during the final days of the war with Tanzania, but not before its last CO, Lt Col Andrew Mukooza, was appointed the C-in-C UAAF.

At some point in the mid-1970s, during the worst period of political instability in Uganda, a UAAF fighter jet unit named 'Suicide Strike Command' was presented to the public by Idi Amin. This reportedly consisted of MiG-21 pilots that declared them-selves willing to fly their aircraft into selected targets when the government in Kampala confronted the US. Except for its name, no details of a specially trained squadron of this kind are known.

In spring 2001 the UPDF/AW established an entirely new fighter squadron to operate ex-Polish MiG-21s from Entebbe AB. This unit originally consisted of six pilots and eight technicians and engineers that received their basic training in Israel, before completing additional courses in Bulgaria and Ukraine. Meanwhile, additional pilots and technicians were trained in Uganda on L-39s flown by the Panther Squadron too, but their exact number remains unknown.

Subsequent operations by the MiG-21 Squadron in Uganda have been supported by foreign contract personnel, primarily Russian and Ukrainian, but also Israeli. Foreigners remained present until at least 2008. However, most were forced to leave after they became involved in two different accidents over Lake Victoria, in 2003 and 2006, both of which resulted in losses of MiG-21s: at least one of these was caused by a Russian pilot still hungover after a fight with his girlfriend the night before.

The sole UPDAF unit flying MiG-21s is now simply known as the 'Fighter Squadron (MiG-21)'. Entebbe remains the main base, but recently the formerly disused Nakasangola air base, as well as the airfield in Gulu and a number of minor, dirt strips in northern and northwest Uganda have been used for temporary deployments of MiG-21s and other UPDAF aircraft.

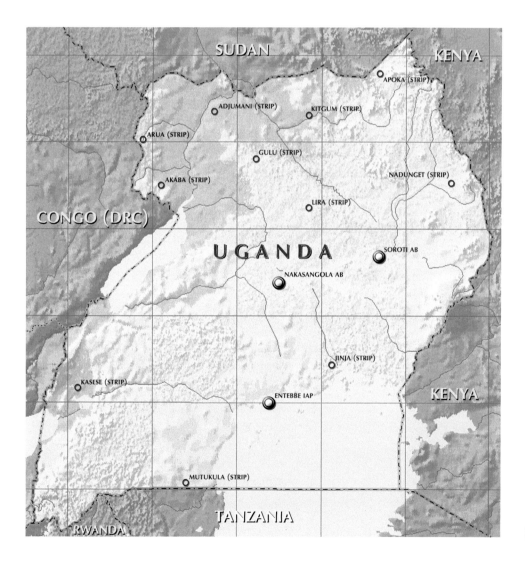

Map of Uganda

National markings

The original UAAF national markings consisted of a roundel with concentric rings of black, yellow, red and black, with a white centre. The white centre carried an illustration of the white-crested crane, Uganda's national emblem. Such roundels were worn in six positions – including the fin – and no roundels were ever applied on the fuselages of Ugandan MiGs. Although some other UAAF aircraft and helicopters used to wear an additional fin flash (this consisted of a total of six stripes in the Ugandan national colours, with the crane symbol in its centre), this was never applied on any MiGs during the 1960s and 1970s.

MiG-21s acquired since the late 1990s initially wore the Ugandan national flag as their fin flash, and did not receive roundels. In the course of their overhaul in Israel they received slightly modified fin flashes only. The two MiG-21bis and a single MiG-21UM two-seater acquired from Ukraine in more recent years appear to wear roundels on their fins only.

Su-30MK2s delivered in 2011 wear roundels similar in appearance to those applied on MiG-21s acquired from Ukraine, and applied in four positions, but also exhibit an entirely different fin flash in the form of the national flag.

Camouflage colours and serial numbers of Ugandan MiGs

Influenced by their Israeli instructors, Uganda camouflaged its first batch of MiG-15UTIs and MiG-17Fs using a variant of the standard IDF/AF camouflage pattern. This consisted of blue (similar to RAL 5008) and brown (similar to RAL 8000) on the upper surfaces, with light grey (similar to RAL 7044) on the lower surfaces. On most photographs that show UAAF aircraft camouflaged in this way, the brown colour appears slightly lighter, sometimes almost tan, but this was probably caused by the effects of Uganda's tropical climate.

There are reports that some UAAF MiG-15UTIs and MiG-17Fs wore a camouflage pattern of different colours, namely reddish-brown (similar to FS30117) and dark sand (similar to FS33351) on the upper surfaces, with lower surfaces in a shade of

In more recent times, this MiG-15UTI, painted sand and dark grey on top surfaces, and wearing a black serial number 'U-618' was posted as a second gate guard at Entebbe AB. (via Pit Weinert)

grey similar to US 'neutral grey' (FS36270). This cannot be confirmed using available photographic reference.

It is possible that later during their career, the surviving MiG-15s and MiG-17s were over painted in dark grey overall, perhaps in combination with sand.

All MiG-15s and MiG-17s wore large serial numbers on their forward fuselage, applied in yellow and starting with the prefix 'U' (for details of known serial numbers, see the table below). On aircraft seen painted in dark grey or in sand and dark grey overall, serials were applied in black.

MiG-21MFs delivered to Uganda in the mid-1970s were painted 'air superiority grey' overall, while MiG-21UMs appear to have been delivered in 'natural metal' overall, but some were later over painted in the same colour as the MiG-21MFs. These aircraft wore serial numbers on their forward fuselages ranging from U901 to U912, applied in orange or red and prefixed with a 'U'. Seven MiG-21s provided as replacements in 1977 received serial numbers from U913 to U919.

Ex-Polish Air Force MiG-21bis acquired in the late 1990s were originally delivered painted in metalcote overall and wore their original Polish serial numbers applied in red on the forward fuselage. Following their overhaul in Israel, the MiG-21bis were camouflaged in light blue-grey and blue-grey on the upper surfaces, with light grey lower surfaces. Each of the two MiG-21UMs received a different camouflage pattern (see artworks for details). Except for the MiG-21UM acquired from the Georgian TAM company, all wore serial numbers applied in red on their forward fuselage.

One of the two MiG-21bis destined for Uganda and observed in Ukraine (and subsequently also identified in Uganda) received only a coat of light grey on the upper surfaces, with RLB lower surfaces. The aircraft wears a small serial number applied in black on the forward fuselage.

The first two Su-30MK2s delivered in July 2011 wear a newly designed disruptive camouflage pattern consisting of olive green and dark earth on the upper surfaces, with RLB lower surfaces. All dielectric panels on the fuselage, wings and the fin tops are painted in grey, while the radome is white. The Su-30MK2s received serial numbers applied in black on the forward fuselage, on the fins and on the lower surfaces of both wings (alongside the roundels applied here).

A still from a video taken in the mid-1970s, showing a row of UAAF MiG-21s, either at Gulu or Entebbe. The two aircraft in the foreground are both MiG-21UM two-seat conversion trainers, the nearest wearing the serial number U901.
(Albert Grandolini Collection)

Table 37: Known serial numbers of UAAF and UPDF/AW MiGs, 1964–2009

Aircraft type	Serial number	c/n	Remarks
MiG-17F	U601		
MiG-17F	U602		
MiG-17F	U603		
MiG-17F	U604		
MiG-15UTI	U605		
MiG-15UTI	U606		
MiG-17F	U607		
MiG-17F	U614		Gate guard at Entebbe AB, 2006
MiG-15UTI	U618		Gate guard at Entebbe AB, 2007
MiG-21UM	U901		Wrecked at Entebbe, 1979, dumped at local scrap yard
MiG-21UM	U902		
MiG-21UM	U903		Wrecked at Entebbe, 1979, dumped at local scrap yard
MiG-21	U904		
MiG-21MF	U905		
MiG-21MF	U906		Wrecked at Entebbe, 1979, dumped at local scrap yard
MiG-21MF	U907		Last sighted in January 1976
MiG-21MF	U908		Wrecked at Entebbe, 1979, dumped at local scrap yard
MiG-21MF	U909		Wrecked at Entebbe, 1979, dumped at local scrap yard
MiG-21MF	U910		
MiG-21MF	U911		
MiG-21MF	U912		
MiG-21MF	U913		
MiG-21MF	U914		
MiG-21MF	U915		
MiG-21MF	U916		Damaged at Entebbe, 10 April 1979, fate unknown
MiG-21MF	U917		
MiG-21MF	U918		
MiG-21MF	U919		Wreck at Entebbe, 1995
MiG-21UM	–	516999393	Purchased via TAM; camouflaged example wearing no serial number; last seen 2011
MiG-21bis	9211	N75089211	Former WLiOPL 9211; last seen Entebbe, 2006
MiG-21UM	9307	516999307	Former WLiOPL 9307; probably crashed on 15 June 2006
MiG-21bis	9799	N75089799	Former WLiOPL 9799; last seen Entebbe, 1999
MiG-21bis	9801	N75089801	Former WLiOPL 9801
MiG-21bis	9802		Origin unknown; last seen before redelivery from IAI, 2004
MiG-21bis	9811	N75089811	Former WLiOPL 9811; last seen Entebbe, 2008
MiG-21bis	9818	N75089818	Former WLiOPL 9818; last seen Entebbe, 2008
MiG-21bis	AF-973	N75089307	Ex-QJJ; last seen after overhaul by Odesaviaremservice, 2009
Su-30MK2	AF-011		Delivered 6 July 2011; last seen 12 July 2011
Su-30MK2	AF-015		Delivered 6 July 2011

MiG fighter operations in Uganda, 1971–76

While no details concerning operations by UAAF MiGs in the 1960s are known, it is certain that by the early 1970s the policies of the government in Kampala had brought the country on a collision course with numerous enemies inside and outside Uganda. Above, all Tanzania was a threat, and an increasing number of Ugandan dissidents were living there. Indeed, it seems that the major reason for the expulsion of Israeli advisors from Uganda was Israel's refusal to lend 24 F-4E fighter-bombers to Kampala. The government wanted to use these jets for an invasion of Tanzania, with the objective of obtaining a corridor to the Indian Ocean.

Such threats prompted the government of Tanzania to side with the Ugandan dissidents and support their plans for a counter-coup in Kampala. This saw the insertion of a heavily armed group into Kampala, while several other brigades of the Tanzanian Army were to advance from the Tanzanian border towards Entebbe, accompanied by Ugandan insurgents.

On 13 September 1972, the Kenyan Directorate of Security Intelligence (colloquially known as the 'Special Branch') reported to Kampla that it received intelligence about Tanzanian troops and Ugandan insurgents planning an invasion of Uganda. This report was dismissed and thus the attack took the Government and Ugandan military by surprise.

Only two days later, on 15 September 1972, a group of armed Ugandans hijacked a Douglas DC-9 airliner of Kenya's East African Airways at Arusha airport. The airliner was flown to an isolated airstrip near Kilimanjaro, where the insurgents planned to pick up another group of armed dissidents before continuing for Kampala, with the intention of capturing or assassinating the Ugandan president Idi Amin. However, the DC-9 was damaged during the landing in Uganda, and this part of the plan had to be aborted.

News of this failure did not reach the ground units before they crossed the border, and these advanced on Mbarara, only to clash and suffer heavy losses in the Battle of Kalisizo, two days later, when the Ugandan Army Simba Battalion Mbarara and Suicide Regiment nearly routed them. Simultaneously, the UAAF was ordered to carry out reprisal air raids on Tanzanian towns, and Bukoba and Mwanza were bombed and rocketed several times by MiG-17s, eventually forcing the government in Dar-es-Salaam to call for a ceasefire.

Despite this success, the government in Kampala found itself facing riots in the capital as well as in Jinja and called for assistance from Libya. On 18 September, five LAAF C-130 transports carrying 300 Libyan Army troops appeared deep inside Sudanese airspace while under way to Uganda. They were intercepted and forced to land by two Sudanese Air Force MiG-21s. Following brief negotiations, an agreement was reached for the C-130s to return to Libya. Once airborne, however, the entire Libyan formation turned around and quickly escaped into Ugandan airspace.

Reinforced by Libyan troops, the government unleashed a counteroffensive against the insurgents that were still active along the border to Tanzania. On 18 September 1972, UAAF MiG-17s and Magisters flew several attacks against various depots and roads in the area of the border town of Bukoba. These attacks were repeated on the following day, and on 22 September two UAAF MiG-17s bombed Mwanza airfield.

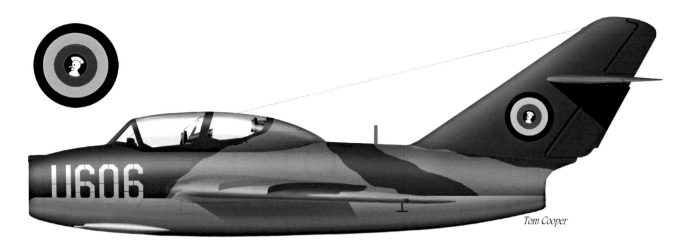

A reconstruction of MiG-15UTI U606 as seen at Entebbe in the late 1960s. This unusual camouflage pattern was based on that used by the IDF/AF at the time. The inset shows a reconstruction of the roundel as applied on this aircraft in at least two positions (on the fin).

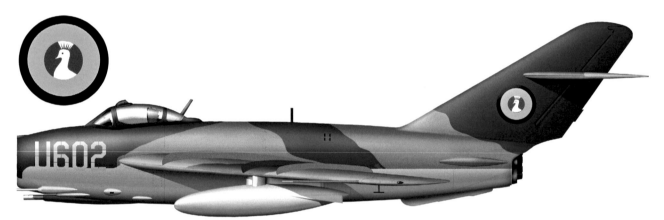

A reconstruction of a Ugandan MiG-17F as seen in Entebbe in the late 1960s, when their camouflage consisted of blue (close to RAL 5008) and brown (close to RAL 8000, which tended to look like dark tan in bright sunlight) on top surfaces, and either 'bare metal' or light grey (close to RAL 7044) on the lower surfaces.

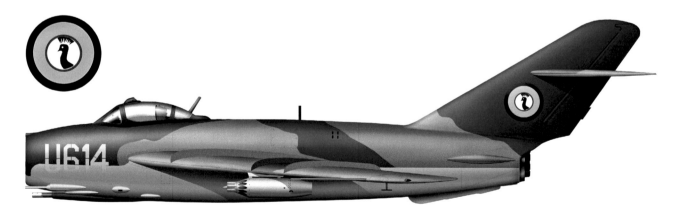

A reconstruction of a Ugandan MiG-17 as seen in the early 1970s. While wearing the same camouflage pattern as the MiG-15UTIs and MiG-17Fs delivered at an earlier date, this aircraft apparently received a different roundel on the fin. U614 survived all subsequent wars and unrest, and is now posted as a second gate guard at Entebbe.

By that time, reports indicated that the UAAF was left with only a few operational MiG-17s, and that a number of LAAF Mirage 5 fighter-bombers had been deployed in Uganda to bolster the air force. Some sources indicate that the above-mentioned strikes were actually flown by these fighters, manned by Egyptian Air Force pilots. However, no such deployments can be confirmed with the aid of Egyptian sources, and with hindsight it appears that reports of 'Mirages' were based on the deployment of French-made Magisters of the UAAF.

Early in 1973, Radio Uganda broadcast several reports alleging that a combined force of Tanzanian Army and Ugandan insurgents, estimated to be 10,000 in number, had been assembled for a new invasion of Uganda. The Ugandan Army deployed own units along the border and put the UAAF on alert. However, after reconnaissance and intelligence provided no evidence about a possible Tanzanian military build-up, no order for a pre-emptive attack was issued.

The Ugandan Army managed to put down this revolt and surviving dissidents withdrew into Tanzania. Tensions remained high, nevertheless, particularly due to Tanzanian concerns of a possible Ugandan invasion, as well as the decision of the government in Kampala to force thousands of Ugandans of Asian origin to leave the country, while submitting the remainder of the population to severe oppression.

Eventually, these developments resulted in both Tanzania and Uganda acquiring more advanced MiG fighters during the mid-1970s, but also in Uganda increasingly siding with Libya and Palestine and eventually breaking its relationship with Israel and the USSR. In turn, when an armed Palestinian group hijacked an Air France Airbus A300B2 under way from Tel Aviv to Paris on 27 June 1976 and forced it to land in Entebbe, Uganda found itself on the receiving end of an Israeli military intervention. Once on the ground in Uganda, all 256 passengers and 12 crewmembers were disembarked from the Airbus and brought to the main building of Entebbe IAP, the Palestinians demanding the release of 53 inmates of Israeli prisons. Israel entered negotiations in order to buy the time required to organise a rescue operation.

Launched on 3 July 1976, this included four IDF/AF C-130H transports carrying members of the West German and Israeli special forces, two Boeing 707 tankers and top cover provided by several F-4s. These aircraft deployed from Sharm el-Sheikh airfield, in the southern Sinai, which was then under Israeli control, flying over the Red Sea to a position off the coast of Djibouti. From there, the C-130s continued over Ethiopia and arrived over Entebbe by night. Upon landing, the first Hercules disgorged a group of Israeli paratroopers and a black Mercedes sedan similar to that known to be used by Idi Amin, together with several Land Rovers. The other three C-130s followed in a similar manner, minutes later. The Israeli and West German operatives quickly overwhelmed most of the hijackers and brought the hostages to the waiting transports. Meanwhile, several Israeli operatives planted explosive devices on four UAAF MiG-17s and seven MiG-21s present nearby, and detonated these. This action rendered all the MiGs present at Entebbe unserviceable and thus incapable of pursuing the slow transports as these began their return journey to Israel. Three of the MiG-17s disabled at Entebbe were subsequently brought to Nakasangola, where their wreckage can be found to this today.

Wreckage of a Ugandan MiG-21 destroyed by Israeli commandos at Entebbe, on 3 July 1976. The MiG-21UM in the background appears to have survived in largely undamaged condition. (Pit Weinert Collection)

This scene from Entebbe AB, on 10 April 1979, after this air base was captured by Tanzanian troops, shows the MiG-21MF U906 or U916 in damaged condition. The fact that the ejection seat appears to have been fired and the avionics bay in front of the cockpit was ripped open, points at sabotage by withdrawing Ugandan personnel. (Pit Weinert Collection)

The flag of the UPDAF presently in use in the form of fin flashes on recently delivered Su-30MK2s, and as a patch worn on the flying suits of Ugandan jet pilots.

Squadron patch of the sole Ugandan squadron flying L-39 jet trainers, nicknamed 'Puma Squadron'.

Patch worn by the pilots of the MiG-21 Squadron, UPDAF.

MiG fighter operations in Uganda since 1999

The story of the end of MiG fighter operations in Uganda in the late 1970s is provided in detail in Chapter 20 (United Republic of Tanzania). Suffice to say, the UAAF was completely destroyed in the course of that conflict and the Ugandan military had to make do without any combat aircraft and with very few helicopters for most of the 1980s.

Following the establishment of the UPDF/AW in the 1980s, and after training sufficient pilots and ground personnel, in the late 1990s the Ugandan government decided to acquire an interceptor capability. This requirement was born out of a requirement to intercept and shoot down Sudanese Air Force bombers and transports that frequently operated over northern Uganda, and often on behalf of insurgents of the Lord's Resistance Army (LRA), renowned for its maniacally destructive behaviour. Correspondingly, in 1998 the Ugandan government purchased five ex-Polish Air Force MiG-21bis and one MiG-21UM through the Israeli company Silver Shadow, run by the infamous arms dealer Amos Golan. The same Israeli company apparently also negotiated the acquisition of 100mm (3.94in) calibre KS-19 anti-aircraft guns from North Korea. An additional MiG-21UM was obtained via the Georgian TAM company. The KS-19s were rushed into action in northern Uganda in December 1998 and January 1999, but failed to achieve any kills due to their poor technical condition.

Service entry of the ex-Polish MiGs appears to have been marred by technical problems, since rumours surfaced of local pilots refusing to fly them as a result of missing technical documentation. One of the newly delivered MiGs crashed soon after delivery, on 15 July 1999, killing its pilot.

As early as October 1999, three Ugandan MiGs were shipped to Israel for an overhaul and upgrade of their weapons systems and other avionics by Israel Aircraft Industries (IAI). Simultaneously, Silver Shadow signed another contract with Kampala, worth USD13 million, covering the training of between 15 and 17 Ugandan fighter pilots and technical personnel in Israel. Whether these projects were ever entirely realised remains unknown. IAI reportedly charged between USD20 and USD25 million for the overhaul and upgrade of the ex-Polish MiGs, which was to result in them being brought up to an equipment standard known as 'MiG-21-2000'. However, when the first two UPDF/AW MiG-21s arrived back in Uganda in early 2001, they showed no indications of having being upgraded to this standard. Furthermore, the Ukrainian contract personnel operating the fighters experienced technical problems that persisted upon the re-delivery of the three other aircraft reworked by IAI, in 2002. Two of these reportedly developed serious mechanical faults and had to be returned to Israel for servicing, while the third crashed shortly after take-off from Entebbe AB into Lake Victoria on 15 July 2003, killing a Russian contract pilot.[6]

Meanwhile, during the spring of 2001, reports surfaced indicating acquisition of at least one additional MiG-21 from Belarus. Subsequent reports from Israel indicated that, due to financial reasons, some of the Ugandan MiG-21s had been impounded in that country pending payment for the work completed by IAI so far.[7] Correspondingly, the UPDF/AW MiG-21 fleet remained incomplete until at least 2004, when the last two aircraft were returned to Uganda – this time apparently with some support from contracted Israeli pilots and ground personnel.

The MiG-21s of the UPDF/AF flew their first known combat sorties in the course of Operation Iron Fist, launched in early May 2011. Iron Fist was the first 'external'

One of the ex-Polish MiG-21bis as seen relatively shortly after delivery to Uganda, in late October 1999. Of interest is the original serial number and a fin-flash, both of which were applied before delivery. (via Robert Szombaty)

offensive by the Ugandan military launched against the insurgents of the Lord's Resistance Army (LRA), active in northern Uganda since 1987. This is not only one of Africa's longest-running conflicts, but also one of the most violent, with the insurgents repeatedly being accused of extraordinary human rights violations.

In the course of Operation Iron Fist, which was undertaken in agreement with the government in Khartoum, UPDAF MiG-21s hit five insurgent camps up to 60km (37 miles) within what is now South Sudan. Their raids were followed by heliborne assaults, and then a massive operation launched by at least two mechanised brigades of the Ugandan Army. In the process, Kampala reported the capture of arms caches worth more than USD2 million. However, the UPDF forces suffered heavy losses, while the insurgents scattered, leaving the Ugandans with no choice but to leave Sudan by 18 May, as originally agreed with Khartoum.

The first group of six pilots and eight technicians that began their training in Israel returned to Uganda and were officially declared as qualified in a small ceremony at Entebbe on 27 May 2005. On 17 June 2006, another UPDF/AW MiG-21 – this time a two-seat conversion trainer – crashed into Lake Victoria, near Buwu Island, some 20km (12 miles) south of Entebbe. The crew, reportedly consisting of an Israeli contract pilot named Capt Yotam, and a 'Russian' pilot named Anatoliy, ejected safely.

Despite such problems, the UPDF/AW (subsequently renamed as the UPDAF), eventually managed to establish a small fighter unit, centred on a handful of Ugandan

In the course of their overhauls and upgrades in Israel, the Ugandan MiG-21bis received a small white GPS antenna on top of the forward fuselage, an unknown aerial in front of the windshield, and a chaff and flare dispenser below the rear fuselage. (A.T. via Chuck Canyon)

Probably the first MiG-21 delivered to Uganda was this MiG-21UM conversion trainer. As far as known, it arrived painted in bare metal overall, and subsequently received only roundels in two positions and its full serial.

Of interest on MiG-21MFs delivered to Uganda from the USSR in the 1970s is that part of the rear fuselage was not camouflaged, but painted in dull aluminum colour, as this was the practice on Nigerian and Somali examples as well.

A reconstruction of one of several UAAF MiG-21MFs captured in sabotaged condition at Entebbe, on 10 April 1979. Contrary to contemporary assumptions based on poor photographs, they did not receive any kind of anti-glare panel in front of the cockpit, but this appeared to have been applied due to the removal of the avionics bay cover.

pilots that underwent very intensive training. In the course of their basic flying training in Israel, in 2000 and 2001, these pilots soloed on Cessna 152s and Cessna 172s, as well as L-39s, before continuing with supersonic fighter pilot courses. Additional training provided until 2006 included an advanced jet fighter operations course, live-firing exercises and an advanced evasion and rescue course. A few of the pilots even completed an advanced life-support and casualty evacuation course. As such, this unit was finally ready for intensive operations by 2006 and subsequently became deeply involved in the war against the LRA.

After repeated attempts at negotiations have all failed, together with an attempt to assassinate the leader of the LRA, undertaken by a group of US-trained Guatemalan special operations operatives, in 2006 the UPDAF began launching a series of highly effective raids against LRA bases in northern Uganda.[8] Usually based on carefully collected intelligence – often gathered with help from the US – these caused heavy destruction and losses to the insurgents. Frequently followed by heliborne landings of Ugandan special forces, these attacks effectively forced the LRA to vacate all of its bases inside Uganda and flee to the Central African Republic (CAR) and the northern Democratic Republic of the Congo (DRC) by the end of the same year.

This MiG-21UM was delivered to Uganda more recently and in addition to seven ex-Polish MiG-21s acquired in the late 1990s. It lacks various modifications and aerials added in the course of works undertaken in Israel, but has a slightly different roundel applied on the fin.
(AT via Chuck Canyon)

Between 2006 and 2008, a complex series of negotiations – known as the Juba talks – between the Ugandan government and the LRA sparked optimism for peace in the region. The counterparts reached a final peace agreement that was ready to be signed in 2008. To the great embarrassment of the negotiators and politicians that organised the event, however, the insurgent leadership failed to attend the signing ceremony and subsequently accused the mediators of manipulating the negotiations. However, the main reason for the failure concerned the arrest warrant issued by the ICC for the leader of the LRA. In reaction, the government in Kampala decided to put down the violent insurgency by military means.

On 14 December 2008, Uganda – this time not only with approval from the government of the Democratic Republic of the Congo, but also in cooperation with its military, as well as the military of South Sudan – launched Operation Lightning Thunder against the LRA camps inside the densely forested Garamba National Park, in northeast DRC.

Operation Lightning Thunder was carefully prepared, with Ugandan military intelligence tracking LRA commanders for several months with the help of advanced eavesdropping equipment provided by the US. This enabled Uganda to exactly triangulate the individual hut at Suke, inside Garamba National Park, in which the LRA leadership was sleeping. A plan was prepared according to which this hut, as well as surrounding AAA positions, were to be hit by UPDAF MiG-21s. For this purpose, the MiGs were to take off from Nakasangola AB, in northern Uganda, hit their target and land at Isiro, an airstrip in the DRC, some 300km (186 miles) from the Ugandan border, to refuel. This initial air strike was to be followed by an attack by UPDAF Mi-24s, which were then to land commandos inside the LRA camp. Finally, two Army brigades with more than 4,200 troops, supported by MBTs, APCs and plenty of supplies, were to launch a ground offensive out of the Koboko area, in northwest Uganda. This latter assault was to be launched immediately after the air raids began, and in coordination with the Army of the DRC, in order to block possible escape routes.

Eventually, bad weather prevented the MiGs from participating in the opening strike, and only the Mi-24s attacked, but were unable to drop commandos due to fierce AAA fire from positions that had not been softened up by the MiGs as originally planned.

A reconstruction of the camouflage pattern applied on the left-hand side of the MiG-21UM acquired by Uganda from Ukraine in the late 2000s. The inset shows the roundel applied on the aircraft, which differs in several details to that applied on MiG-21bis overhauled and upgraded in Israel.

This ex-Polish MiG-21UM was overhauled in Israel in the early 2000s, and then painted in a camouflage pattern consisting of grey (similar to RAL 7044) on top surfaces and sides, and white or a very light blue-grey shade on undersurfaces. Insert shows the roundel as applied in Israel.

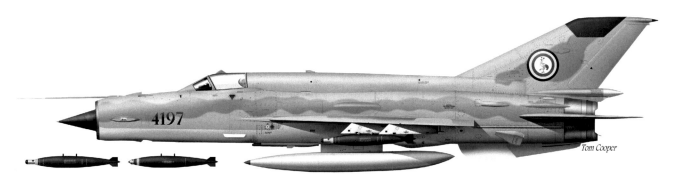

A reconstruction of the one of rarely-seen Ugandan MiG-21bis as it appeared early following an overhaul and upgrade in Israel. Since their re-delivery to Uganda, these aircraft appear to be also armed with a selection of low-drag Israeli- or South African-made 250kg (551lb) bombs based on the Mk 82 design (from the US).

An UPDF/AW MiG-21bis rolling down the apron at Entebbe AB, following a training sortie in the early 2000s. Notable is the UB-32-57 rocket pod under the inboard underwing pylon (though lacking its rear cover). (AT via Chuck Canyon)

When the Mi-24s were forced to withdraw in order to refuel, surviving LRA insurgents were able to regroup, collect their equipment and abandon their bases. Two days later, when the ground component of the Army finally reached the LRA camps in Suke and Pilipili, they found them empty – with the exception of considerable stocks of food the insurgents had been unable to take with them. The Army then launched a pursuit operation, supported by air-to-ground attacks by MiGs and Mi-24s, but this offensive eventually faltered. Although the insurgents ran into several ambushes set up by the Ugandans and the Congolese, most of them managed to trickle out of the combat zone. Furthermore, the UAF suffered a painful blown on 24 December 2008 when, while taking off from Isiro for another sortie in reaction to one such engagement, a MiG-21bis crashed just 1.5km (0.9 miles) from this airfield, killing the pilot, Lt John Bosco Opio Okorom.[9]

Operation Lightning Thunder continued through January and was declared 'completed' in late February 2009. However, the operation had soon become characterised by dozens of massacres committed by the LRA against the local population while retreating towards the border with the CAR, as well as the limited success on the part of the Ugandan military. Although the Army claimed to have killed over 200 insurgents and killed or captured several of its top leaders, the majority of the LRA escaped. The LRA thus not only remained active, but also sparked another insurgency in northern Uganda, where an armed group known as the Uganda People's Front (UPF) became active in June and July 2009.

After the loss of 28 December 2008, the UPDAF MiG-21 fleet should have been reduced to only three aircraft, and it is therefore hardly surprising that recent reports indicate the acquisition of replacement aircraft from Ukraine.[10] Reports also suggest that the remaining UPDAF MiG-21 fleet has meanwhile been overhauled again – this time the work was undertaken in Uganda with the help of the Ukrainian company Odesaviaremservice.

During 2009 and 2010, the UDF continued launching attacks on LRA camps inside the Garamba forest. Often operating from dirt strips around northern Uganda or primitive airfield s inside the DRC, the Ugandan MiG-21s and Mi-24s successively hit targets near Nyere, Fuke, Piripiri, Baoute and Bawesi, causing some losses to the insurgents. Reinforced by several anti-LRA operations by the Congolese Army, the government in Kampala eventually felt safe enough to declare northern Uganda as secure from LRA attacks. However, the insurgents reacted with harsh reprisals against civilians in the DRC, killing more than 1,200 and displacing up to 318,000 people within barely three weeks.[11] Even though by the end of 2009 the UPDF claimed to have killed 305 and

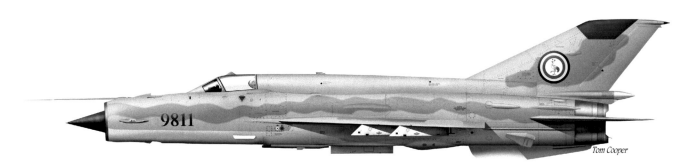

A reconstruction of the camouflage pattern applied on the left-hand side of this UPDAF MiG-21bis. This appears to consist of grey (FS36320) or French blue (FS35626) and a shade similar to RAF medium sea grey on the upper surfaces. The undersides appear to be painted in white, or a very light blue-grey.

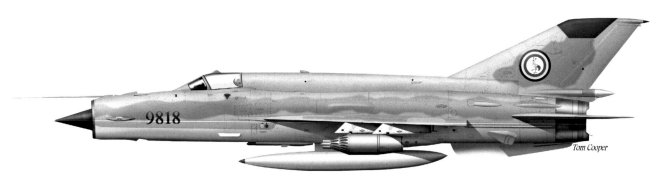

Except for Israeli and South African weapons, Ugandan MiG-21s can be armed with much cheaper and more readily available Soviet/Russian weapons, like the UB-32-57 rocket pod shown here. They are regularly carrying 800-litre drop tanks under the centreline, and 400-litre drop tanks under outboard underwing pylons.

This ex-Algerian MiG-21bis, purchased from Odesaviaremservice in Ukraine, in recent years, is painted in a very unusual pattern consisting of light grey on the upper surfaces and sides, and light blue on the undersides. As usually, the roundel – which is again slightly different to that used on earlier aircraft – appears to have been applied in two positions, on the fin only.

One of the latest additions to the UPDAF is this ex-Algerian MiG-21bis, overhauled by Odesaviarem and sold to Uganda in recent years. Available reports indicate that additional aircraft followed. (Odesaviaremservice)

captured 41 insurgents while freeing 513 hijacked civilians, and the LRA presence in the DRC was reduced to less than 90 fighters scattered in small pockets, the major goal of all these enterprises – the capture of the LRA leadership – was not achieved. Part of the reason was that the UPDAF continued experiencing significant problems with its MiG-21s when deploying these to hit distant insurgent bases. The type lacked range, endurance and the capability to carry guided air-to-ground ammunition, and its cockpit proved too cramped for extended combat operations, some of which lasted for up to eight hours and included several landings and take-offs on primitive airfields.

Therefore, the UPDF continued pursuing the remaining insurgents into the CAR into early 2010, by which time its entire 4th Division was deployed inside that country. While this operation resulted in several large groups of insurgents laying down their arms, what was left of the LRA – around 200 fighters – escaped once again.

Some remnants of the LRA are still active inside the CAR, where the UPDF and Chadian forces are still involved in minor operations against them, while most of the insurgents reportedly meanwhile fled to southern Darfur.

In addition to fighting the war against the LRA, the UPDF became involved in border strife with Kenya. On 20 February 2009, UPDAF Mi-17s and Mi-24s deployed a force of Ugandan commandos of the Presidential Guards Brigade, the Marines and Police on Migingo Island, claimed by Kenya. Taken by surprise, the nine local Kenyan police officers swiftly gave up and were all arrested. These officers had supposedly provoked this action through hoisting the Kenyan flag, despite a mutual agreement between Kampala and Nairobi. At least two MiG-21s flew a CAP while the force was landed, but no reaction on the part of the Kenyan Air Force was observed.

It was in light of the war against the LRA and tensions with Kenya, but especially due to the increasingly tense relations between Uganda and its former ally, Rwanda (the troops of the two countries clashed in a number of bitter battles during the latter stages of the Congo War in 1998–2001) that Kampala made the decision to purchase

six Sukhoi Su-30MK2 fighters in 2010. Acquisition of the new fighters was also seen as necessary to secure the development of Uganda's emerging oil industry.

By the time the Su-30MK2s began to arrive, the UPDAF had gathered considerable experience in operating fighter jets, and completed the training of a new generation of pilots with the aid of three L-39 jet trainers, acquired in recent years.

The Su-30MK2 is a modern, twin-engined, multi-role fighter-bomber capable of carrying up to 6,000kg (13,228lb) of weapons over a range of more than 2,000km (1,243 miles). Originally designed for and sold to China, the Su-30MK2 is a two-seat aircraft with an impressive combat capability. Centred on a passive electronically scanned array radar with a range of 170km (106 miles) and capable of simultaneously tracking 15 airborne targets, its weapons system is compatible with a wide range of guided air-to-air and air-to-ground weapons. The type is therefore capable of fulfilling a wide range of tactical and operational missions, varying from air defence to counter-air, suppression of enemy air defences, air interdiction, close air support and maritime strike. Additionally, the Su-30MK2 can perform early warning tasks and exercise command and control over groups of other fighters and helicopters performing joint missions. On top of that, the fighter is equipped with very advanced electronic systems with 'open architecture', enabling it to be adapted to a wide range of targeting pods and additional weapons. As such, Ugandan Su-30MK2s are vastly superior to practically any other fighter presently in service in sub-Saharan Africa.

The conversion process of Ugandan pilots and ground personnel to the Su-30MK2 began in March and April 2011, and was undertaken in Russia. Due to the complexity and diversity of this aircraft's equipment and weapons, operational training was likely to continue well into 2012. For similar reasons, and also due to warranty-related issues, a number of Russian pilots and instructors arrived in Uganda together with the brand-new Su-30s, and were planned to remain there for at least six months.

The second Su-30MK2 delivered to Uganda, serial number AF 015, in the process of pre-flight inspections, in mid-August 2011. In the course of subsequent weeks, the UPDAF launched a very intensive process of completing the training of its pilots and ground personnel on this type.
(Melting Tarmac Images)

Ugandan Su-30MK2s wear a unique camouflage pattern of dark earth and olive green. While the radome is painted white, all other dielectric panels are grey. Of interest is the application of roundels on the upper surfaces of both wings – in addition to fin flashes in the form of the national flag.
(Melting Tarmac Images)

Bottom view of the Su-30MK2 'AF 011' while this was in the process of flying a display for Ugandan President, on 25 July 2011.
(Melting Tarmac Images)

The appearance of the first two Su-30MK2s at Entebbe on 6 July 2011 came as something of a surprise and was largely missed by the international media – probably the result of the controversy surrounding their purchase. The most potent fighter-bomber in sub-Saharan Africa therefore experienced a relatively discrete service entry in Uganda.
(Melting Tarmac Images)

1   Based on Rwehururu, *The Cross to the Gun*; Petermann, 'Die Flieger des Julius Nyerere', *Fliegerrevue Extra*; Flintham, *Air Wars and Aircraft* and interviews with some of the individuals involved, granted on condition of anonymity. Additional sources, foremost those concerning recent operations of the Ugandan Air Force, are mentioned separately.

2   Kazan Helicopters, *Flight Goes On*.

3   'Musseveni Probes Tank Purchase', *New Vision*, 2 January 1999 and 'Uganda Buys Arms', *Post of Zambia*, 2 February 1999.

4   The replacement of all the Mi-8MTV-2s acquired in the 1990s was necessary due to their heavy attrition – during the war in Congo and subsequent operations against the LRA. While exact circumstances of these losses remain unknown, it is highly interesting that they were 'hidden' through the application of their serial numbers on newly-purchased Mi-17MTV-5s, that are presently in service!

5   'Uganda Pilots Fly Libya MiGs', *New Vision*, 30 April 2001.

6   Although usually reported as being Russian, the pilot in question was apparently Ukrainian or Belarusian, since the ministry of defence of the Russian Federation denied the presence of any kind of Russian instructors in Uganda at that time. For details, see *Scramble* magazine, Vol. 268, September 2001.

7   'Museveni Shopped for Arms in Belarus', *The East African*, 30 April 2000 and 'Ugandan AF tests MiG Fighter Jets', *New Vision*, 21 March 2001.

8   'Hard Target', *Newsweek*, 16 May 2009.

9   'UPDF Air Force Pilot Killed in MiG Accident', *Sunday Vision*, 27 December 2008 and 'Reclusive Kony: UPDF's Tactics Under Spotlight', *Sunday Monitor*, 1 January 2009.

10 MiG-21s delivered to Uganda from Odesaviaremservice in Ukraine appear to be former Algerian examples, delivered to Ukraine within an extremely complex deal between Moscow and Algiersm, which saw a write-off of most of Algerian debts to Russia, return of Algerian MiG-21s, concessions for Russian companies and gas-deliveries to Russia and Ukraine, in exchange for Algerians ordering Su-30s and MiG-29s. Signed in 2006, this deal nearly collapsed in late 2008, when Algerians realized that the MIG RSK is delivering over-hauled MiG-29s to them, manufactured back in the early 1990s, instead of brand-new examples, as cited in the contract. For details about this affair see 'Algerian Fighter Deal Threatened', Combat Aircraft magazine, Volume 9/Issue 1 (January 2008) & 'Wie MIG und Irkut Kunden verprellen', Fliegerrevue magazine, Volume 09/2010.

11 'Resisting the Lord's Army', *International Relations and Security Network*, 3 September 2009

Chapter 22

REPUBLIC OF ZAMBIA

Overview

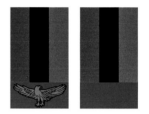

The former British protectorate of Northern Rhodesia gained independence as the Republic of Zambia on 24 October 1964.

Originally established as the Northern Rhodesia Air Force on 1 March 1964, the future Zambian Air Force (ZAF – renamed as such on 24 October 1964) came into being as a transport and liaison arm, consisting of two squadrons and depending heavily on British and Rhodesian support. No. 1 Squadron operated four C-47s and two Percival Pembrokes (received from Southern Rhodesia), while No. 2 Squadron operated eight de Havilland Canada DHC-2 Beavers for liaison purposes. Upon gaining independence, the recruitment of British officers remained standard practice. Some additional equipment – including six DHC-1 Chipmunk trainers that enabled the formation of a Flying Training School, as well as five DHC-4A Caribous – were granted or sold by the UK in subsequent years. Although British aid enabled expansion of the ZAF through the second half of the 1960s, from 1966 'Zambianisation' of the entire military had become a matter of national policy. As a result, acquisition of additional equipment foremost from Italy and Yugoslavia became more common. It was during this period that the ZAF established its first helicopter squadron, equipped with Agusta-Bell AB.205s.

By the early 1970s, the ZAF, then numbering around 1,000 personnel, was strengthened through the acquisition of SF.260 trainers (many of which were subsequently lost and then replaced by SAAB MFI-15-200 Safaris) and MB.326GB light attack aircraft, as well as SOKO G-2 Galeb and J-21 Jastreb jet trainers and light attack aircraft. Ties to China became ever more important during the late 1970s, and resulted in the delivery of Chinese-made supersonic jet fighters, sometime between 1976 and 1978. Ever since, precise reports dealing with additional acquisitions and operations have become

A very poor but extremely rare photograph of ZAF pilots and ground personnel together with their Chinese advisers, posing in front of a single FT-5 (background, left) and one F-6, in 1995. The FT-5 appears to have worn a camouflage pattern in sand, dark earth and dark olive green on the upper surfaces, and dark RLB on the lower surfaces and within the intake. The F-6 was also camouflaged, but no details are clearly visible.
(via Pit Weinert)

The only clear photograph of any Zambian F-6 that is presently available shows this example, serving as a gate guard at the Technical Training School (TTS). It is painted in sand, dark earth and dark olive green, but due to poor light, the colours appear much darker than they actually are.
(via Pit Weinert)

extremely scarce. However, it seems that the ZAF experienced very little in terms of new acquisitions and further development in the last 30 years, until it began to purchase transport and training aircraft from China in the late 1990s.[1]

Deliveries of Shenyang and MiG fighters to Zambia

Deliveries and operations of Shenyang and MiG fighters in Zambia remain a matter of great secrecy. The reasons for this are apparently twofold: firstly, due to the country's clandestine, sometimes indirect involvement in various conflicts in Africa, and secondly due to tensions with some of its neighbours.

The first 12 Shenyang F-5s and FT-5s, as well as 12 F-6s are likely to have arrived between 1976 and 1978, supposedly to serve as a deterrent against regular incursions by Rhodesian Air Force aircraft into Zambian airspace. Their actual value in this regard was probably minimal, since Rhodesia is known to have flown a number of attacks against the bases of armed African nationalists inside Zambia nevertheless. In so doing, Rhodesia also openly warned against the ZAF becoming involved. It remains unknown as to whether Zambian F-6s participated in any of the fighting in Mozambique, in support of the deployment of the Zambian military during the war against RENAMO in the early 1980s.

Negative experiences with the F-6 resulted in the decision to reinforce the ZAF through the acquisition of at least 16 MiG-21bis and 2 MiG-21UMs from the USSR, together with a number of SA-3 SAMs, considerable quantities of AAA pieces and other equipment. Deliveries began in September 1980 after over 300 ZAF personnel underwent conversion training in the Soviet Union. ZAF MiG-21s were shown to the public for the first time during celebrations marking the 20th anniversary of Zambian independence, on 24 October 1984. At least three of these fighters were lost in various accidents, including one example that crashed in May 1989. In 1997, 12 or 13 survivors were sent for a major overhaul by Israel Aircraft Industries; however, their planned upgrade to MiG-21 Lancer standard was apparently not realised. Zambian MiG-21s remained in service until early 2009, when official sources confirmed that all had been retired from active service.[2]

Force structure

The ZAF is known to have retained the squadron structure introduced by the British during the 1960s, although the exact designation of any of the units that used to fly MiGs and Shenyangs remain unknown, primarily because these are still considered 'top secret'.

A number of modern airfields were constructed on the basis of those existing from earlier times, and some of these also assumed their former roles. Mumbwa air base, northwest of Lusaka, is reportedly the main training base and housing units flying K-8s and MB.326s. During its history, the same base might also have been the home of one or at least half a fighter squadron.

Mumbwa is believed to have been the main MiG-21 base, but most aircraft stationed there have not flown for many years.

Mbala air base was the home to Jastrebs and Galebs, but the unit based there has been disbanded. Finally, Ndola air base, in northern central Zambia, was regularly used by MiGs, while all transport assets are based at Lusaka IAP.

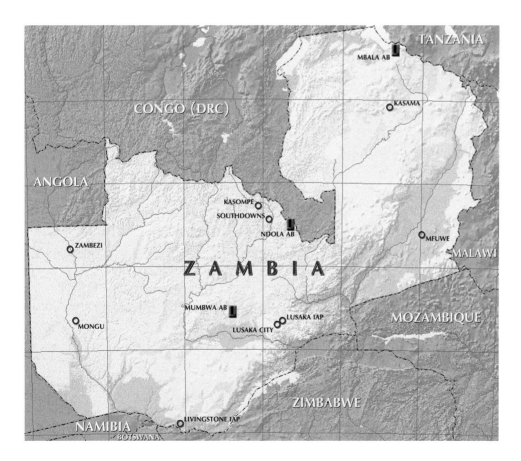

Map of Zambia

Showing four MiG-21s 'stored' at Lusaka, this photograph reveals that MiG-21bis delivered to Zambia once wore two entirely different camouflage patterns. One was reminiscent of that applied on MiG-21MFs at the Znamya Truda Works in the 1970s. The other was a modification of the standard camouflage pattern as applied on examples exported in the 1980s. (Rwandanflyer)

National markings

The Zambian national colours of green, red, black and orange also feature in the roundel applied to ZAF aircraft. The roundel has a white eagle superimposed over its centre. ZAF roundels appear to be applied in four positions on the wings, but have never been clearly seen on any of MiGs or Shenyangs.

At least the Zambian MiG-21s are certainly known to have received a fin flash, which is also consisting of national colours, and includes a white or golden eagle.

Camouflage colours and serial numbers

Practically no definite details are known of the camouflage colours of ZAF Shenyang F-6s, except that an example withdrawn from service and painted in sand, dark earth and dark olive green is positions as a gate guard near the entrance to Lusaka City Airport.

A still from a video showing the cockpit section of a ZAF MiG-21bis painted in the standard camouflage pattern in the 1980s. Of interest is the fact that this included a dark brown shade, in addition to the more usual combination of beige, light grey, and dark olive green on the upper surfaces. (via Pit Weinert)

In the mid-1990s, Zambia and Israel signed a contract for the overhaul and upgrade of several ZAF MiG-21s by Israeli Aircraft Industries. This photograph offers a top view of of the MiG-21bis (foreground, probably AF930) inside the IAI hangars. (via Pit Weinert)

Reported details of the camouflage colours of ZAF MiGs vary widely, but photographs indicate the use of two different camouflage patterns. One of these was apparently the same pattern as applied on all MiG-21bis delivered to Angola, with beige and dark olive green on the upper surfaces, and RLB on the lower surfaces. The other pattern seems to be the same as that applied on MiG-21bis exported in the mid-1980s to Mali, Mozambique and Nigeria, albeit modified through the addition of fields of dark brown on the upper surfaces, with RLB on the lower surfaces. Three-digit serial numbers in the 901-930 range, prefixed by 'AF', were applied in red on the rear fuselage, with the 'last two' repeated on the forward fuselage.[3]

Table 38: Known serial numbers of ZAF fighter jets, 1978-2009

Aircraft type	Serial number	c/n	Remarks
F-6	Unknown		Gate guard at TTS
MiG-21bis	AF9xx		Stored at Lusaka IAP; aircraft wearing a dark camouflage pattern
MiG-21bis	AF912		Reported as 'AF612' after sighting at Lusaka IAP, February 1986
MiG-21UM	AF923	516999318	Stored at IAI's compound at Lod IAP, since 2005
MiG-21UM	AF924	516999319	Reported as 'AF824' in 1986; stored at IAI's compound at Lod IAP since 2005
MiG-21bis	AF930	N75086175	Stored at IAI's compound at Lod IAP since 2005
MiG-21UM	AF9xx		Stored at Lusaka IAP, 2009

Crest of ZAF

A Zambian MiG-21UM
undergoes work at IAI. Due to
a lack of finances, IAI stopped
working on ZAF MiGs and at
least three of these were thus
left stranded at Ben Gurion IAP.
Curiously enough, the involved
IAI personnel were said to be
working on 'Namibian MiGs'.
(Wim Das, Dutch Aviation
MEDIA BV)

ZAMBIA

Patch with the national flag
as usually worn by ZAF fighter
pilots.

Patch of the ZAF as usually
worn by Zambian pilots.

Official insignia of the Fighter
Command ZAF.

Shenyang and MiG fighter operations in the Republic of Zambia

Up to four Zambian F-6s were observed airborne simultaneously during several Rhodesian attacks against the bases of various armed African nationalists groups inside Zambia, in the late 1970s. One example of such sightings is the attack on a camp near Chikumbi on 19 October 1978. However, the F-6s never successfully intercepted any Rhodesian aircraft. On the other hand, Zambian F-6s did succeed in intercepting and shooting down an Angolan Yak-40FG (registration D2-TYC) on 8 June 1980, under as of yet unknown circumstances.

ZAF MiG-21s apparently never flew any type of combat sortie, and no details concerning training of their pilots are known. During the mid-1980s, ZAF MiG-21s might have been deployed in Mozambique, during joint operations with Tanzanian and Zimbabwean forces against the insurgents of RENAMO (see Chapter 15: Republic of Mozambique). However, evidence to back up such reports is not forthcoming.

Beginning in early 1999, several reports surfaced concerning deliveries of MiG fighters to Zambia from Ukraine or Russia. Most of these indicated the arrival of several MiG-23s and up to 250 Ukrainian pilots and ground personnel planned to serve as an air force for UNITA insurgents in Angola. All aircraft and foreign contract personnel disappeared soon after their appearance became known in the public.

In subsequent years, ZAF MiG-21s were probably maintained at high readiness rates during tensions with Namibia. This would have been the case especially after it became known that the government in Lusaka had repeatedly provided support to the UNITA insurgents in Angola that operated inside Namibia, and that Zambia also supported armed separatists in Namibia's Caprivi Strip (for details, see Chapter 16: Republic of Namibia). According to official reports from Zambian diplomatic sources, the entire MiG-21 fleet was withdrawn from service in early 2009.[4]

1   Dupuy, *The Almanac of World Military Power*, p277 and Brent, *African Air Forces*, pp205–207.

2   Ibid. and 'Zambia: President Kaunda Celebrates 20 Years in Power', Reuters, 25 October 1984; detail concerning retirement of remaining ZAF MiG-21s from active service was provided by the Embassy of the Republic of Zambia in response to an inquiry by authors.

3   Serial numberss reported to be in the range AF6xx actually belong to ZAF aircraft used for VIP transport.

4   Holger Müller, 'MiG-21 in Schwarzafrika und Amerika', *Fliegerrevue Extra*, Vol. 25/June 2009.

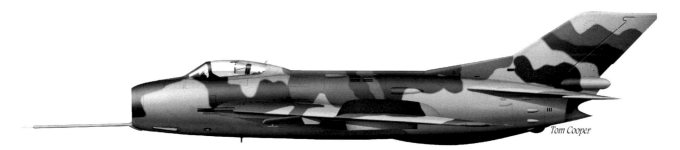

A reconstruction of the camouflage pattern applied on ZAF F-6s in the late 1970s, consisting of sand, dark earth and dark olive green on the upper surfaces (and which appears to have been applied in a symmetrical fashion on either side of the fuselage), with RLB lower surfaces. Sadly, no details of the national markings are known.

The first batch of Zambian MiG-21bis was apparently painted in this camouflage pattern, more often applied on MiG-21MFs during the 1970s. This consisted of beige and dark olive green on the upper surfaces, with RLB on the lower surfaces. The only national markings known to have been applied were fin flashes.

Zambian MiG-21UMs appear to have been painted in a camouflage pattern similar to that of the F-6s, perhaps suggesting that both were camouflaged locally.

Several Zambian MiG-21s, probably the aircraft belonging to the second batch of this type delivered in the mid-1980s, were delivered wearing the standard camouflage pattern for MiG-21bis exported in the mid-1980s, but modified through the addition of fields painted in dark brown.

Another variant of the same camouflage pattern as sighted on MiG-21bis AF926 contained not only fields in brown, but also much larger fields in dark olive green. Note that the fin flash on this aircraft was applied in a straight fashion, instead of being inclined towards the rear.

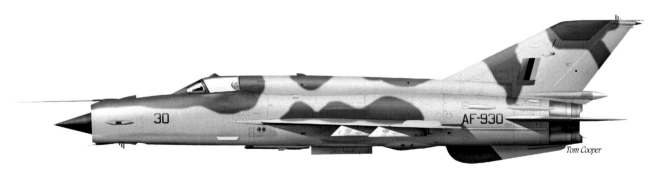

One of the few facts known about Zambian MiG-21s is that they had their serial numbers applied in dark red on the rear fuselage, including the prefix 'AF'. The 'last two' were usually repeated on the forward fuselage. No national insignia is known to have been applied on either the upper or lower wing surfaces.

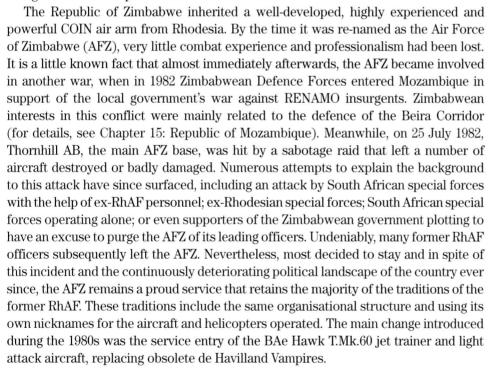

Chapter 23

REPUBLIC OF ZIMBABWE

Overview

Zimbabwe came into being as part of the British crown colony of Rhodesia, a country ruled by a white minority that declared its unilateral independence in 1965. After a long and debilitating civil war between Rhodesian security forces and no less than three different African nationalist insurgent movements, supported by almost all of Rhodesia's neighbours except South Africa, the first general elections were organised in April 1979. Elections led to a reorganisation of the entire country and its international recognition as the Republic of Zimbabwe in 1980.

The Republic of Zimbabwe inherited a well-developed, highly experienced and powerful COIN air arm from Rhodesia. By the time it was re-named as the Air Force of Zimbabwe (AFZ), very little combat experience and professionalism had been lost. It is a little known fact that almost immediately afterwards, the AFZ became involved in another war, when in 1982 Zimbabwean Defence Forces entered Mozambique in support of the local government's war against RENAMO insurgents. Zimbabwean interests in this conflict were mainly related to the defence of the Beira Corridor (for details, see Chapter 15: Republic of Mozambique). Meanwhile, on 25 July 1982, Thornhill AB, the main AFZ base, was hit by a sabotage raid that left a number of aircraft destroyed or badly damaged. Numerous attempts to explain the background to this attack have since surfaced, including an attack by South African special forces with the help of ex-RhAF personnel; ex-Rhodesian special forces; South African special forces operating alone; or even supporters of the Zimbabwean government plotting to have an excuse to purge the AFZ of its leading officers. Undeniably, many former RhAF officers subsequently left the AFZ. Nevertheless, most decided to stay and in spite of this incident and the continuously deteriorating political landscape of the country ever since, the AFZ remains a proud service that retains the majority of the traditions of the former RhAF. These traditions include the same organisational structure and using its own nicknames for the aircraft and helicopters operated. The main change introduced during the 1980s was the service entry of the BAe Hawk T.Mk.60 jet trainer and light attack aircraft, replacing obsolete de Havilland Vampires.

Following a period during which new personnel had to be trained in order to replace former RhAF officers that left after 1982, and in which the AFZ required some foreign assistance (mainly from Pakistan), by 1988 the AFZ was completely self-sufficient in regards to all aspects of pilot training, and all courses were organised locally. It was towards the end of the 1980s that the AFZ acquired a batch of 12 Chengdu F-7IIs direct from China. Subsequently, during the early 1990s, Pakistani aid was limited to fighter

In order to ease the process of converting Zimbabwean pilots to supersonic F-7s, China leased two FT-5s to the AFZ during the late 1980s. These had been withdrawn from service and returned to their owners by the mid-1990s.
(Albert Grandolini Collection)

pilot training, and only two or three PAF exchange pilots flew with the AFZ on average, usually supporting conversion courses for Hawks and F-7s. Some of the Pakistani pilots that served in Zimbabwe brought with them a huge amount of air-to-air combat experience, having even encountered Soviet pilots over Afghanistan.

The AFZ reached its zenith during its deployment to the Democratic Republic of the Congo (see Chapter 5: Democratic Republic of the Congo), and foremost during the Battle of Kinshasa in August 1998, and the pitched battles fought over the expanses of the eastern Congo up until 2001. Subsequently, most aircraft of Western origin had to be grounded due to a lack of spare parts caused by an EU arms embargo.

The FAZ found a solution for such problems, acquiring Mi-35 helicopter gunships with Libyan aid, followed by Chinese-made K-8 trainers and light attack aircraft. The quality of training provided to AFZ personnel is still so high that even South African Air Force has used it for training its own pilots and maintenance personnel in recent years.

Deliveries of Chengdu F-7 fighters to Zimbabwe

Reports from the early 1980s concerning the possible acquisition of Shenyang F-6 from China proved wrong. Similarly, reports of deliveries of up to 48 F-7s proved exaggerated. In fact, it was in 1983 that a Zimbabwean delegation led by President Robert Mugabe and Minister of Security Emmerson Munangagwa first attempted to acquire aircraft of Soviet or similar design – during a visit to Prague, in Czechoslovakia. On that occasion, they demanded delivery of L-39 jet trainers and provision of training services to the AFZ – free of charge. The government in Prague flatly declined this request.[1]

The AFZ thus eventually obtained only 12 F-7IIs and F-7IINs from a batch manufactured in 1986. The aircraft arrived by sea from China and then by train through the Beira Corridor in Mozambique. They were then assembled by Chinese and Zimbabwean technicians at Thornhill AB. The first group of AFZ pilots and technicians for the F-7 were trained entirely in China. Additionally, two FT-5 two-seat conversion trainers were acquired to ease the conversion process of AFZ pilots. The FT-5s were later replaced by two FT-7BZs, a two-seat conversion trainer variant of the F-7II.

In 1989 Zimbabwe placed an order worth USD300 million with the USSR for a squadron of MiG-29s. Some AFZ personnel even travelled to Russia to begin their conversion courses, but the entire deal was first postponed and then cancelled in

For the first 10 years of their careers, AFZ F-7s served painted white overall. Roundels were applied on the upper and lower wing surfaces, quite far inboard. (Albert Grandolini Collection)

1992, in light of South Africa withdrawing from Angola and Namibia and the general stabilisation of the entire region.

During the Second Congo War in the DRC in 2000, Libya donated several MiG-23s to Zimbabwe, but their operations are still shrouded in secrecy and the type was shown only once in public.

Renewed negotiations with Moscow for the acquisition of MiG-29SMTs were reported in 2004, but an accompanying deal was never completed. Similarly, a reported order for Chengdu FC-1/JF-17 Thunder fighters from 2005 never materialised.

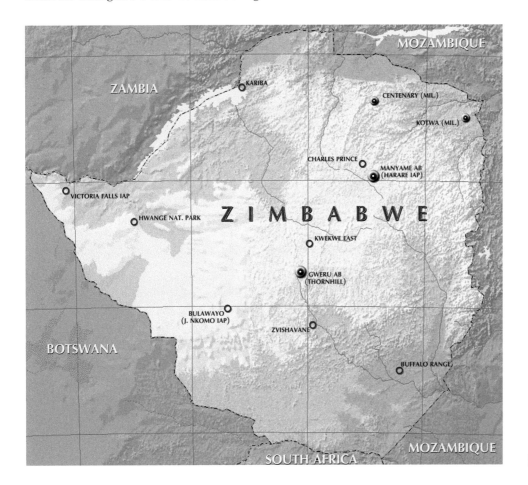

Map of Zimbabwe

Force structure

The AFZ force structure has remained fairly stable over the last 30 years. The AFZ consists of the Engineering Wing (responsible for maintenance and aeronautical inspection services, mechanical, electrical and ground equipment services, and running the School of Technical Training), the Administration Wing, the Flying Wing (which includes eight flying units – see table below – as well as the Flying School and the Parachute Training School), and the Regimental Wing (which includes the now defunct Nos 201, 202 and 203 Squadrons responsible for guarding air force personnel and installations). Originally operating Canberra B.Mk 2 bombers, No. 5 Squadron was disbanded in 1983 when that type was retired from service. The unit was reformed in 1986 to operate F-7s from Thornhill AB, where it remains stationed until this day.

Table 39: AFZ force structure, 1980–2009

Unit	Type operated pre–1980	Type operated since mid–1980s	Remarks
No. 1 Squadron 'Panzer'	Hunter FGA.Mk 9 and T.Mk 81	Hunter FGA.Mk 9 and T.Mk 81	Deactivated in January 2002
No. 2 Squadron 'Cobra'	Vampire FB.Mk 9 and T.Mk 55	Hawk T.Mk 60, K-8E Karakorum	Including Hawk OCU
No. 3 Squadron 'Falcon'	C-47, Cessna 402, BN-2A Islander	C-212-200, BN-2A Islander, Il-76, B720, BAe 146, Gulfstream III, Yak-40	
No. 4 Squadron 'Hornet'	AL-60F5, FTB-337G, SF.260W	FTB-337G, O-2A	
No. 5 Squadron 'Arrow'	Canberra B.Mk.2 and T.Mk.4	F-7II, F-7IIN, FT-7BZ, MiG-23MS	
No. 6 Squadron 'Tiger'	Provost T.Mk.52, SF.260M/TP	SF.260M/TP	Flying School
No. 7 Squadron 'Scorpion'	SA.315B, SA.316B	SA.316B	
No. 8 Squadron 'Spider'	AB.205	AB.412SP, Mi-35, AS.532 Cougar	

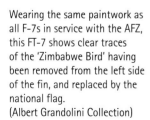

Wearing the same paintwork as all F-7s in service with the AFZ, this FT-7 shows clear traces of the 'Zimbabwe Bird' having been removed from the left side of the fin, and replaced by the national flag.
(Albert Grandolini Collection)

National markings

After the former RhAF was renamed as the Air Force of Zimbabwe, the previous Rhodesian markings were removed, but no new national markings were applied until 1982. The new national insignia consists of the Zimbabwe Bird (or 'Soapstone Bird') sitting on the walls of Great Zimbabwe, applied in yellow, and outlined and stencilled in black. This marking was applied on the fin of all aircraft and on the fuselage of helicopters. No roundels were applied on aircraft's wings.

Since 1994, this marking has been carried only on the starboard side of the fin. On the port side a fin flash was introduced in pan-African colours, this consisting of (from top to bottom) green, yellow, red, black, red, yellow and green. At the same time, all aircraft received roundels on the fuselage – the forward fuselage in the case of the F-7II – and in all four positions on the wings. These roundels consist of green, yellow, red, black and white rings.

Camouflage colours and serial numbers of FT-5s, F-7IIs and FT-7BZs in AFZ service

AFZ F-7s were originally delivered painted in dull white overall, with black panels in front of their cannon. All the usual dielectric panels – including the radome and the front part of the ventral fin – were painted dark green. During their first major overhaul, starting in the late 1990s, the entire fleet received a wraparound coat of camouflage. Colours consisted of grey and light grey. Dielectric panels remained in green. The engine exhausts are left in their 'natural' colour of 'bare gun metal', while the rear part of the fuselage is painted matt silver.

Zimbabwean FT-5s and FT-7BZs were originally painted in dull white overall. Since the late 1990s, at least one FT-7BZ has been sighted wearing the same camouflage as the rest of the F-7 fleet. Known serial numbers of these aircraft are as follows:

Table 40: AFZ FT-5, F-7II and FT-7BZ fleet, 1988-2009

Aircraft type	Serial number	c/n	Remarks
F-7II	700		Crashed on 14 November 1994
F-7II	701		Last seen 2008

Sometime around the turn of the century, surviving AFZ F-7s were overhauled and have since worn this unique camouflage pattern consisting of dull white and grey. Note the roundels are applied on the lower surfaces of both wings, very close to the fuselage.
(SAAF)

F-7II	702	Last seen 2003 wearing new camouflage
F-7II	703	Last seen 1994
F-7IIN	704	Last seen May 1995
F-7IIN	705	Last seen September 2005 wearing new camouflage
F-7IIN	706	Last seen 2003 wearing new camouflage
F-7IIN	707	Last seen May 1995
F-7IIN	708	Last in 1998
F-7IIN	709	Last seen 1994
F-7IIN	710	Last seen September 2005 wearing new camouflage
F-7IIN	711	Last seen 2003 wearing new camouflage and 'personalised' insignia
FT-7BZ	730	Last seen 2003 wearing new camouflage
FT-7BZ	731	Last seen February 1998
FT-5	795	Wfu early 1990s
FT-5	796	Wfu early 1990s

Chengdu fighter operations in the Republic of Zimbabwe

Official crest of No. 5 Squadron

Unofficial crest of No. 5 Squadron, developed by several pilots in the early 2000s

The original group of AFZ pilots trained to fly F-7s underwent their conversion courses in China. Ever since, all AFZ F-7 pilots first have to pass the Hawk OCU before converting to the F-7, which means that most of them remain current on both types. To aid training of its personnel, the AFZ initially obtained two FT-5s, Chinese-built two-seat conversion trainers based on the MiG-17 fuselage. These two aircraft were later replaced by two FT-7BZ two-seat conversion trainers, roughly similar to the original MiG-21US – also in so far that they have only one underwing hardpoint per wing, and carry no cannon in the lower fuselage.

In order to support the introduction of F-7IIs to service and their operations, in 1990 the AFZ also acquired several CEIEC 408-C and JY-14 early warning radars. New radar sites were established in Harare, Gweru, Chegutu, Chivhu, Hwange and four other locations, supported by 12 communications centres that integrate them within a complete C3 network connected to command centres at Harare and Gweru, as well as a Command Maintenance Centre. This network was reportedly upgraded in 2006, and now possibly includes several SAM sites of Chinese origin.

Since the F-7II possesses only very limited operational capabilities when operated without the ground support offered by such a system and contrary to countless reports ever since, the type was not deployed to the Democratic Republic of Congo during the Second Congo War. AFZ participation in that war (see Chapter 5: Democratic Republic of the Congo for details) varied significantly in intensity and scale, but foremost as a result of the vastness of the battlefield, the staggering numbers of combatants and its conventional nature. Under such conditions, Zimbabwe preferred to deploy its Hawks and some other aircraft and helicopters to the Congo.

Nevertheless, during the war in the DRC in 2000, Libya donated at least two, or more likely three or four MiG-23MS and MiG-23UB fighters to Zimbabwe. Very little is known of their presence in the country, and there are now some doubts as to whether these are not the same aircraft donated to Congo. Although two examples conducted a flypast over Harare in 2003, none have been seen in operational condition since. The fleet is either stored at Thornhill AB or was returned to the DRC.

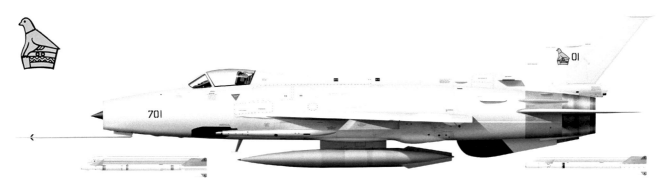

The first Zimbabwean 'MiG' was this Shenyang F-7NI, a variant that had only one underwing pylon per wing. At the time they entered service, AFZ F-7s were armed only with obsolete PL-2 AAMs (right lower corner) and wore the original national insignia – the 'Zimbabwe Bird' (inset) – on either side of the fin. PL-2s were soon replaced by PL-5s (left lower corner).

Most Zimbabwean F-7s belong to the slightly more advanced F-7NII variant, which has four underwing pylons. Sometime during the late 1980s, the Zimbabwe Bird applied on the left side of the fin was replaced by the Zimbabwean national flag. When deployed as interceptors, these aircraft usually carry either one 'supersonic' drop tank under the centreline, or one under each of the outboard underwing pylons.

The second of two FT-7s delivered to Zimbabwe wore the serial number 731. Notable on all AFZ F-7s is that the rear fuselage and underwing hardpoints are painted in a heat-resistant silver-grey colour. All maintenance stencils are in English and are applied in enamel blue or dark red.

Since the early 2000s, surviving AFZ F-7s have worn this camouflage pattern, consisting of dull white and dark grey, with slight differences from aircraft to aircraft. National markings and other insignia remained the same, although serial numbers are now applied in a slightly larger size. The type has meanwhile been adapted to carry many different weapons, including (from left to right): MDB multiple ejector racks for FAB-150 and OFAB-100-120 bombs, FAB-250M-54 and FAB-500M-54 bombs of Soviet/Russian origin, Argentine BR-250 and BR-500 general-purpose bombs, and British-made BL.755 cluster bombs.

Following their overhaul in the early 2000s, AFZ F-7s were modified to carry additional air-to-air weapons, including Soviet/Russian-made R-60MKs (inset left) and Chinese-made PL-7s (inset right). The latter represent reverse-engineered copies of the French Matra R.550 Magic 1.

In addition to various air-to-air missiles and bombs, Zimbabwean F-7s have meanwhile been armed with different types of launchers for unguided rockets, including (from left to right), French-made Matra F4s, Soviet/Russian made UB-16-57s and (shown on the aircraft) UB-32-57s. The inset shows the top view of the camouflage introduced after the entire fleet was overhauled in the early 2000s.

Around 2001, this F-7NII was decorated as the personal aircraft of the CO No. 5 Squadron, Flt Lt Michael Enslin, famous from the war in Congo, in which he flew Hawks. Of interest is the twin-rail launcher for R-60MK missiles, installed on the outboard pylon, increasing the total capacity to six AAMs.

Although mainly serving as advanced trainers and for conversion of new pilots to the type, Zimbabwean FT-7s have an important secondary ground-attack role. For this purpose, they can also be armed with S-24B unguided rockets. When under way on air-to-ground missions, the F-7s carry slightly larger drop tanks of Chinese origin under the centreline. These are limited to subsonic speeds.

The status of Zimbabwean MiG-23MS fighter remains something of a mystery. Delivered directly from Libyan stocks, they apprently have arrived in Zimbabwe wearing a fresh coat of camouflage, albeit applied according to the pattern usually found on aircraft of this type exported to the Middle East and Africa. Next to nothing is known about their markings, but it appears that at least one of the recently sighted aircraft might have received a fin flash and a small serial number (13), applied in black.

At least two AFZ F-7IIs have been lost, including one in a crash that occurred on 14 November 1994. Another example was lost in January 2001, during a much-publicised – yet very brief – non-combat deployment to the DRC in order to participate in the burial ceremony for the local president. Indeed, this incident revealed not only how demanding F-7 is to fly (particularly on instruments only and when not supported by a well-established ground control network), but also why the AFZ never deployed any of its supersonic fighters to the DRC for combat purposes. In order to reach Kinshasa, a formation of four aircraft was to make refuelling stops in Lubumbashi and Kananga, in the DRC. The loss occurred under way from Kananga to N'Djili IAP, when the formation entered a tropical thunderstorm, and the lead F-7, flown by a pilot with the rank of squadron leader, was struck by lightning that disabled the attitude indicator and power supply. The pilot became disoriented and ejected some 15 minutes after taking off from Kananga – still in the middle of the storm. The pilot landed safely and was rescued after making contact with local villagers. The wreckage of his F-7 was never found.

A second accident occurred on the return trip from N'Djili to Kananga. The No. 3 F-7 in formation – flown by a wing commander short of recent experience on the type – made a wheels-up landing at Kananga and blocked the runway. The No. 4 found himself without enough fuel to divert and did an excellent job in landing literally over the belly-landed No. 3, using just over half of the remaining runway. However, he overshot, damaging the starboard underwing tank on a small tree and suffering some light damage to the wing. Worse yet, the pitot tube – mounted under the nose – was bent. Both of these F-7s were subsequently recovered by AFZ repair teams and flown back to Zimbabwe, where the belly-landed jet received extensive repairs in order to be made operational again.

1   Information based on original Czechoslovak documents, kindly provided by Martin Smisek.

APPENDIX I:
AIR ORDERS OF BATTLE

Current as of the date of publication (September 2011), the air orders of battle that follow are provided for the 23 countries featured in both volumes of this work and which have, through the years, operated MiG, Sukhoi, Chengdu, Shenyang and Nanchang fighters.

1. Angola

Força Aérea Nacional de Angola (FAN)

C-in-C   Chefe do Estado Maior FAN   *Gen Francisco Lopes Alfonso Concalves 'Hanga'*
Deputy C-in-C   Chefe do Estado Maior-Adjunto FAN   *Gen Mário Joáo Venáncio Paiva*
Deputy Air Defence   Comandante DAA   *Gen Manuel Massague Neto*

Zona Aérea Centro

Regimento Aéreo de Transportes (RAT), Base Aérea N°1 Luanda

Unit	Aircraft	No.	Remarks
Esquadra VIP	Boeing 707	1	D2-MAN
	Yak-40	2	D2-MAS
	Bombardier BD-700	1	D2-ANG
	Embraer EMB-135BJ	1	T-501
	Embraer EMB-120	1	T-500; crashed 14 September 2011
Esquadra de Transportes	Il-76	4	D2-FCN, T-905, T-907, T-909
	An-72	2+	D2-MBX, T-703; additional aircraft stored
	An-74	2+	D2-MBE; additional aircraft stored
Esquadra de Transportes	An-12	5-6	D2-FDB, D2-MAZ, D2-MBH, D2-MDB, T-300, T-315
	An-26	4	D2-END, D2-TAE, T-253, T-255,
	An-30A	1	D2-MBO
	An-32	2-3	T251, T-252, T-256; additional aircraft stored
Esquadra de Reconhecimento	EMB-312	7-12	R-452, R-454, R-455, R-459, R-461
	Dornier Do 28	1-2	R-614 stored, all other Do-28 phased out unit possibly an independent training asset or actually assigned to the EMFAL (see below) but stationed in Luanda

Regimento Aéreo de Helicópteros (RAH), Base Aérea N°3 Negage (BAN)

Unit	Aircraft	No.	Remarks
Esquadra do Bomber	Mi-24, Mi-25	6-8	H-376, H-377, H-384, H-389; additional helicopters stored (H-380, H-381)
Esquadra de Bell 212	Bell 212	8-9	H-801, H-806

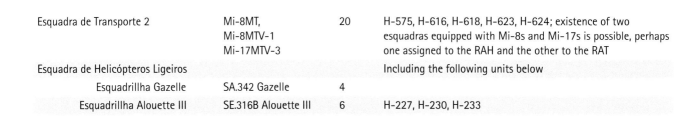

Esquadra de Transporte 2	Mi-8MT, Mi-8MTV-1 Mi-17MTV-3	20	H-575, H-616, H-618, H-623, H-624; existence of two esquadras equipped with Mi-8s and Mi-17s is possible, perhaps one assigned to the RAH and the other to the RAT
Esquadra de Helicópteros Ligeiros			Including the following units below
Esquadrillha Gazelle	SA.342 Gazelle	4	
Esquadrillha Alouette III	SE.316B Alouette III	6	H-227, H-230, H-233

Regimento Aéro de Caça-bombardeiros (RACB), Base Aéra N°5 Catumbela (BAC)

Unit	Aircraft	No.	Remarks
Esquadra de Caça-bombardeiros	Su-22M-4K	10	C503, C507, C509, C516, C517, C518, C522, C521, C550, C551 C510 w/o 15 September 2011
	Su-22UM-3K	4	I-34, I-35, I-36, I-38
Esquadra de Caça-bombardeiros	Su-24	1	B-615, stored
	Su-25	5-6	all stored, unit disbanded
Esquadra de Trinamento Avançado	L-29	4-6	L-80, L-8?; plus up to 8 L-29 stored
	L-39	6	I-51, I-52, I-53, I-54, I-55, I-56

Escola Militar de Formação Aeronaútica (EMFAL), Base Aéra N°4 Lobito

Unit	Aircraft	No.	Remarks
Esquadra de Instrução de Pilotagem	Zlin 242	5	I-131, I-132, I-133, I-134, I-135; plus 1 simulator
	Cessna T-41	4	I-114, I-119
	Pilatus PC-7	2	R-422, R-423
	SA.316B Alouette III	4	

It is possible that the EMFAL is further subdivided within Esquadrillha Zlin, Esquadrillha Cessna and Esquadrillha Alouette, but no corresponding information is available

Zona Aérea Norte
Peacetime HQ in Catumbela, but no units assigned

Zona Aérea Sul
Peacetime HQ in Huambo, but no units are permanently assigned to that air base (only helicopter units have regular, temporary assigned detachments deployed in Huambo

Regimento Aéreo de Caças (RAC), Base Aérea N°2, Lubango (BAL)

Unit	Aircraft	No.	Remarks
Esquadra de Caças	Su-27UB	1	I100, usually stored
	MiG-23MLD	8-10	C-470, C-471, C-474, C-475, C-482
	MiG-23UB	3-4	I-26, I-30, I-31

Escola de Formação Militar e Tècnica, Namibe
Namibe/Jury Gagarin air base was an official air base in the late 1980s and early 1990s, but is not considered as such any more and appears not to have seen any major deployments in recent years

Zona Aérea Leste
No units permanently assigned. This HQ controls only ground personnel and installations on two airfields. It is possible that helicopter units deploy on a temporary basis either to Base Aérea Saurimo or Base Aérea Luena

2. Burkina Faso

Armée de l'Air Burkinabé (AAB)

C-in-C	(Chef D'état-Major de l'Armée de l'Air)	*Col Maj Abraham Raore*
Deputy C-in-C	(Chef D'état-Major de l'Armée de l'Air par interim)	*Col Gustave Palenfo*

Brigade Aérienne

Base Aérienne 511 Ouagadougou
HQ 1° Région Aérienne
Escadron de l'Armée de l'Air

Unit	Aircraft	No.	Remarks
Gouvernement	Boeing 727-282	1	XT-BFA
Escadrille de Transport	HS.748 Series 2A/320	1	XT-MAL
	CASA CN235	1	XT-MBE
	Beech King Air 200	3	XT-MAX, XT-MBA, XT-MBD
Escadrille d'Hélicotères	Mi-35	2	BF0504, BF05??
	Mi-17	2	BF9001, BF9202
	AS.350 Ecureuil	2	XT-MAV, XT-MAW
	Mi-8S	1	XT-MAU, stored
Escadrille d'Aviation Legere d'Appui	Piper PA-34	1	XT-MAZ
	Air Tractor AT-802A	1	XT-MBB
	Air Tractor AT-802	1	XT-MBC
	M.S.893E Rallye 180GT	1	XT-MAY
Ministère de la Sécuritè	Celier Xenon RST gyrocopter	2	XT-MFA, XT-MFB

Base Aérienne 5?? Bobo Dioulasso
HQ 2° Région Aérienne

Unit	Aircraft	No.	Remarks
Escadrille d'Aviation Legere	SF.260W	3-5	BF8423, BF8425, BF8626, BF8627, BF8639

3. Republic of Chad

Armée de l'Air Tchadienne (AAT)

CoS Armée Tchadienne	supervising the AAT	*Gen Alain Mbajodenandé Dionadji*
Deputy C-in-C		

Base Aérienne N'Djamena

Unit	Aircraft	No.	Remarks
Escadrille de Transport	Gulfstream II	1	TT-AAI
	Beech 1900	1	TT-ABB
	Boeing 737-74Q	1	TT-ABD
	An-12	1	TT-PAF?
	An-26	1+	TT-LAO, TT-LAP; TT-LAM, TT-LAN phased out 2007
	C-130H-30	1	TT-AAH
Escadrille d'Appui	Su-25	4	TT-QAI, TT-QAL, TT-QAN, TT-QAO
	Su-25UB	2	TT-QAH, TT-QAM
	PC-9	1	TT-QAG
	PC-7	1	TT-QAB, status unclear
	SF.260	1	TT-QAK
Escadrille d'Hélicotères	Mi-24	2	wrecks, stored[1]
	Mi-35	3	TT-OAQ, TT-OAR, TT-OAS
	Mi-8MTV	2	TT-OAJ/4320, TT-OAK/4321; rebuilt
	Mi-171	2	TT-OAN/7344, TT-OAO/7415
	SA.316B Alouette III	1	TT-OAH
	AS.550C2 Fennec	2	TT-OAT, TT-OAU

The delivery of two ex-AdA EMB-312 Tucanos is expected by late 2011/early 2012. These are likely to replace two PC-7/9s and serve as training aircraft[2]

Base Aérienne Abéché
Forward operating base; no permanently assigned units but frequent deployments of PC-7/9s, Su-25s and various combat helicopters have been observed

4. Republic of the Congo (Brazzaville)

Armée de l'Air du Congo (AAC)

| C-in-C | Chef d'état-major de l'armée de l'Air | *Col Jean Baptiste Philippe Tchicaya* |
| Deputy C-in-C | | |

Base Aérienne 01/20 Brazzaville

Unit	Aircraft	No.	Remarks
Escadrille d'Hélicotères	Mi-24	3	TN-359, TN-3??, TN-3??
	Mi-8T	1	TN-355
	Mi-17	2	TN-354, TN-358
Escadrille de Chasse	Mirage F.1	2	delivery reported by South African company
Escadrille de Transport	An-32	1	TN-227
Gouvernement	SA.365N Dauphin	1	TN-AES
	MD-83	1	SX-IFA; leased by the Government of the Congo
	Il-76TD	1	TN-AFS
Police Nationale	Mi-2	3	TN-657, TN-658, TN-659; possibly assigned to the Escadrille d'Hélicotères

Base Aérienne 02/20 Pointe-Noire

Unit	Aircraft	No.	Remarks
Escadrille de Chasse	MiG-21bis	5	509, 511, 513, 515, 525; all stored

Base Aérienne 03/20 Makua

No aircraft known to be permanently assigned or active and status of BA03/20 is presently uncertain

5. Democratic Republic of the Congo

Force Aérienne Congolaise[3] (FAC)

C-in-C   Chef d'État-Major de la Force Aérienne   *Maj Gen Rigobert Masamba*

Deputy C-in-C

Groupement Aérien

Base Aérienne Kinshasa-N'Djili

Unit	Aircraft	No.	Remarks
Groupe de Vol de Transport	An-12	4	9T-TCH, 9T-TCO, both are An-12BP 9T-TCI, 9T-TCM
	An-26	2+3	9T-TAE, 9T-???; 9T-TAA, 9T-TAB, 9T-??? stored
	C-130H	1	9T-TCB, stored
	Boeing 727-100/-22C	3	9T-TCK; 9T-TCJ, 9T-TCL
Groupe d'Appui	Su-25	2	FG-500, FG-502; seldom flown
	MB.326K	3	FG-478, FG-479, FG-481; all stored
	MiG-23UB	2	FG-2000, FG-2001; all stored
	SF.260	1	stored
Groupe de Vol d'Gouvernment	Boeing 727	2	9Q-CDC, 9Q-CDJ
	Mi-8PS	2	3X-GCN, S9-HEA

Base Aérienne Kinshasa-Ndolo

Unit	Aircraft	No.	Remarks
Groupe d'Hélicoptères	Mi-24V	8	9T-HM2, 9T-HM3, 9T-HM4, 9T-HM12, 9T-HM14; rarely flown
('Simba Squadron')	Mi-8T	2	9T-HM20, 9T-HM21; both operational
	Mi-2	2	9T-HT12, 9T-H??[4]
Ecole de Pilotage			inactive
Group d'Entrenement	Cessna 150		all stored
	Cessna 310R		all stored

Base Aérienne Kamina

Used for forward deployments of helicopters and transports[5]

Base Aérienne Kitona

Base not operational, but up to 12 MB.326GB/K stored at this site

Base Regionale Lumumbashi

Used for forward deployments of helicopters. 2 Mi-8, 1 Mi-26 (9T-HM15), 1 SF.260MC and a number of Cessna 310Rs are all stored

Goma International Airport
Used for forward deployments of helicopters and Su-25s; 1 Mi-8MT (9T-HM7) is seldom flown

Gbadolite Airport
Not operational; 5 MiG-21, 2 J-21, 1 G-2 and 2 Mi-24 all derelict

 # 6. Republic of Equatorial Guinea

Fuerza Aérea de Guinea Ecuatorial (FAGE)

C-in-C   *Unknown*
Deputy C-in-C

FAGE probably under direct control of the President and C-in-C Armed Forces, Brig Gen (ret.) Teodoro Obiang Nguema Mbasogo. No unit structure is known, but the air force is equipped as follows:

Malabo IAP

Unit	Aircraft	No.	Remarks
Transport aircraft	An-32	1	3C-5GE
	An-72	1	3C-CMN
	An-72P	1	032
	Boeing 737	1	3C-EGE
	ERJ-145EP	1	3C-QQH
	Dassault Falcon 900	2	3C-ONM
	Dassault Falcon 50	1	3C-LGE
	Il-76TD	1	3C-HHV
Combat aircraft	Su-25	2	028, 029
	Su-25UB	2	026, 027
Helicopters	Enstrom 480B	2	015, 017
	Mi-172	2	3C-LLD, 3C-LLE
	Mi-24V	3	010, 011, 012
	Mi-24P	3	020, 021, 022
	Mi-26	1	30
Training aircraft	L-39C	2	024, 025

 # 7. State of Eritrea

Eritrean Air Force (ERAF)

C-in-C   *Maj Gen Teklai Habteselassie*
Deputy C-in-C   *unknown*

Asmara IAP

Unit	Aircraft	No.	Remarks
No. 1 Squadron	IAI Westwind 11258P	1	non-operational
	Canadair CL-601-3A	1	
No. 2 Squadron	Valmet L-90TP Redigo	6	202, 205, 206
No. 3 Squadron	Mi-8	2	306
	Mi-17	1	
	Mi-35	1	
No. 4 Squadron	MB.339CE/FD	5	403, 405, 407, 408, 409
No. 5 Squadron	MiG-29	8	502, 503, 505, 506, 507, 508, 509, 512
	MiG-29UB	1	501
No. 6 Squadron	Su-27S	2	608, 609
	Su-27UB	2	601, 602
No. 7 Squadron	Bell 412	2	701, 702
No. 8 Squadron	Harbin Y-12	3	801; 802 taken over by civilian operator
	Shaanxi Y-8	2	reported, but not confirmed

8. Federal Democratic Republic of Ethiopia

Federal Democratic Republic of Ethiopia Air Force (FDREAF)

C-in-C	*Maj Gen Abebe Teklehaimanot*
Deputy C-in-C	*unknown*

Debre Zeit AB

Unit	Aircraft	No.	Remarks
No. 5 Squadron	Su-27	8+	1951, 1961
	Su-27UB	2	1907
No. 12 Squadron	Mi-35	15	2128, 2133; detachments for United Nations outside Ethiopia
No. 14 Squadron	Mi-8	20	
	Mi-17		2011, 2013; further helicopters stored
No. 21 Squadron	An-12B	6	status unknown
	C-130B	2	all stored
	Yak-40	1	status unknown
No. 33 OCU	L-39	6	1707, 1725; further aircraft stored

2 gyrocopters, for observation purposes

Bahir Dar AB

Unit	Aircraft	No.	Remarks
No. 44 Squadron	MiG-23BN		1285; status unknown, many aircraft stored
	MiG-23UB	2	

Dire Dawa AB

Unit	Aircraft	No.	Remarks
No. 31 Flight School	SF.260TP	5-6	153, 157, 159, 160
Temporary Detachments	Mi-8, Mi-17, Mi-35	2-4	involved in operations inside Somalia

9. Republic of the Gambia

Gambian National Guard (GNG)

C-in-C   *unknown*
Deputy C-in-C   *unknown*

Bangui IAP

Unit	Aircraft	No.	Remarks
	Su-25	1	81
	Air Tractor AT-802A	2	C5-DOA, C5-KSB
	Il-62M	2	C5-RTG, C5-GNM; phased out and stored
	Boeing 727-95	1	C5-GAF 'Kanilai'

Only VIP transports are presently operational

10. Republic of Guinea (Conakry)

Armée de l'Air Guinée (AAG)

C-in-C   Chef d'État-Major de l'armée de l'Air   *Col Kadjali Conté*
Deputy C-in-C   Chef d'État-Major de l'armée de l'Air Adjoint   *Col Mamadou Labo Barry*

Base Aérienne principale de Conakry
Division Vol et Opcration (Opcrational Command AAG)

Unit	Aircraft	No.	Remarks
Government	AS.350B Ecureuil	1	3X-GBF
	SA.330L	1	3X-GVC
	AW139	1	3X-???
Escadrille de Chasse	MiG-21bis	3	
	MiG-21UM		
Escadrille d'Hélicoptères	Mi-17	2	FAG-1008, FAG-1009
	Mi-24	3	FAG-995, FAG-1003, FAG-1004
	MD500	2	FAG-??? and FAG-999; status unclear; sent to Ukraine in 2006

Bataillon Autonome des Troupes Aéroportées (BATA)
CO: Lt Col Aly Traoré
XO: Lt Col Ousmane Cissé
Airport authority at Faranah, Labe and Boke without any flying equipment

Centre d'instruction de l'école de l'armée de l'air (CIEA), Conakry
Technical education facility without any flying equipment; organisation wise independent of Base Aérienne Conakry

11. Republic of Guinea-Bissau

Armée de l'Air Guinée (FAGB)

C-in-C	Chefe de Estado-Maior da FAGB	*Brigadeiro General Ibraima Camará*
Deputy C-in-C	Vice-Chefe de Estado-Maior da FAGB	*Coronel Carlos Bampuque*

Base Aérea No. 1 Bissalanca

Unit	Aircraft	No.	Remarks
	C-212	1	J5-GZZ; used for VIP transport is operational

No other active aircraft is known

12. Republic of Côte d'Ivoire (Ivory Coast)

Force Aérienne de la Côte d'Ivoire (FACI)

C-in-C	Chef d'état-major de l'armée de l'Air	*Col Brindou M'Bia et Aka*
Deputy C-in-C		*unknown*

Base Aérienne de Abidjan

Unit	Aircraft	No.	Remarks
	BAC 167 Strikemaster	2	TU-VRA, TU-VRB; unserviceable condition
	Su-25	2	02, 03; unserviceable condition
	Su-25UB	2	21, 22; unserviceable condition
	An-12	1	TU-VMA; unserviceable condition
	Gulfstream III, IV	1+1	TU-VAF, TU-VAD
	Cessna 402	1	TU-VAL; unserviceable condition
	IAR-330	2	TU-VHM, TU-VHP; unserviceable condition
	Mi-24	3	TU-VHO, TU-VHQ, TU-VHR; unserviceable condition
	SA.365 Dauphin	1	TU-VAV; in airworthy condition

Due to rigid sanction by UN, FANCI aircraft are not operational. Even the smallest maintenance work is strictly forbidden by UN observers.

Base Aérienne de Bouake
Not operational

13. Malagasy Republic (Madagascar)

Armée de l'Air Malgache (AdAM)

| C-in-C | Chef d'état-major de l'armée de l'Air | *unknown* |
| Deputy C-in-C | | *unknown* |

Base Aéronavale d'Ivato Antananarivo (BANI)

Unit	Aircraft	No.	Remarks
Escadrille l'Aviation Légère	ULM Joker 300	3	5R-MNM, 5R-MNN, 5R-MNO
	ULM Tetras	1	5R-MNR
	SOCATA Rallye	1	5R-MNL
Escadrille d'Hélicoptères	SA.318 Alouette II	3–4	including ex-Belgian A-39
			all other helicopters either phased out or stored

All aircraft and helicopters mostly operated on behalf of the Protection Civile and Gendarmerie Nationale

Base Aérienne Tactique d'Arivinimamo (BATAC)
Not operational

Base Aéronavale d'Antsiranana (BANA)
Forward operating base

Government

Unit	Aircraft	No.	Remarks
Air Force I	Boeing 737-300		5R-MRM; transferred to Air Madagascar
Air Force II	Boeing 737-700		5R-MAP; now serving as Air Force I

14. Republic of Mali

Force Aérienne de la République du Mali (FARM)

| C-in-C | Chef d'état-major de l'armée de l'Air | *Gen Mamadou Togola* |
| Deputy C-in-C | | *unknown* |

Base Aerienne 101 Bamako-Sénou

Unit	Aircraft	No.	Remarks
Escadrille l'Aviation Légère	Cessna 172	1	TZ-392
	ULM Tetras	3	TZ-406, TZ-408, TZ-410
	Cessna O-2	3	TZ-387; all stored
Escadrille de Chasse	MiG-21bis/UM	5–7	all stored
	MiG-21MF	2	TZ-356, TZ-357
	MiG-21UM	2	TZ-375, TZ-358

226

Escadrille le Transport	An-26	1	TZ-399
	Basler BT-67	1	TZ-391
	BN-2A	1	TZ-389
Escadrille d'Hélicotères	Mi-24D	4	TZ-404, TZ-405, TZ-406, TZ-407
	Harbin Z-9	1	TZ-394
	AS.350 Ecureuil	1	TZ-374
Ecole Pilotage Aérienne	ULM Tetras	4	TZ-395, TZ-396, TZ-397, TZ-402
Gouvernment	Boeing 707	1	TZ-TAC
	Boeing 727	1	TZ-MBA
	BAC One-Eleven	1	TZ-BSB

Base Aérienne 102 Mopti-Sévaré
Forward operating base

Following airfields are technically under the military management: Base Aérienne de Dogofry, Base Aérienne de Tombouctou, Base Aérienne de Gao, Base Aérienne de Kayes

15. Republic of Mozambique

Forca Aérea Moçambicana (FAM)

Comandante do Ramo da Força Aérea	*Major-General Luís Raul Dique*
Comandante da Força Aérea	*General José Beca Chagua*

The air force, practically nonexistent by the early 1990s, began to be re-established from 2009. Personnel have undergone training in flight safety, telecommunications and administration in Brazil, Portugal, Russia and elsewhere. At the time of writing a number of pilots and ground personnel were undergoing training with Portuguese assistance on Cessnas at Maputo. Additionally, an Aviation Medicine Centre is under development in Nampula.
On 3 March 2011, two ex-Portuguese Air Force Reims-Cessna FTB-337Gs (the former 13729/0030 and 13713/0014) were delivered to Maputo. Equipped with upgraded avionics, they are expected to be used for pilot training, light transport, medevac and maritime surveillance. Both aircraft were disarmed prior to delivery.

Base Aérea da Maputo

Unit	Aircraft	No.	Remarks
Esquadra de Transporte	An-26	1+	Last known active aircraft FAM-022; stored
	Mi-8	2	FAM-???; stored
Escola Prática de Aviação	FTB-337G	2	FAM-547, FAM-548
	Cessna 150	2	FAM-???; status unknown
	Cessna 182	1	FAM-545
	Piper Seneca	1	FAM-546

Unit report to the Academia Militar 'Samora Marchel', AM Nampula

Base Aérea da Nacala
Taken over by civilian administration

Base Aérea de Beira
Escola Aeronáutica, responsible for theoretical and technical traing; no flying equipment. Reports to the Academia Militar 'Samora Marchel', AM Nampula

The air force is expected to become responsible for technical maintenance of airfields in Chingodzi, Cuamba, Marrupa and Mueda

 # 16. Republic of Namibia

Namibiese Lugmag (NL)

C-in-C   *Maj Gen Pinehas*
Deputy C-in-C   *unknown*

Air Defence Wing
CO: Lt Col Teofilus Shaende

Grootfontein AB

Unit	Aircraft	No.	Remarks
No. 23 Squadron	F-7NM	12	0310, 0311, 0312, 0313, 0314, 0315, 0316, 0317, 0318, 0319, 0320, 0321
	FT-7	2	0330, 0331
No. ?? Squadron	An-26	1	NAF-3-644
	Y-12	2	NAF-97-600, NAF-97-639
No. ?? Squadron	Mi-24	2	
	Mi-8MT	1	H-802
	Cheetak	2	H-/04, H-???
No. ?? Squadron	O-2A	6+	602, 605, 640
Air Wing Training Squadron	K-8E	4	NAF-6-502, NAF-6-504, NAF-6-506, NAF-6-608

Detachments from from transport and helicopter units are frequently observed operating from Windhoek IAP

Karibib AB
Base under construction; to become home of the Flying School's Air Wing Training Squadron

 # 17. Federal Republic of Nigeria

Nigerian Air Force (NAF)

Chief of Air Staff   CAS   *AM Mohammed Dikko Umar*
Air Officer Commanding Tactical Air Command   AOC TAC   *AVM Gabriel Babatunde Odesola*
Air Officer Commanding Training Command   AOC TC   *AVM Ibrahim Salihu*

101 Presidential Fleet (PAF)

Unit	Aircraft	No.	Remarks
Presidential Air Wing	AW139	2	NAF-540, -541
	Cessna Citation 550	2	NAF-550, 5N-AYA
	Dassault Falcon 7X	2	5N-FGO, 5N-FGU
	Boeing 737-7N6 BBJ	1	5N-FGT
	Gulfstream 550	1	5N-FGS

Training Command (TC, HQ Kaduna)

301 Flying Training School (301 FTS), Kaduna

Unit	Aircraft	No.	Remarks
Primary Flying Training Wing (PFTW)	RV-6A Air Beetle	12	NAF-071, -076, -094, -098, -099; additional aircraft stored
	Dornier Do 128-6	4	NAF-023, -025; additional aircraft stored
	Do 228	4	NAF-027, -028, -032

303 Flying Training School (303 FTS), Kano

Unit	Aircraft	No.	Remarks
Advanced Flying Training Wing (AFTW)	MB.339CD	12	undergoing overhaul
	L-39ZA	8	NAF-360, -361, -362, -363; additional aircraft stored

305 Flying Training School (305 FTS), Enugu

Unit	Aircraft	No.	Remarks
Basic Helicopter Flying Wing (BHFW)	Hughes 300C	6+	NAF-587, -588, -589; phased out and sold
	Mi-34C	6	NAF-551, -552, -555; phased out and up for sale
	AW109	13	NAF-570, -571, -574, -575; on process of delivery

Tactical Air Command (TAC, HQ Makurdi)

64 Air Defence Group (64 ADG), Makurdi

Unit	Aircraft	No.	Remarks
	F-7NI	11	balance following two crashes
	FT-7NI	2	NAF-812, -813, -814; one w/o 11 May 2011
	MiG-21MF/bis/UM	19	NAF-693 (MF, preserved); all stored and in process of being phased out
	SEPECAT Jaguar	14	all stored and offered for sale

204 Wing (204 W), Maiduguri

Unit	Aircraft	No.	Remarks
	MiG-21bis/UM	4	all stored and in process of being phased out and offered for sale

75 Strike Group (75 STG), Yola
No aircraft known to be permanently assigned

81 Air Maritime Group (81 AMG), Benin

Unit	Aircraft	No.	Remarks
	ATR-42-500MP	3	NAF-930, NAF-931
	Do 228	2	NAF-831; operational

88 Military Airlift Group (88 MAG), Ikeja

Unit	Aircraft	No.	Remarks
221 Wing (221 W)	C-130	2	Based at Ikeja; 6 stored at Lagos; two more stored
227 Wing (227 W)	G.222	5	Based at Ilorin; NAF-953, -954; stored at Lagos

99 Air Weapons School (99 AWS), HQ Kainji

Unit	Aircraft	No.	Remarks
909 Tactical Fighter Training Wing (909 TFTW)	Alpha Jet	4	Based at Ikeja; operational, following overhaul

97 Special Operations Group (97 SOG), Port Harcourt

Unit	Aircraft	No.	Remarks
206 Wing (206 W)	Alpha Jet	6	non-operational, awaiting overhaul
207 Wing (207 W)	Mi-24P/V Mi-35P	7	NAF-536, - 537, -538
	Bo.105	5	phased out
	AS.332M1 Super Puma		NAF-568, -569; undergoing overhaul
225 Wing (225 W)			Based at Ikeja; no aircraft known as assigned

Forward operational bases (with no permanently assigned aircraft): Calabar, Ibadan, Sokto

Note: Naval Aviation of the Nigerian Navy appears to have been disbanded. The Agusta A.109 and Westland Lynx Mk 89 helicopters previously operated by its No. 101 Squadron were probably distributed among 81 AMG and 97 SOG.

18. Republic of Somalia

C-in-C	*unknown*
Deputy C-in-C	*unknown*

No air force known to exist as an operational branch of the military. A paramilitary aviation service exists in the Republic of Somaliland (including the parts of northern Somalia formerly under the Italian mandate in the 1950s) and operates a few light aircraft. Although run by a democratically elected government supported by Ethiopia and Italy, the independence of Somaliland has so far failed to find wider international recognition.

19. Republic of the Sudan

Al Quwwat al-Jawwiya As-Sudaniya (SuAF)

C-in-C   *Maj Gen Abbas Yusuf Ahmed Al-Badri*
Deputy C-in-C   *unknown*

Wadi Sayyidna AB

Unit	Aircraft	No.	Remarks
No. 1 Fighter Squadron	A-5C	8–9	401, 402, 403, 404, 405, 406, 407, 409, 410
	F-6C/FT-6	1+1	764; additional overhauled F-6Cs in storage
No. 2 Fighter Squadron	MiG-29SEh	12–16	601, 606, 614, 623, 624
	MiG-29UB	1	602
No. 3 Fighter-Attack Squadron	Su-25	11+	201, 202, 203, 204, 205, 206, 207, 208, 209, 210, 211, 212, 213, 214; two landing accidents are known
	Su-25UB	3	215, 216, 217
	MiG-23MS	4	phased out and stored
No.? Jet Training Squadron	K-8S	12	800, 802, 804, 806, 807, 808, 810, 812
No. 1 UAV Squadron	al-Qods UAV		

Khartoum AB

Unit	Aircraft	No.	Remarks
No. 1 Transport Squadron	Il-62M	1	ST-PRA
	Falcon 50	1	ST-PSR
	An-74-100D	4	ST-BDT, ST-GFF, ST-PRB, ST-PRD
No. 3 Transport Squadron	An-12BK	1	ST-ZNN
	An-26	4+	7705, 7715, 7716, 7722, 7755
	An-30A-100	1	7704
	Il-76	1	SAF1106
No. 1 Helicopter Squadron	Mi-35	12+	913, 918, 920, 921, 924, 925, 928, 929, 932, 933, 935, 938, 939, 941, 944, 947, 948; up to 15 additional helicopters stored (including 902, 910, 912, 915, 916, 930, 931, 936), some presently undergoing overhaul 909, 945, 946, 947
No. 2 Helicopter Squadron	Mi-8PS	1	502
	Mi-8MT	1	525
	Mi-171Sh	5	534, 535, 536, 537, 538
	Mi-17MTV-5	3+	528, 531, 533
	Mi-172	1	ST-GFK; up to 10 additional helicopters stored, some presently undergoing overhaul

Port Sudan AB

Unit	Aircraft	No.	Remarks
No. 1 Flight School	PT-6	8+	25?,257,264
	Safat 01	2	
	Safat 03	1	
No. 2 Flight School	FT-5	2–4	

20. United Republic of Tanzania

Jeshi la Wananchi la Tanzania/Usafirashaji wa Anga (JWTZ/UA)

C-in-C   *Maj Gen Festo Ulomi*
Deputy C-in-C   *unknown*

Jeshi la Anga la Wananchi wa Tanzania (Tanzania Air Force Command, TAFC)

Usafirshaji wa Anga (Air Wing)
601 Kikosi cha Jeshi (601 Brigade)

Dar-es-Salaam AB

Unit	Aircraft	No.	Remarks
Transport aircraft	Y-8F200	2	JW 9034, JW 9035
	Y-12II	2	JW 9029, JW 9030
	An-28	1	JW 9031
	Cessna 402	2	JW 9026, JW 9028 (stored)
	HS.748	1	JW 9010
Helicopters	AB.205A	1	JW 9502
	AB.412EP	2	JW 9505, JW9506

Morogoro AB (Ngerengere)

Unit	Aircraft	No.	Remarks
Fighters	F-7	4	JW 9242, JW 924?, in process of delivery
	F-6A/ F-6C	6	JW 9204, JW 9205, JW 9211, JW 9236; additional F-6s in
	F-6A/ F-6C		storage
Jet Training	FT-6	2	JW 9124, JW 912?
	FT-5	4–6	JW 9102, JW 9118, JW 9120; additional F-5s in storage
	FT-7	2	JW 9125, JW 9126
Basic Training	PT-6	8	JW 9136, JW 9137, JW 9138

Mwanza AB

Unit	Aircraft	No.	Remarks
Fighters	MiG-21	7	stored since 1993
	MiG-21UM	3	stored since 1993

602 Kikosi cha Jeshi (602 Brigade)
Technical support and maintenance

603 Kikosi cha Jeshi (603 Brigade), Dar-es-Salaam
Operating ground-based air defence systems

Government, Dar-es-Salaam IAP

Unit	Aircraft	No.	Remarks
Government Flight	Gulfstream IV	1	5H-ONE, 'Air Force I'
	Fokker 50	1	5H-TGF, 'Air Force II'

Unit	Aircraft	No.	Remarks
Police Air Wing	Bell 412EP	1	5H-TPA

21. Republic of Uganda

Uganda People's Defence Air Force (UPDAF)

C-in-C   *Maj Gen Jim Owoyesisigire*
Deputy C-in-C   *Brig Sam Turyagyenda*

Entebbe AB

Unit	Aircraft	No.	Remarks
Government Flight	Gulfstream IVSP	1	5X-UEF
MiG-21 Squadron	MiG-21bis	5	AF-973
	MiG-21UM	1	camouflaged without serial number
	Su-30MK2	6	AF-011, AF-015; in process of delivery
Puma Squadron	L-39ZO	6	151, AF-70?, AF-703, AF-709, AF-735
	AS.202	1	status unknown
	Tempco P-92	?	status unknown
Attack Squadron	Mi-24	7–8	AF-802, AF-803, AF-811
Helicopter Squadron	Mi-172	1	AF-6??
	Mi-17MTV-5	12–14	AF-601, AF-603, AF-605, AF-607, AF-611, AF-620, AF-639
Helicopter Squadron Bell	AB.206	4	AF-317, AF-321?, AF-325, AF-329; rest has been phased out by 2010
	AB.412s		phased out by 2010
Uganda Air Cargo Corporation (operated on behalf of AF)	Y-12A	2	5X-UYX, 5X-UY?
	L-100	1	5X-UCF, 'The Silver Lady'

22. Republic of Zambia

Zambian Air Force (ZAF)

C-in-C   *Maj Gen Andrew Sakala*
Deputy C-in-C   *Brig Gen Monta J. Chileshe*

Tactical Air Command

ZAF Mumbwa

Unit	Aircraft	No.	Remarks
No. 1 Squadron	MB.326	4	AF-812, AF-817, AF-81?,
No. 43 Squadron	K-8E	8	AF-824, AF-825, AF-826, AF-827, AF-828, AF-829, AF-830
No. ?? Squadron	MiG-21bis	?	all stored, unit status unclear
	MiG-21UM	?	

ZAF Lusaka (Lusaka IAP)

Unit	Aircraft	No.	Remarks
No. ? Squadron	MA-60	2	AF-607, AF-608
	HS.748	1	AF-602
	Yak-40	2	stored
No. 22 Squadron	Y-12A	5	AF-214, AF-217, AF-220, AF-221
No. ?? Squadron	AB.205	6	AF-701, AF-768, AF-769, AF-770, AF-771, AF-772; possibly additional examples available
	Bell 212	1	in VIP configuration
No. ?? Squadron	AB.206	2	at least two operational
	AB.47G-4A	2	status unclear
Former No. 2 Squadron	Do 27		In open storage
	Do 28		
No. ?? Squadron	MiG-21	5–6	In open storage

ZAF Mbala, 'Samora Machel AB'

Unit	Aircraft	No.	Remarks
No. ?? Squadron	SOKO G-2 Galeb		all phased out and stored, unit disbanded
	SOKO J-21 Jastreb		
No. ?? Squadron	SOKO G-2 Galeb		all phased out and stored, unit disbanded
	SOKO J-21 Jastreb		

The 'Samora Machel AB' has been disbanded and is in the process of being reconstructed into an IAP

Ndola IAP
Forward operating base with detachments of K-8s and transport aircraft

Training Command, HQ Mbala

ZAF Livingstone (Livingstone IAP)

Unit	Aircraft	No.	Remarks
Flying Training School (FTS)	MFI-15	8	AF-519, AF-520, AF-522, AF-523, AF-526, AF-528, AF-529, AF-531
Zambia Air Force Academy (ZAFA)	no aircraft assigned		

ZAF Mumbwa
Technical Training School (TTS)

Lusaka City AP
Used only for VIP flights by the ZAF and the Government Flight

23. Republic of Zimbabwe

Air Force of Zimbabwe (AFZ)

Commander AFZ	*AM Perence Shiri*
Chief of Staff Operations	*AVM Shebba Brighton Shumbayaonda*

Administration Wing
Responsible for accounting, stores, recruiting and purchases

Engineering Wing
Responsible for aircraft maintenance, aeronautical inspection services, mechanical, electrical and ground equipment services

Flying Wing

Gweru-Thornhill AB

Unit	Aircraft	No.	Remarks
No. 2 Squadron 'Cobra'	K-8Z	10	2017U, 2021C, 2104E, 2106G, 2017H, 2068N,
	Hawk T.Mk 60	7	601, 604, 605, 606, 610, 611, 612; stored
No. 4 Squadron 'Hornet'	FTB.337G	8	1144, 3144, 3322, 3407,
No. 5 Squadron 'Arrow'	F-7IN/IIN	7	702, 704, 706, 707, 708, 710, 711
	FT-7N	2	730, 731
	MiG-23MS	2	
	MiG-23UB	1+	status unknown
No. 6 Squadron 'Tiger'	SF.260M	6	3260, 3262, 3266, 3268, 3625, 3629, 6105, 6107, 6324, 6336,
	SF.260C/W	12	9039, 9098, 9194, 9901, 9906, 9911
	SF.260TP/F	5	
Historic Flight	Provost T.Mk 1	1	
	Provost T.Mk 52	1	
Zimbabwe Park and Wildlife Management Authority	O-2A	2	

Harare-Manyame AB

Unit	Aircraft	No.	Remarks
No. 3 Squadron 'Falcon'	C-212-200	7	800, 802, 804, 806, 808, 810, 812
	BN-2A	5	7136, 7213, 7323
	SF.260TP	1	
No. 7 Squadron 'Spider'	SA.316B Alouette III	7	including G-Car and K-Car variants
	Eurocopter AS.532UL	2	
	Mi-8	2	
No. 8 Squadron 'Scorpion'	AB.412SP	7	
	Mi-24P	6	01, 02, 03, 04, 05, 06

Regimental Wing
Responsible for protecting air force personnel, equipment and installations

Unit	Aircraft	No.	Remarks
201 Squadron			Based at Gweru-Thornhill AB
202 Squadron			Based at Harare-Manyame AB

1 Two Mi-25s obtained from Libya in the 1990s (TT-OAL/03010 and TT-OAM/03028) have been derelict at N'Djamena IAP since the early 2000s. The second Mi-35 purchased in early 2008 (TT-OAR) was shot down in an engagement with insurgents near Abéché in June 2008. Another Mi-24 or Mi-35, flown by a South African pilot and Ukrainian gunner, was reported shot down on 17 September 2006, and a third example was reported shot down on 17 January 2008.

2 SF.260 TT-QAL/334 was shot down in an engagement with insurgents in December 2006.

3 The FAC cannot presently be described as an operational air force. Most of its aircraft and helicopters have been stored and not regularly maintained for more than 10 years. Only a very few transport assets are regularly active, all flown by contracted foreign personnel. The DRC has an agreement with Angola for the deployment of the FANA on local air bases and airfields to protect Kinshasa in case of foreign invasion.

4 Six Mi-24s, two Mi-8s, one An-26 and one Boeing 727 took part in the flypast commemorating the 50th anniversary of independence, on 30 June 2010. This is probably the maximum in terms of aircraft and helicopters the FAC can simultaneously put into the air.

5 Unconfirmed reports cite the presence of '2 Tactical Air Group', consisting of Pursuit and Attack Wings, and a Tactical Transport Wing, with a total of four squadrons. However, no first-hand accounts concerning any activity at Kitona air base are available. Other reports appear to be based on the units stationed at that base prior to the outbreak of the civil war in 1996, and which have not been operational for some time.

APPENDIX II

The deployment of transport aircraft for combat purposes, specifically as 'bombers', is not unique to the wars in Sudan but became one of the characteristics of that little-known air war. Considering the close relation between this topic and the combat deployment of MiG and Sukhoi fighters in Sudan during the last 30 years, it is clear that some additional information about 'Antonov bombers' is of great relevance.

Due to the sheer size of Sudan, and its relatively poor land communications, transport aircraft are of immense importance for the SPAF and the SuAF, moving men and materiel to various locations around the crisis areas. During the war with the SPLA in the 1990s, and realising the deficiencies in terms of range and payload of its available fighter jets, the SuAF began modifying its An-12s and An-24s as makeshift bombers. Already equipped for dropping paratroopers, but foremost because they have large loading/unloading ramps below the rear of the fuselage, these aircraft actually required a minimum of modifications: they can simply unload bombs through these doors while in flight.

Early on, at least, it is perfectly possible that these aircraft usually carried standard Soviet-made bombs from the FAB and similar series of 'general purpose' weapons. However, available reports indicate that, over time, SuAF technicians began to develop a number of much cheaper and more readily available 'homemade' bombs, most of which resemble empty fuel drums filled with explosives and metal pieces. Reportedly, An-26s – which saw deployment for such purposes for the first time in the mid-1990s – can carry up to 16 or 17 such drums; the larger An-12s can carry up to two twice as many. It should be noted that the An-26 was equipped from the outset with equipment to deliver bombs, although the 'bombsight' installed was originally developed for aiding the deployment of paratroopers.

Over time, Sudan began deploying not only SuAF transport aircraft for offensive purposes, but also transports chartered from various domestic airfreight companies, including those leased by Sudanese enterprises such as Ababeel Aviation Company, Air West, AZZA, Sarit Airlines, Sudanese States Aviation, United Arabian. Others were provided by different Russian companies operating in Africa, often with dubious backgrounds.

This 'business' of outsourcing military transport and bombing operations became particularly obvious during the later stages of the war in South Sudan, in the early 21st century, when such aircraft flew hundreds of bombing attacks,. In particular, they gained notoriety for attacking well-known humanitarian relief sites. The following photographs and table offer a review of 'Antonov bombers' and other 'civilian' transport aircraft known to have been used during the wars in South Sudan and Darfur.

In the late 1960s, the SuAF purchased at least five An-24TVs from the USSR. Serial numbers 900, 911, 922, 933 and 944 saw lengthy careers with the SuAF, including deployments as makeshift bombers in the course of the war against the SPLA. The last few ended their service in the late 1990s, on the military side of Khartoum IAP. (Claudio Tosselli Collection)

In the mid-1990s the SuAF purchased two Shanxi Y-12 transports (Chinese-built An-12s) from China, and they saw extensive service during the war against the SPLA. Curiously enough, both aircraft ended their carriers at Wau, where their wreckage was photographed in April 2007 (note that the registration ST-ALU was subsequently applied on a Sudanese An-26s). (Melting Tarmac Images)

This SuAF An-12B (sadly, the serial number is no longer visible) ended its days at el-Geneina airfield, sometime during the early stages of the war in Darfur. Its wreckage was photographed in July 2007. (Melting Tarmac Images)

A trace of the Iraqi presence: this An-12B once served with the Iraqi Air Force, as serial number 988, before being taken over by Iraqi Airlines as YI-AER. Sometime in the 1990s it made an emergency landing at Wau, in West Bahr al-Ghazal State, where it was photographed in March 2007. (Melting Tarmac Images)

This An-26 served with the SuAF as serial number 7755 before it received the civilian registration ST-ALU –as previously worn by one of two Y-12s acquired from China. It was abandoned at Raga airfield, in West Bahir al-Ghazal State, and was seen there in April 2007. (Melting Tarmac Images)

Another An-26 to see service with the SuAF as both transport and bomber, this example was photographed at el-Fasher in March 2007. The airframe shows all sorts of 'dual-use' markings, as often seen on SuAF transports in recent years. Contrary to plenty of media complaints at the time, however, its registration UN-26563 does not disguise it as a 'UN aircraft', but points at its origin: Kazakhstan. The SuAF serial number 7705 is applied much smaller on the fin.[1] (UN)

An-26 ST-APO apparently also served with the SuAF before being taken over by Air West. Its career ended under unknown circumstances at Wau airfield, where its wreckage was photographed in April 2007. (Melting Tarmac Images)

Seen at Sharjah in 2006, this An-26B of the Sudanese Ababeel Aviation Company is registered as ST-AQM. Only a year later, the same aircraft was leased to West Cargo, and was sighted while delivering weapons and ammunition to Sudanese ground forces units in Darfur. (Georg Mader)

S9-PSE was one of two An-32s operated by el-Magal Aviation Services during the 2000s. It was photographed while undergoing overhauls at Khartoum IAP in November 2007. An-32s painted white overall were sighted on several occasions in action over Darfur. (Christian Laugier)

United Arabian An-12 ST-ADE was leased to AZZA Transport when it made a crash-landing at el-Geneina on 24 February 2007. By coincidence, a helicopter full of UN observers passed by shortly after and its occupants were able to take this photograph. (UN)

Ever since the late 1990s, aircraft belonging to various Sudanese airlines have repeatedly been seen undergoing maintenance at Sharjah IAP in the United Arab Emirates. In this case the aircraft is Sudanese States Aviation An-12B ST-ABQ. Considering the close relations between the government in Khartoum and various Russian arms dealers, the appearance of such aircraft outside Sudan is almost 'logical'. (Georg Mader)

These two Sudanese An-12s were photographed in Sharjah in 2006: a Sarit Airlines example (ST-SAR) and an aircraft belonging to United Arab Airlines (in the background on the right). As well as transport duties, these aircraft were repeatedly used as makeshift bombers. (Georg Mader)

This An-26 (construction number 8109, former CCCP-26666) made an emergency landing at an airstrip that used to exist in Gogrial after being hit by SPLA ground fire, in 1997. The serial number 7711 was applied in Western-style on the port side of the fin. (Melting Tarmac Images)

This view of the military side of Khartoum IAP, taken in March 2007, documents the close association of several Sudanese and foreign civilian air freighters with the Sudanese military. As well as a number of SuAF Mi-8s and Mi-17s, Mi-35s and four C-130Hs, it also shows a Faso Airways Il-76 (from Burkina Faso) and two AZZA Il-76s in the foreground, together with one An-12 of Sudanese States Aviation. (Melting Tarmac Images)

The sole Il-76TD of Faso Airways (XT-FCD) was sighted several times in 2007 unloading heavy weaponry for the SPAF on different airfields in Darfur. (Georg Mader)

A chartered gunrunner: in July 2007, this An-12B, registered as ST-ASA with Sudanese States Transport, was photographed while unloading weapons at el-Junaina, Darfur, in breach of UN Resolutions.
(Melting Tarmac Images)

Barely six months later, An-12 ST-ASA appeared low over Khartoum in the new colours of AZZA Transport.
(Melting Tarmac Images)

Table 41: Civilian aircraft operated by airlines known to have supported the SPAF and SuAF, and SuAF transports, 2003–08

Company	Aircraft Type	Registration	Remarks
Ababeel Aviation Company	An-24B	ST-ARP	c/n 37308809
	An-26	ST-ARL	c/n 2606
	An-26B	ST-ARO	Crashed in el-Geneina, 7 June 2004
	An-26	ST-AQM	c/n 1404; Khartoum, March 2007, leased to West Cargo
	An-26	ST-AWT	c/n 3508
	Il-76TD	ST-WTA	c/n 0093495863; leased to Click Airways in January 2008
	Il-76TD	ST-WTB	Crashed 30 June 2008, Khartoum, due to technical malfunction

Company	Aircraft Type	Registration	Remarks
Air West East/ West Cargo	An-12B	ST-AWU	c/n 8345804
	An-26	ST-APO	c/n 12792678011005 or 7309805; wreck at Wau, April 2007
	B707-3J8C	ST-AFA	Khartoum, April 2007
	B737-200	ST-SDA	Khartoum, January 2008, leased to Nova Airlines
	B737-200	ST-SDB	Khartoum, January 2008, leased to Nova Airlines
	Il-76TD	ST-AWR	c/n 0033447365; wearing titles of United Arabian as of January 2008
	Il-76TD	ST-EWB	c/n 23438122; crashed west of Khartoum 3 February 2007
	Il-76TD	ST-EWC	Khartoum, January 2008, missing two engines
	Il-76TD	ST-EWD	Khartoum, January 2008, not operational
	Il-76TD	ST-EWX	Khartoum, January 2008
	Il-76TD	ST-WTB	Crashed 30 June 2008, Khartoum, due to technical malfunction
AZZA Transport	An-12BK	ST-DAS	c/n 7345209; subsequently possibly taken over by SuAF in 2009
	An-12	ST-ASA	Khartoum, December 2007; ever since taken over by SuAF
	B707-330C	ST-AKW	c/n 20123/788; Khartoum March 2007
	B707-384C	ST-JCC	c/n 18948/495
	Il-76TD	ST-APS	c/n 1023409316, Khartoum, January 2008
	Il-76TD	ST-AQB	c/n 0053460975
El-Magal Aviation Services	An-12A	ST-SIG	c/n 1400101; crashed near Dalang, 11 May 2004
	An-26	ST-HIS	Khartoum, November 2007
	An-32	ST-NSP	c/n 2109 (ex S9-BOI, formerly ER-AZW), Khartoum, October 2007
	An-32B	S9-PSE	c/n 2803 (formerly UR-48053); Khartoum, November 2007
Juba Air Cargo	An-12TB	ST-JUA	Formerly EK-11010; crashed Khartoum, 11 August 2007
	An-12TB	ST-ARN	Khartoum, January 2008, waiting for inspection due to crash of ST-JUA
Marsland	An-24	ST-ARP	Khartoum, March 2007; subsequently returned to owner in UAE
	An-24	ST-ARQ	Khartoum, March 2007; subsequently returned to owner in UAE
	An-24	ST-WAL	c/n 69901004 (ex UN-47736); crashed Khartoum on take-off to el-Fasher, 2 June 2007
Sarit Airlines			Company ceased operations in late 2007 and became Badr Airlines, which took over only one aircraft
	An-12	ST-SAA	c/n 5342905; crashed near Wau, 17 November 2003
	An-12	ST-SAD	Crashed Khartoum, 19 October 2004
	An-12	ST-SAF	Crashed near Heglig, 5 October 2004
	An-12	ST-SAR	c/n 402102; crashed Wau, 24 September 2003
	An-12	ST-SAT	c/n 5343502; crashed Wau, 26 June 2004 due to bird strike
	An-12BP	EK-11997	c/n 6344407; crashed el-Geneina, 3 November 2003
	An-26B	ST-SAL	11907
Sudan Air Force	Y-8	ST-ALU	Wreck at Wau as of April 2007
	An-12BP	988/YI-AER	c/n 5908; wreck at Wau as of March 2007

Company	Aircraft Type	Registration	Remarks
	An-30A-100	7704/ST-GFD	Khartoum, 2011
	An-26	7705/UN-26563	current; last seen SAFAT 2010
	An-26-100	7711	Crash-landed Gogrial, 1997, wreck sighted 2009
	An-26	7716	Last seen el-Ubayyid AB, July 2011
	An-26	7755/ST-ALU	Wreck at Raga, April 2007
	An-26	ST-ZZZ	Bomber, sighted at different locations over Darfur, March 2007
	An-26	ST-ZZZ (2nd example)	Crashed el-Fasher, 7 August 2006
	An-12	700	Destroyed el-Fasher, 25 April 2003
	An-12	711	Whereabouts unknown
	An-12	722	current
	An-12	733	Whereabouts unknown
	An-12	744	Whereabouts unknown
	An-24TV	900	c/n 1022803; wreck in Khartoum, January 2007
	An-24TV	911	c/n 1022804; wreck in Khartoum, January 2007
	An-24TV	922	c/n 1022807; wreck in Khartoum, January 2007
	An-24TV	933	c/n 1022808; wreck in Khartoum, January 2007
	An-24TV	944	c/n 1022809; wreck in Khartoum, January 2007
Sudanese States Aviation and Sudanese States Transport	B707	ST-ARI	Khartoum, January 2008 (although reported as w/o at Sharjah IAP, 2006)
	An-12	ST-ABQ	Sharjah, 2006
	An-12	ST-ADE	Crashed near el-Geneina, 24 February 2007
	An-12BP	ST-AQQ	c/n 9346504
Trans Arabian Air Transport	B707	ST-AME	Khartoum, March 2007
	B707-321C	ST-AMF	c/n 19367/637
	B707-321C	ST-ANP	Wreck in Juba, January 2008
Trans Attico	An-12B	ST-AQF	c/n 11008
	An-12B	ST-AQP	c/n 1404
	An-26B	ST-AQD	c/n 8345504
	An-26	ST-AQM	c/n 4342305
	Il-76TD	ST-AQR	c/n 0043454575; Nyala, March 2007
	Il-76TD	ST-CAC	c/n 0023437076
United Arabian	An-12BP	ST-ADE	c/n 01400106; crashed el-Geneina, 24 February 2007, while on lease to Sarit
Faso Airways	Il-76TD	XT-FCB	

1   The sighting of this aircraft caused a controversy when the Amnesty International – followed by the UN – complained that the SuAF transport aircraft
     would be wearing the 'UN insignia'. Actually, the prefix 'UN' is used by all civilian aircraft registered in Kazakhstan.

BIBLIOGRAPHY

ANTUNES, J. F., *A Guerra De Africa*, 1961-1974 (Lisbon, Temas e Debates, 1996),
ISBN 972759039X

BALL, R., *Camouflage & Markings No.3: The Israeli Air Force, Part One, 1948 to 1967* (Luton,
Guideline Publications/Scale Aircraft Monographs, 2001), ISBN 0-9539040-1-6

BARLOW, E., *Executive Outcomes: Against all Odds* (Alberton, Galago Publishing, 1999),
ISBN 978-1-919854-19-9

BRENT, W., *African Air Forces* (Freeworld Publications, 1999)

BRIDGLAND, F., *The War for Africa* (Gibraltar, Ashanti Publishing Ltd, 1990)
ISBN 187480012X

BUGAKOV, I. S.; IVANOV, B. V.; KARTASHEV, V. B.; LAVRENTEV, A. P.; LIGAV, V. A. & PASHKO, V. A.,
Kazan Helicopters: Flight Goes On (Vertolet Publisher and Kazan Helicopters, 2001)

BUTANDU, R. N., *Forgotten War: The Criminal Invasion of the Democratic Republic of Congo –
the International Conspiracy Unveiled* (Baltimore, PublishAmerica Ltd, 2004),
ISBN 1-4137-3082-5

CHILLON, J., 'Military Aircraft Registers of Former French Africa', *AirBritain Digest* magazine,
September/October 1984

COOPER, T., BISHOP, F. & HUBERS, A., 'Bombed By Blinders: Tupolev Tu-22s in Action', *Air Enthu-
siast* magazine, Volume 116/March/April 2005 (UK)

COOPER, T., 'Algerian Fighter Deal Threatened', *Combat Aircraft* magazine, Volume 9/Issue 1
(January 2008)

COOPER, T., 'Flanker Sobre Badme', *ASAS* magazine, Volume 22/December 2004/January 2005
(Brazil)

COOPER, T., 'Krieg um Kinschasa', *Fliegerrevue Extra* magazine, Volume 15/March 2007
(Germany)

COOPER, T., 'Schwarze Falken' im Sudan', *Fliegerrevue Extra* magazine, Volume 20/June 2008
(Germany)

COOPER, T., 'Wie MIG und Irkut Kunden verprellen', *Fliegerrevue* magazine, Volume 09/2010

COOPER, T. & MATOS J., 'Ginas' über Afrika', *Fliegerrevue Extra* magazine, Volume 24/March
2009 (Germany)

COOPER, T., NADEW, S. & CANYON, C., 'Fishbed gegen Tiger II – Der Luftkrieg über Ogaden', *Fliegerrevue Extra* magazine, Volume 28/March 2010 (Germany)

COOPER, T., CANYON, C. & GRANDOLINI, A., 'Libyens Luftwaffe – von König Idris bis Oberst Gaddafi', *Fliegerrevue Extra* magazine, Volume 29/June 2010 (Germany)

COOPER, T., 'Sudan's Air Force', *Scale Aircraft Modelling* magazine, October 2008 (UK)

COOPER, T., '45 Years of Wars and Insurgencies in Chad', *Truppendienst* magazine, Volume 6/2009 (Austria)

COOPER, T., 'Tschad: Hintergründe', script for briefing on situation in Chad, delivered to the Offiziersgesellschaft Wien, 3 April 2008 (Austria)

DEL PINO, R., *Proa a La Libertad: La Historia de una vida heroica consagrada a la más alta causa de la humanidad – la libertad* (Planeta, México, D.F., 1991), ISBN 968406294X

DRAPER, M. I., *Shadows: Airlift and Airwar in Biafra and Nigeria, 1967–1970* (Aldershot, Hikoki Publications Ltd, 1999),   ISBN 1-902109-63-5

DUPUY, T. N. (Col, US Army, ret.), and BLANCHARD W. (Col, US Army, ret.) *The Almanac of World Military Power* (Dunn Loring/London, T. N. Dupuy Associates/Arthur Barker Ltd, 1972) ISBN 0-213-16418-3

FLINTHAM, V., *Air Wars and Aircraft: a Detailed Record of Air Combat 1945 to the Present* (London, Arms and Armour Press, 1989), ISBN 0-85368-779-X

GEORGE, E., *The Cuban Intervention in Angola, 1965–1991: From Che Guevara to Cuito Cuanavale* (Frank Cass, London/New York, 2005), ISBN 0-203-00924-X

GLEIJESES, P., *Conflicting Missions: Havana, Washington, and Africa, 1959–1976* (Chapel Hill, The University of North Carolina Press, 2002), ISBN 0-8078-2647-2

HAMMOND, DR P., *Holocaust in Rwanda* (Newlands, Frontline Fellowship, 1996)

HAMMOND, DR P., *In the Killing Fields of Mozambique* (Newlands, Frontline Fellowship, 1998)

HEITMAN, HELMOET-ROMER, *War in Angola* (Gibraltar, Ashanti Publishing Ltd, 1990)

HEITMAN, HELMOET-ROMER & HANNON P., *Modern African Wars 3: South-West Africa* (Osprey, 1991), ISBN 185532122X

ICG, *Congo at War: A Briefing on the Internal and External Players in the Central African Conflict*, ICG Congo Report No. 2, 17 November 1998

ICG, *Scramble for the Congo: Anatomy of an Ugly War*, ICG Africa Report No. 26, 20 December 2000

LAFFIN J., *The World in Conflict; Contemporary Warfare Described and Analysed, War Annual 7* (London, Brassey's, 1996), ISBN 1-85753-196-5

LORD, D., *Vlamgat: The Story of the Mirage F1 in the South African Air Force* (Oak Tree House, Covos-Day Books, 2000), ISBN 0-620-24116-0

LOUW, M. & BOUWER S., *The South African Air Force at War* (Melvile, Chris van Rensburg Publications, 1989), ISBN 0-8646-09-2

Marcus, G. P., *A History of Ethiopia* (Berkeley, University of California Press, 1994), ISBN 0 520 22479 5

Möller, H., *DDR und Äthiopien: Unterstützung für ein Militärregime (1977-1989)* (Berlin, Dr Hans-Joachim Köster Verlag, 2003), ISBN 3-89574-492-1

Newdick, T. & Cooper, T., *Modern Military Airpower, 1990-Present* (London, Amber Books Ltd., 2010)

Nordeen, L. & Nicolle, D., *Phoenix over the Nile* (Washington: Smithsonian, 1996) ISBN 1-56098-826-3

O'Ballance, E., *The Secret War in the Sudan* (London: Faber & Faber, 1977), ISBN 0-571-10768-0

Petermann W., 'Die Flieger des Julius Nyerere', *Fliegerrevue Extra* magazine, Volume 27/September 2009 (Germany)

Rogers, A., Guest, K. & Hooper J., *Flashpoint! At the Front Line in Today's Wars* (London, Arms and Armour Press, 1994), ISBN 1-85409-247-2

Roslag, L., *Fort Leclerc: Von Tunis Nach Sebha* (Horitschon, Novum Verlag, 2004) ISBN 3-900693-04-08

Rwehururu, B., *Cross to the Gun* (Kampala, Monitor, 2002), ISBN 9789970411658

Sonck, J.-P., 'History of the Congolese Air Force', unknown magazine (France), unknown volume

Sonck, J.-P., 'L'Aermacchi MB 326 sous le ciel Zairois', *Jets* magazine (France), unknown volume

Stanik, J. T., El Dorado Canyon: Reagan's Undeclared War with Qaddafi (Annapolis, Naval Institute Press, 2003), ISBN 1-55750-983-2

Stockwell J., *In Search of Enemies: A CIA Story* (Bridgewater, Replica Books, 1997) ISBN 0-7351-0012-8

Sweetman, B., *The Hamlyn Concise Guide to Soviet Military Aircraft* (London, The Hamlyn Publishing Group Ltd/Aerospace, 1981), ISBN 0-600-34968-3

Thompson, Sir R. (editor), *War in Peace: An Analysis of Warfare since 1945* (London, Orbis Publishing, 1981), ISBN 0-85613-341-8

Turner, J., *Continent Ablaze: The Insurgency Wars in Africa, 1960 to the Present* (London, Arms and Armour Press, 1998), ISBN 1-85409-128-X

Venter, Al J., *War Dog, Fighting Other People's Wars: the Modern Mercenary in Combat* (Havertown, Casemate, 2006), ISBN 1-932033-09-2

Venter, Al J., *War in Angola* (Hong Kong, Concord Publications, 1992) ISBN 962-361-030-0

Venter, Al J., *The Chopper Boys: Helicopter Warfare in Africa* (Gibraltar, Ashanti Publishing Ltd., 1994), ISBN 1-85367-177-0

WHEELER, B. C., *An Illustrated Guide to Aircraft Markings* (London, Salamander Books Ltd, 1986), ISBN 0-86101-206-2

WILLIS D. (editor), *Aerospace Encyclopaedia of World Air Forces* (London, Aerospace Publishing Ltd, 1999), ISBN 1-86184-045-4

'FAPA – A Force Alone', *Air International Magazine*, February 1993

'Força Aérea Populaire de Angola, Angolan People's Air Force', *World Air Power Journal*, Volume 19

The Air Force of Zimbabwe Magazine, various volumes since 2006

National Defence of Ethiopia: Patterns of Progress, (Addis Ababa, Ministry of Information, 1968)

INDEX

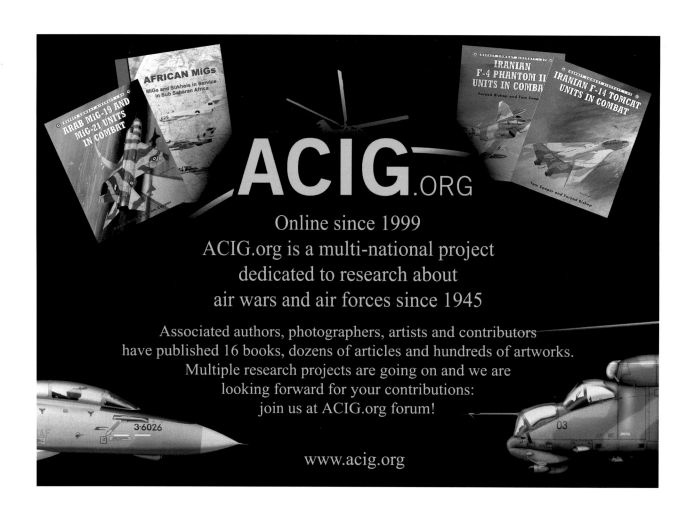

Dutch Aviation Society

P.O.Box 75545
1118 ZN Schiphol
The Netherlands
Fax: +31 (0) 84 - 738 3905
E-mail: info@scramble.nl
www.scramble.nl

DUTCH AVIATION SOCIETY

The **Dutch Aviation Society** is a non-profit organisation run totally by volunteers. For those of you who have never heard of us, we will briefly explain our activities.

The main activities of the **Dutch Aviation Society** are:

- The publication of the monthly magazine **'Scramble'**.
- Maintaining the aviation website www.scramble.nl.
- To organise spotter conventions.
- Maintaining an aviation information database.
- Publishing from an aviation information database.

The production of the magazine, **Scramble**, is our core business. The magazine averages around 144 pages and more than 100 photographs from all over the world. It is published in the English language. It covers all aspects of civil and military aviation worldwide in many separate sections:

- Extensive civil airport and military airbase movements from the Netherlands;
- Civil and military movements from many European airports and airbases;
- Civil aviation news word wide (general news, jetliners, propliners, commuters, bizjets, bizprops, helicopters, extensive Soviet coverage, vintage aircraft, wrecks & relics);
- Dustpan & Brush (Stoffer & Blik), in depth reports about accidents and incidents worldwide;
- Military aviation news world wide (general news, procurement plans, unit changes, updates, orders of battle, vintage aircraft, wrecks & relics);
- Timetables and other information on shows, deployments, exchanges and other aviation events;
- Radio Activity (new frequencies, call signs);
- Show reports (full reports in all major aviation events);
- Fokker news (all about Fokker aircraft, including the Fairchild F-27 and FH-227);
- Full coverage of the Dutch Civil Aircraft Register;
- Trip reports from all over the world;
- A mix of large and small, civil and military articles.

If you would like a subscription, or more info on our magazine, please check out www.scramble.nl/subscribe.htm or send an E-mail to subscribe@scramble.nl

You are welcome to visit the official website. The website is in English and free for everybody. You can find more information about **Scramble** in the "Magazine" section of the Internet site. As **Scramble** Magazine covers both civil and military aviation, we have created sections for every interest. For a growing number of countries you will find an extensive Order of Battle on the site with unit-badges, database, base-overview, maps, pictures and links. For a considerable and growing number of countries you can access our database for your own reference. Scramble-subscribers even have more privileges and can get more information out of our databases. We hope you will enjoy our site. The pages are updated on a regular basis, so come back often to our website!

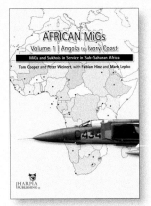

African MiGs Vol. 1 | Angola to Ivory Coast – MiGs and Sukhois in Service in Sub-Saharan Africa
Tom Cooper and Peter Weinert, with Fabian Hinz and Mark Lepko
256 pages, 28x21cm, softcover
35.95 Euro   ISBN 978-0-9825539-5-4
This second, expanded and fully revised edition of the groundbreaking book *African MiGs* examines the role and deployment history of MiG- and Sukhoi-designed fighters – as well as their Chinese derivatives – in no fewer than 23 air forces in Sub-Saharan Africa. This first volume, covering 12 air arms from Angola to Ivory Coast, will be followed by a second volume in 2011. In order to ensure precise documentation of every airframe delivered to and operated by the various air forces, special attention is given to illustrations as well as extensive tables of known serial numbers and attrition. The new volume is updated with much exclusive information, photographs and artworks. As such, it provides the most comprehensive and reliable source on the background of each of the features air forces, their organisation and unit designations, deliveries of fighters built by MiG, Sukhoi, Chengdu and Shenyang, camouflage, markings and combat deployment.

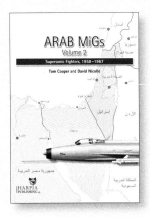

ARAB MiGs Volume 2, Supersonic Fighters, 1958–1967
Tom Cooper and David Nicolle
256 pages, 28x21cm, softcover
35.95 Euro   ISBN 978-0-9825539-6-1
Largely based on original, previously unavailable documentation from official archives, as well as interviews with participants and eyewitnesses, the second volume is an unprecedented study of the developments of six air forces during the late 1950s and 1960s. The authors present the main topic – the introduction of supersonic fighters such as the MiG-19 and MiG-21 – against the geopolitical back-drop. For the first time, the authors explain how and why specific air forces developed in the way they did, why they received specific aircraft types, and also why they suffered a defeat with such dramatic consequences during the June 1967 War with Israel. The volume is completed by an in-depth study of the application of early MiG-21 variants in combat, development of tactical combat methods in Syria during the mid-1960s, and finally an order of battle for the Egyptian Air Force as of 4 June 1967.

Latin American Mirages – Mirage III/5/F.1/2000 in Service with South American Air Arms
Santiago Rivas and Juan Carlos Cicalesi
256 pages, 28x21cm, softcover
35.95 Euro   ISBN 978-0-9825539-4-7
For more than four decades, different versions of the classic Dassault Mirage fighter have served as one of the most potent combat aircraft in Latin America. Equipping seven South American air forces in significant quantities, the delta-winged jets have seen action in various different wars and inter-nal conflicts, and they continue to fulfil their mission with a number of operators. This book tells the story of all the members of the Mirage family in service with Latin American air arms, with indi-vidual histories of the air arms and their constituent units that have operated the Dassault-designed fighter, as well as its Israeli and South African derivatives. The volume provides a comprehensive collection of colour photographs and profile artworks that cover all the variants, plus maps, and tables that illustrate the individual stories of all the aircraft, their units and their various weapons.